The southern poor white is one of America's oldest and most enduring folk figures. His stereotypical blend of extreme poverty with slyness and folly, sloth and random violent activity, has provided a stimulus to both the artistic and social consciousness of our country, resulting in a rich literary tradition. As a literary character, the southern poor white accumulated at first a reputation for comic vulgarity and absurd violence; then, in the late nineteenth century, he was typified as a quaint peasant, praiseworthy for his archaic loyalties to region and religion. By the 1920s, the proponents of proletarian literature began to visualize the possible Marxist transformation of this backward peasant into a revolutionary proletarian.

Although there have been earlier studies of poor white humor and gothicism, little has been done in the analysis of the political uses of this folk character. In this volume, Sylvia Jenkins Cook examines the ways in which a popular image like that of the southern poor white may be altered by dramatic changes in the social milieu and the political allegiances of his chief chroniclers.

the difficult transformation of peasants into revolutionary proletarians in novels based on the 1929 strike of textile workers in Gastonia and analyzes the works of three other major southern writers who tried to reconcile private, aesthetic visions of the poor white with the public, contemporary record of his plight.

Sylvia Jenkins Cook teaches English at the University of Missouri at St. Louis.

From Tobacco Road
to Route 66

From Tobacco Road
to Route 66

The Southern Poor White
in Fiction

Sylvia Jenkins Cook

*The University of
North Carolina Press
Chapel Hill*

Copyright © 1976 by
The University of North Carolina Press
All rights reserved
Manufactured in the United States of America
ISBN 0-8078-1264-1
Library of Congress Catalog Card Number 75-35822

Library of Congress Cataloging in Publication Data

Cook, Sylvia Jenkins, 1943–
    From Tobacco Road to Route 66.

    Bibliography: p.
    Includes index.
    1. American fiction–Southern States–History and criticism. 2. American fiction–20th
century–History and criticism. 3. Poor in literature. I. Title.
PS261.C57   813'.03   75-35822
ISBN 0-8078-1264-1

To my MOTHER
and FATHER

CONTENTS

PREFACE

The southern poor white is one of America's oldest and most enduring folk figures. His image is an elusive one, compounded of popular prejudice, a rich literary tradition, and myriad sociological investigations; but most typically it derives from the alliance of extreme material deprivation with slyness, sloth, absurd folly, and random violence. The actual prevalence of people of this nature in the South has long been a sore point with the region's defenders, who have argued persistently and convincingly that the vast majority of the white population there neither are, nor have been, wealthy exploiters or miserable trash. Instead they emphasize the "plain folk," "sturdy yeomen," and "good old boys": expressions that suggest solidity and self-sufficiency rather than shiftlessness and want. However, the fascination of poor whites has never lain in the magnitude of their numbers. Originating in the familiar ethnic and cultural background of the Anglo-Saxon pioneers who settled the South, they represent the obverse reflection of the most revered values of that tradition; their curious, alien, and debased lives challenge all complacency about such an inheritance. Poor whites, by their capacity to provoke both compassion and ridicule, have provided a perennial stimulus to the artistic consciousness and social conscience alike. These, in turn, have constantly reshaped and redefined their qualities in response to both personal and public imperatives.

The poor whites' recorded history stretches back at least to the early eighteenth century, and a partial listing of the various synonyms by which they have been known indicates not only their diverse geographic distribution but also their changing characteristics and occupations: lubbers, crackers, dirt eaters, woolhats, river rats, piney-woods tackies, po buckra, sandhillers, hillbillies, tarheels, lintheads, and factory rats. The attributes implied by these names are not necessarily consistent. The difficulty of discovering any satisfactory synthesis of qualities that compose the term "poor white" is a consequence partly of the cultural diversity of the groups to which it is applied and partly of the use of the term as a moral, as well as economic and sociological, label. Indeed, one scholar who attempted a definitive essay on the subject and was continually forced to qualify his assertions made what is perhaps the only valid generalization there is. "It soon became clear that the poor whites appear as a problem to everyone, including themselves."[1]

The earliest reports refer to isolated rural people who displayed indolence and indifference toward any material improvement of their lot. A. N. J. Den Hollander has sketched a model of the type. "He lives in a dilapidated log cabin and ekes out a wretched existence by the half-hearted cultivation of a few corn rows, by hunting squirrels in the pine woods, and by fishing for catfish around the cypress stumps of sluggish streams. There is something wrong with him, something inferior, possibly, in his blood."[2] Eventually, most of these people were forced away from their own very limited resources to become sharecroppers and tenants on cotton and tobacco plantations. They moved from a pattern of backwoods subsistence on hunting and farming, such as that described by Den Hollander, to complete dependency on others. They now had employers on whom to focus both loyalty and resentment and a clearly apparent position in a highly structured society—at the bottom. Yet despite this considerable change in their mode of life, the absorbing problem for their chroniclers continued to be what was "wrong" with them that they had neither the ability nor, more significantly, the will to lift themselves out of their despised status. Writers continued to describe with relish the shocking living conditions of these southern "peons"—almost always in conjunction with their personal theories on the causes of such degeneracy. Debates flourished over the relationship of physical debility to intelligence, morality, and ambition; gradually, even major differences in the locale and occupation of the poor white subjects became blurred in the enthusiasm with which the broader philosophical questions were discussed.

The declining importance of the cultural differences among various groups of the poor in the face of the overwhelming effects of poverty itself is attested by the readiness with which the label "poor white" was affixed to the mountain dwellers of the southern Appalachians. Travelers began to report in the late nineteenth century on the brutal and archaic lives these people led in what they themselves sardonically referred to as "the land of want." The contrasts between the mountain people and the plantation and lowland poor whites are plentiful: the former were depicted as proud, energetic (though not necessarily at work), independent, hospitable, and intensely loyal to their mountain homes while the latter, since they were so frequently forced to move, had a reputation for abject and inert sullenness and indifference to the claims of any one place. Yet, because of the mountaineers' acquiescence in their remote and seemingly deprived existence and the admixture of their familiar ancestry with alien codes of conduct, they provoked the same kind of speculation as the sharecroppers and tenants on the effects of heredity and environment.

At least one other distinct group of southerners came to have the appellation "poor white" casually attached to them despite even greater differences between their ways of life and those of the sharecroppers and mountaineers. These were the textile workers who crowded into the factories of the Piedmont district of North Carolina after the Civil War. Although their numbers were made up largely of sharecroppers and tenants from neighboring rural areas, along with some yeomen farmers and mountaineers hoping for a new life in the towns, they soon evolved a unique and often wretched urban culture of their own on the mill hills. Since southern textile manufacturers supplied housing for their workers in mill villages on the outskirts of towns and adopted a generally paternalistic attitude to their employees, these people were most easily isolated and stigmatized by the rest of the community. However, this most public exhibition of the shame and squalor of their lives also provided the opportunity for the first time for a sense of communal solidarity to develop among these urban poor whites, though their capacity for any real improvement without outside intervention was doubtful.

All of the preceding groups, from the earliest squatters to the urbanized factory workers, were the most likely breeding grounds for the types of people called poor whites. However, when social scientists began to attempt to survey and document poor whites as a class, they found that not only did the term imply a host of perplexingly diverse qualities but that its usage often revealed as much about the labeller as about the people labelled. Thus, the more prosperous people were, the more likely they were to use the expression "poor white" for *all* poor people; further down the economic and social scale, people tended to make much finer discriminations between "worthy" poor and "trash," while at the lowest level the derogatory terminology began to have a reverse application to the more successful.[3] In the light of so much confusion, some of the most sensitive observers of the southern poor, like James Agee and Robert Coles, have chosen in their documentaries to abjure categorization and present instead individual case studies that are closer in approach to the work of artists than social scientists. In these more personal studies, the difficulty of making satisfactory generalizations about poor whites becomes an advantage, giving the author freedom to explore variety rather than compelling him to impose unity. Similarly, the sociologists' problems were in many ways the novelists' great attractions; the ironies and incongruities of poor white behavior became an essential part of the rich fictional tradition that flourished alongside the reportorial one. Each of these traditions reached a peak during the years of the depression when the national crisis threatened a greater number of Americans than ever before with the exigencies of poverty. Then the poor white's image was more extensively revised and rejuvenated than at any time in his long-recorded history. This process resulted not only from a leftward swing in the allegiance of many American writers and their attempt to find appropriate subjects for a native proletariat but also from the remarkable flowering of literary talent in the South that drew on regional material there and expanded it far beyond the earlier, often sentimental pieties of "local color" writing.

This book attempts to trace both the attractions and problems for writers, primarily of fiction, who handled the paradoxical poor white stereotype in the 1930s. It surveys first the origin of the literature in colonial Virginia and North Carolina and indicates some of the complex interaction between writers' social and political sympathies and their fictional accounts in the nineteenth century. After the Civil War, poor white fiction fell into temporary abeyance, but there were plenty of reflections in the nonfictional reports that the image was accumulating and thriving. The grotesque reputation of the poor white suited neither the proponents of the New South at this time nor the sentimentalists of the Old, but in the twentieth century his propensities for extreme behavior and shocking conditions were no longer such obstacles. In the 1920s and

30s the revival of southern fiction was accompanied by a national interest in the possibilities of an American radical literature and also an expansion of documentary techniques that grew concomitantly with the extraordinary experiences of the depression. All of these focused interest once again on the poor white and the challenge he presented to conventional ways of viewing southern society and culture.

His behavior had always been incongruous with pathos; now, in this new era, there was a chance to test its capacity to stir anger. Yet the same qualities that made the poor whites appealing—the comic folklore, extravagant vulgarity, obsessive (and frequently self-serving) illogicality—were likely to be major stumbling blocks in the depiction of them as exploited workers coming to a rational and wrathful awareness of their condition. Six writers attempted this imposing transformation of peasants into revolutionary proletarians in novels based on the 1929 strike of textile workers in Gastonia, North Carolina. One of these six, Mary Heaton Vorse, covered the strike as a newspaper reporter, and her novel parallels the journalistic records so closely that it is treated here in conjunction with them in order to offer a means of comparison between radical journalism and the demands of radical fiction. Another chapter is devoted to three southern women novelists—Fielding Burke, Myra Page, and Grace Lumpkin—who were at least as concerned in their depiction of the strike with the feminist cause of the poor white woman as with the broader economic situation of all southern workers. Of the last two Gastonia novelists, Sherwood Anderson and William Rollins, neither was a native southerner, but Anderson knew the ways of southern factory workers intimately while Rollins was so ill at ease in the southern milieu that he transferred the setting of the strike to the North. Thus his novel demonstrates, by antithesis, the extreme effect of the southern environment on radical literature.

Three major southern writers—William Faulkner, Erskine Caldwell, and James Agee—tried to reconcile more private aesthetic visions of the poor white with the public record of his contemporary plight; and all three produced devastating, though by no means similar, indictments of the modern South. However, the most popularly successful poor white novel of the decade, John Steinbeck's *The Grapes of Wrath*, was neither by a southerner nor did it deal specifically with the southernness of the poor white. Steinbeck achieved the desired combination of folk heroics, humor, and revolutionary anger; but for the satisfactory blending of these qualities, he had to move the poor whites not only to the periphery of their geographic location in the South but also away from the historical process of urban industrialism there. By focusing on a singular ecological catastrophe in Oklahoma, Steinbeck revealed as much by implication and evasion about the peculiar relationship of socially conscious fiction to the southern literary consciousness as did those writers who tried the more complicated task of fusing them around a more genuine image of the southern poor white.

I would like to acknowledge here the particular importance of Shields McIlwaine's book, *The Southern Poor-White: From Lubberland to Tobacco Road*, 1939, in stimulating this study. Not only did it first arouse my interest in the topic, but it also has provided me with more vital information than I can convey by the frequent footnote references to it.

I would also like to thank those faculty members of the University of Michigan who worked with me on the first version of this material, especially Cecil Eby, Robert Sklar, and the late Joe Lee Davis. Finally, I am most grateful to my husband, Richard M. Cook, for constant encouragement, advice, and support.

From Tobacco Road
to Route 66

CHAPTER I

The Development of the Poor White Tradition

In 1728, on orders from the king of England, William Byrd led a technical expedition into the swamps and backwoods of Virginia and North Carolina to chart the precise dividing line between the two colonies. After the first part of the arduous task was over, Byrd compiled a journal of the proceedings which the fellow commissioner of the expedition, Richard Fitzwilliam, refused to sign on the remarkable grounds that it was "too poetical."[1] Indeed Byrd's considerable literary talent had been used to embellish his account of the variety and habits of the wildlife, the legends of the Indians, and the capacity of the soft air and lush scenery to inebriate the explorers. However, one discovery above all others in this remote periphery of Anglo-Saxon society had fascinated and stimulated the imagination of the urbane scholar of Petronius: in roofless cattle pens and bowers covered only with tree bark, Byrd unearthed an array of "indolent wretches" with "custard complexions" who practiced their vices publicly and their virtues in intense privacy; who lived in "a dirty state of nature" and were alternately subject to "gross humors" and "a lazy, creeping habit" that kept them squatting on a frontier. From them Byrd created the first comic portrait of the southern poor white.

The creatures Byrd described were bizarre specimens of moral laxity and physical lassitude. They cohabited like "mere Adamites, innocence only excepted," and subsisted passively on the providence of the land with the occasional aid of a little milk stolen from neighbors' cows. Their freakish appearance—yellow-skinned and nearly noseless—and extreme sloth provoked Byrd's amused contempt, but his inquiring mind also pondered an array of possible explanations for their alien quality. The climate was enervating and the land so abundant that there was little incentive for careful husbandry; a diet of pork, with a little fresh milk, vitiated their constitutions and caused the physical peculiarities, while the proximity of marshes with vast numbers of mosquitoes further impaired their health. In addition, by Byrd's account, North Carolina deliberately encouraged the increase of its population by debtors, criminals, and fugitives. It was a haven for the innately idle. "To speak the truth, 'tis a thorough aversion to labor that makes people file off to North Carolina, where plenty and a warm sun confirm them in their disposition to laziness for their whole lives."[2] Thus, just as Byrd helped form the stereotype of the poor white as idiotic, immoral, and—above all—inert, he also established precedents for the two opposing ethical positions that would later be taken by an array of literary and political partisans. Environmental determinists would blame ecology, climate, disease, and diet, while genetic determinists would argue something closer to inherent depravity.

Since Byrd's time journalists, travel writers, and sociologists have enforced each of these extreme positions with the kind of fervent moral rhetoric that debates on the "redemption" of this subject tend to produce. Thus an investigator for the United States Department of Labor wrote of it in 1891, "Not the shallowest optimist, the most ardent apologist for the present social order, can be content with the benighted and unprogressive attitude of the poor whites, when out of this seemingly unpromising material education, mental, moral, and physical, might evolve the highest order of humanity."[3] However, the opposite attitude was equally prevalent, even seventy years of "progress" later: "The mind of the poor white is feral, fatalistic, bordering on bitterness—unable to improve, and unwilling to relent."[4]

The fiction of the poor white, though frequently used to bolster political propaganda, did not polarize with such ideological distinctness as the nonfictional reports. Humorists and novelists were initially less interested in penetrating the macabre mystery of his evolution, or even the possibilities of his salvation, than in exploring the ambivalent responses he might generate—laughter, pity, discomfort, indignation, revulsion. Thus as a literary figure, the poor white is defined more accurately in terms of the moral, emotional, and intellectual incongruity with which he is perceived than in any objective ranking of his social and economic status. He is of course more likely to be discovered in the last and lowest of the five categories of nonslaveholders into which Frank L. Owsley ranked the white population of the Old South, but sociological classifications are frequently confounded in the fiction. The Walden family in *God's Little Acre*, by Erskine Caldwell, own their land and employ a number of black servants; yet they are indisputably poor whites—notwithstanding the possession of property, which obviously does not bring the concomitant yeoman virtues of thrift, energy, and self-respect.[5] By contrast, in Elizabeth Madox Roberts's *The Time of Man*, Ellen Chesser is the child of an abysmally poor wandering tenant farmer; yet she dreams of a neat farm, "ducks spread out in thrifty processions, brightly whitewashed hen-yards"[6] and readily labels as "trash" many who appear to be clearly her superiors in any standard economic ranking. The difficulty of insisting that the poorest whites are necessarily "poor whites" is apparent even in Byrd's journal, for in fact he cites a preponderance of cases where industry and neatness prevailed in the homes he visited; but stalwart farming and orderly housekeeping could scarcely provide a rival imaginative stimulus to the grotesque comic possibilities of the "lubbers." Thus, a too-discriminating search for social correspondences to the rapidly accumulating literary myth is not always relevant—the fictional stereotype and the social reality of the poor white developed simultaneously but not always in complete harmony.

During the nineteenth century the fictional poor white gained an increasingly firmly established role in southern literature. He was a confirmed object of ridicule in the works of humorists and a stock minor character in many novels, with generally villainous or pathetic tendencies according to the broader ideological sympathies of the author.[7] The work of the humorists, from Longstreet's *Georgia Scenes* in 1835 to Harris's tales of Sut Lovingood in 1867, has as a rule only an incidental concern with the financial and social burdens of the poor white but a major interest in his grotesque appearance and vicious conduct. The writers are intent on unfolding the wonders, extravagances, and outrages of southern frontier life in tales that balance admiration for the tough feats of pioneers with the mock-heroic style of their boastful reports. Poor whites thus rarely prove objects of compassion in these tales, although a modern sensibility might easily overestimate the significance of the economic determinism that may be gleaned from the famous portrait by Longstreet of Ransy Sniffle:

> Now there happened to reside in the county just alluded to a little fellow by the name of Ransy Sniffle: a sprout of Richmond, who, in his earlier days, had fed copiously upon red clay and blackberries. This diet had given to Ransy a complexion that a corpse would have disdained to own, and an abdominal rotundity that was quite unprepossessing. Long spells of the fever and ague, too, in Ransy's youth, had conspired with clay and blackberries to throw him quite out of the order of nature. His shoulders were fleshless and elevated; his head large and flat; his neck slim and translucent; and his arms, hands, fingers, and feet were lengthened out of all proportion to the rest of his frame. His joints were large and his limbs small; and as for flesh, he could not, with propriety, be said to have any. Those parts which nature usually supplies with the most of this article—the calves of the legs, for example—presented in him the appearance of so many welldrawn blisters. His height was just five feet nothing; and his average weight in blackberry season, ninety-five.[8]

Ransy's normal state of torpor can be shaken only by the prospect of witnessing a fight, and in Longstreet's tale he manages to provoke one between two men greatly superior to himself in physical and moral wholesomeness. When the fight ends in ghastly bloodshed and dismemberment, Ransy has his fill of pleasure and escapes unscathed. This wily capacity to survive and even profit from the disasters of others not only undercuts pity for the poor white but also marks his potential as a con man—the victimizer as much as the victim of his society.

Johnson J. Hooper's Simon Suggs, living high off the follies and weaknesses of others by following his motto, "It is good to be shifty in a new country,"[9] epitomizes this type. Suggs has all the immorality and pious hypocrisy of the comic poor white although he is not so physically impoverished. In fact, the only person to penetrate his sanctimonious pose is an even more sly and invincible clay eater, who heckles Suggs's bombastic efforts to promote himself leader of the Tallapoosa Volunteers. The shifty hero is thus forced to resort to the one sure means of overcoming the constitutionally weak—physical violence: " 'Take *that* along, and next time keep your jaw, you slink, or I'll kick more clay outen you in a minute, than you can eat again in a month, you durned, dirt-eatin' deer-face!' " His opponent, though temporarily quelled, exhibits a speedy talent for scoring off his own disadvantages: " 'Keep the children outen the way,' said the little fellow, as he lay sprawling in the farthest corner of the room; 'ef you don't *Cap'en* Suggs will whip 'em all. He's a sight on children and people what's got the *yaller janders!'* "[10]

By showing that the poorest of the trash could ridicule and manipulate other classes, southern humorists could avoid dealing with less amusing aspects of their struggle for survival; or, as in the case of the preposterously named Sut Lovingood, the foulness and bestiality of the subject would almost obscure any need to consider the implications of such a mode of life. Sut, whom Edmund Wilson referred to as "a peasant squatting in his own filth,"[11] certainly managed to offend the more tender critics of the twentieth century; he won from D. W. Brogan the title "horrible hero of odious Southern humour."[12] Capitalizing on his reputation as knave and fool to avoid work, play cruel tricks and avenge himself mercilessly on his enemies, he is certainly the crudest, most villainous, and most repulsive of the poor white con men. The reader's sympathy for Sut as bottom dog is ruthlessly curtailed by his ability to force others—including his own father and, in one absurd incident, his own dog—into that position. No small amount of one's distaste for Sut derives from his obsessive and lingering attention to the physical details of his person; thus he will open a yarn, "Well, one day I wer sittin on the fence in the sunshine, with my trousis rolled up mos' to my pockits, a saftenin' the holts of the dorgticks on my laigs with spittil, so I cud pull 'em off without leavin' thar heads in the hide."[13] Such incidental naturalistic details are not uncommon even in Byrd's account of the dismay of his surveyors, when, on making sexual overtures to a backwoods girl, they find her body to be covered with scabs. However, the horror in this latter situation is not attended with a delight in the disgusting, as is Sut's, who enjoys being as offensive as possible.

The general ideological strain of this southern humor has been interestingly assessed by Kenneth Lynn as an effort to bolster political Whiggery and elegant plantation ideals by emphasizing the chasm between the respectable gentleman narrators who venture into the frontier regions of the Southwest and the vulgar and unpolished natives.[14] The theory is a persuasive one, for the poor whites seemed less sinned against than sinning in these comic episodes, but Harris's creation of Sut Lovingood goes well beyond demonstrating the necessary foxy survival instinct that takes the trash off the conscience of the comfortable. If Sut emphasizes, by contrast to himself, the genteel virtues of the upper class, he is also an ominous warning to the confidence of those people that "ginerily has a pedigree wif one aind tied to thar sturn, an' tother one a-soakin' in NOAH'S flood"(165) and who are "powerful feard ove low things, low ways, an' low pepil" (164). Sut's hideous exploits seem to guarantee that their fears are justified, not only by his personal disruptiveness but also by his revelation of untapped wells of bitterness in the consciousness of the poor white. Sut's hatred of privilege and affectation is not irrational, no matter how absurd and shocking its manifestations may be; it suggests that while the poor whites begged, stole, loafed, and schemed, a long memory of resentment was accumulating in their minds that might appear suddenly in both foolish and ugly forms.

The emergence of the rather subversive Sut Lovingood from a comic tradition that ostensibly gloried in gentlemanly condescension to the colorful vigor of the Old South is an interesting omen for the flexibility of the poor white's literary career and a useful reminder that the fictional strength of the poor whites could often transcend the political partisanship of their creators. It would prove most difficult to detach the comedy and villainy of the poor white from his poverty and low social origin, and equally so to separate pity from more complicated qualifying emotions, without degenerating into mere pathos. Thus the malevolent poor whites who play minor roles in several proslavery novels tend to expose certain ironies that were less than desirable for the defense of the old régime. Specifically, in George Tucker's heavily tendentious *The Valley of Shenandoah*, a surly, poor white wagoner who refuses to give way on the highway to "any whipper-snapper in a fine coat"[15] is appropriately punished by fate for his little display of class consciousness when the wagon crushes his foot; unrepentant of his upstart arrogance, he takes his gentlemen opponents to court and, naturally, loses again. Later in the novel these same gentlemen encounter on the road a poverty-stricken family with eight children who, unable to survive on the proceeds of the man's tenancy, are migrating west. The gentlemen comment on the tenant's flight as an admirable example of the equality of opportunity in an open country, but in conjunction with what we have seen earlier, it gives what one critic calls, "by inference and frank statement . . . a wealth of social truth"[16] that is certainly contrary to Tucker's intentions. Likewise, the most ardent literary defender of the antebellum South, William Gilmore Simms, in depicting poor whites whose roguery and stupidity help to justify the concentration of power and wealth in the hands of a more fitting class, provides incidentally revealing glimpses of their squalid living conditions.

Interestingly, the dichotomy between the gentry and the wretches so favored by the defenders of the Old South is also habitually made by northern abolitionist writers, though the cause and effect are reversed so that the low estate of the poor whites is a result of slavery rather than a vindication of it. Shields McIlwaine, the most comprehensive chronicler of poor white literature, points out that such abolitionist writers as Harriet Beecher Stowe, Richard Hildreth, and John Trowbridge exhibited for their propaganda purposes "only the trashiest of the poor-white-trash."[17] So both the defenders and assailants of the slave system seemed to conspire to perpetuate the myth that there were but two classes of whites in southern society, " 'a wealthy, dominant class, and a wretched, ignorant class, at once insubordinate and servile.' "[18] Journalists and essayists, lured by the more macabre elements of the poor whites which might be shaped into convincing crusading material, followed the fiction writers. The extremes of such rhetoric may be found in the writings of Hinton Rowan Helper, a southerner who had no slaves and therefore chose to consider himself a poor white. Of people such as himself he wrote in 1858: " ' The serfs of Russia have reason to congratulate themselves that they are neither the negroes nor the non-slaveholding whites of the South. Than the latter there can be no people in Christendom more unhappily situated.' "[19] Thus, by the time of the war, the poor white had become not merely a prominent literary type—he had virtually supplanted the plain farmer (who comprised the vast majority of the South's population) in the consciousness of the nation.

The first writer to deflate publicly the exaggerated proportions of very rich and very poor in the South was James R. Gilmore, a northern abolitionist, with an article in *Harper's Magazine* in 1864 entitled "The Poor Whites of the South." Gilmore estimated that there could be no more than half a million "mean whites" or "trash" in the South, while there were at least six and a half million members of the "middle or laboring class" who were "an honest, industrious, enterprising, brave, and liberty-loving people."[20] Gilmore wished to shift the focus of northern propaganda to these "plain folk," who were to come into such prominence in the literature of the South after the war, by winning them with ideas or, more precisely, "with a sword in one hand and a Union newspaper in the other."[21] The prime object of this new method of persuasion was to be the women of the South, a group whose power Gilmore never belittled. It is in fact his sympathy and respect for women that constitute the most innovative aspect of Gilmore's fiction, which is memorable mainly for the creation of Mrs. Bony Mulock, the first poor white comic heroine. His novel, *My Southern Friends*, 1863, contrasts the tragic ruin and death of a northern farm girl, abandoned by her lover, with the brash adventures of Mrs. Mulock, a crude, dirty southern poor white woman, abandoned by her husband. While the northern white woman descends to prostitution and death in high melodrama, Mrs. Mulock refuses to be victimized by the world and takes a comic vengeance on her erring husband. Amid the horrors of a slave market where an anguished young black woman is sold for $1,300, Mrs. Mulock promptly disposes of her worthless white male for $100. Her delight in the deal leaves a fine unspoken irony as to the worth of black women and white men when they are forced to compete in the same stock market. It is noteworthy that despite Gilmore's anxiety in the *Harper's* article to correct misconceptions of southern society, his own abolitionist novel pays no attention to that intermediate class of whites whom he had claimed henceforth "must be the real South." These "plain folk" did not fit the propaganda patterns of either group of prewar partisans particularly well, but after the Civil War they were to come into their literary flower in the local color tradition, whose imperatives largely excluded the squalid horror and degenerate humor of the poor white.[22]

The new emphasis on the folk by southern writers was partly a response to avid northern curiosity about the defeated region, partly an effort to vindicate the savage reputation which the South had acquired. The New South began to recreate an idealized and sentimentalized version of the old: "along with the glittering vision of a 'metropolitan' and industrial South to come there developed a cult of archaism, a nostalgic vision of the past."[23] The poor white did not completely disappear from this literature, but his image was softened to become more picturesque and pathetic. Joel Chandler

Harris created several pitiable and near-tragic poor whites and greatly advanced the characterization of poor white women in the heroic figures of Mrs. Feratia Bivins in *Mingo*, 1884, and Emma Jane Stucky in *Free Joe*, 1887. Mrs. Bivins is as tough-minded in defense of her rights as Gilmore's Mrs. Mulock but much more embittered by what Harris calls "the real or fancied wrongs of a class. . . [that] spring from the pent-up rage of a century."[24] The tale turns on the triumphant struggle by the "pore white trash" woman to affirm her claim over the "quality" woman for possession of their mutual grandchild, in which Mrs. Bivins intimidates her rival with the fierce threat, " ' I'll *grab you by* the goozle an' t'ar your haslet out' " (24). Harris insists that these words issued from "the voice of Tragedy," but the fact that such an authorial intrusion is necessary to affirm the dignity and validity of the poor white's position suggests the difficulty of creating a tragic heroine from the remnants of ridicule and horror. Emma Jane Stucky is more successful in this role though there is a heavy weight of pathos in the piney-woods mother, whose only relic of her dead idiot son is his footprint, enshrined in the mud in her homemade monument, "a little contrivance of boards that looked like a bird-trap."[25] She does reveal, however, a superior strength of character to the southern woman whose food she is forced to beg and to the young northern lady whose pity for her dead son she rejects. It is her one emotional departure from the habitual anesthetized endurance in which she exists: "Whatter you cryin' fer now? . . . You wouldn't a-wiped your feet on 'im. Ef you wuz gwine ter cry, whyn't you let 'im see you do it 'fore he died. What good do it do 'im now? He wa'n't made out'n i'on like me' " (234). Apart from Harris's poor whites and some unsuccessful efforts by Thomas Nelson Page to dredge romance from this class,[26] the decades after the war were in the hands of the local colorists and their plain folk. The comic mode was continued but without the crude vitality of the prewar humorists, e.g., R. M. Johnston's *Dukesborough Tales*, 1871, which are "sketches of ordinary people in situations which are awkward, humorous and often pathetic,"[27] without the exaggerations or obscenity attendant on a Ransy Sniffle or Sut Lovingood.

One new type who came into literary prominence during the local color period was the southern mountaineer, who shared aspects of both the poor white and the plain folk stereotypes. Virtually a mystery before the war (except in tales of humorists, where he was not significantly distinguished from frontier types), the mountaineer first came into prominence for the surprising strength of his Union sympathies. However, by the mid-seventies, local colorists began to discover in the southern Appalachians that nearly ideal combination of picturesque poverty, sturdy independence, and quaint custom that was the essence of the genre. At first the fiction concentrated on the excitement and fear of the life of the mountain people—their illicit distilling, fights, feuds, and romances. Later, around 1889, a new emphasis on the misery, filth, and starvation of such an existence began to appear, particularly in conjunction with increasing journalistic exposés of the more intolerable conditions.[28] This new literature showed the poverty of the mountain people to be often as extreme as that of the poorest lowland whites, but they were fiercely proud, in contrast to the dogged apathy to all emotions (save random frenzy) of the trash. According to their main fictional chronicler, Mary Noailles Murfree, they were ignorant, superstitious, and illiterate but pleased to share their hospitality with strangers.[29] Horace Kephart, who published one of the most fascinating accounts of these people, found them by contrast sullen, suspicious, and sly, trained from their youth to dissimulate. Unlike the lowland poor whites they had abundant physical energy, but unlike the plain folk they did not generally direct it to work. As a rule they were less healthy than their homeland might indicate—miserable and undernourished in the mountains and acutely homesick when they left them for the lure of the cotton mills. Kephart found them fanatical about religion but nevertheless indifferent to its moral sanctions, though the fiction writers—as they strove for approval and compassion rather than reforming zeal—avoided more than hints of their sexual promiscuity.

Of the situation of other poor whites after the war, the fiction is virtually silent, despite the great economic upheavals that were bound to alter radically their old norms of subsistence. Ambitious hopes for the redemption of the southern poor by the abolition of the archaic and inefficient institution of slavery appear to have been unduly optimistic. The infertile land and remote regions on which the poor whites eked out their existence with hunting and begging were swallowed up in the conversion of all land to the great cash crops of cotton and tobacco.[30] Their limited capacity for nutritional self-sufficiency disappeared as these inexperienced tenants were forced into a new kind of peonage to their landlords: a vicious circle of debts for equipment and supplies which they had no capital to finance and which necessitated the repeated placing of a lien on their next year's crop.[31] Even the more prosperous class of small farmers appears to have made dubious material gains from the disintegration of the plantations, which frequently became "conglomerates of independent or semi-independent tenant farms,"[32] where these more respectable whites also became submerged in the problems of cash-crop tenancy. If their luck was bad, they were forced to join the grim exodus of poor whites to the cotton mills.

It is to the nonfictional reports that one must look for the postwar fate of the poor whites and ironically also for the perpetuation of their grotesque reputation. John William DeForest's account of his experiences running the Freedman's Bureau at Greenville, South Carolina, is something of a masterpiece in the comic horror tradition. His tales of the filthy, half-naked hags who haunted his office with their perpetual question, "'Anythin' for the lone wimmen?'" reaffirm vigorously the tradition begun by William Byrd. Starvation, disease, and ignorance are allied to laziness, promiscuity, and stealth; rare energy is poured into false efforts to extort compensation from the bureau—"'They don't call it cheating, Major; they call it tryin' to git'"[33]—and the poor whites have already made considerable advances on the biblical injunction for peace by changing "plowshares into begging-bags, and pruning-hooks into baskets" (69). They refuse all opportunities for work while frequently demanding dourly, "'When's our folks gwine to git the land?'" (64). DeForest— convinced that if they were given a few acres, they would merely squat there and remain vagrants—held out little hope for the salvation of this "indigent, ignorant, stupid, and vicious" class, except in an industrialized society with numerous institutions of control. "The chiefest benefactors of the crackers will be those who shall introduce into the South manufactures, with their natural sequences of villages and public schools" (157). This faith—invested in the cotton mills for the trash, the unlucky tenants, and the mountain people who would join them later—was to suffer many assaults, not least from the evolution on the mill hills of a new species of poor white, in many ways more desperate and degenerate than any of his ancestors.

The new industrialism was represented in the South as an altruistic effort to assist those whites who could not be absorbed as tenants and croppers and also to remove them from direct competition with blacks on the land: it was "'not a business, but a social enterprise. . . . The main thing was the salvation of the decaying community and especially the poor whites, who were in danger of being submerged altogether.' "[34] However, this "social enterprise" depended for its success on the existence of a huge surplus market of cheap labor, which was forced to live and work in the most dehumanizing conditions. Just how deplorable these conditions were was revealed in the powerful studies of a southern woman, Mary Clare de Graffenried, an investigator for the Department of Labor, whose highly colored articles and addresses were instrumental in molding a new national image of the southern industrial poor white.[35] "The Georgia Cracker in the Cotton Mills" appeared in 1891 in the *Century* magazine. Copiously illustrated with many sketches of the tattered rags of humanity, it is both a bitter indictment of the sad paradox that was progress, and also a wry commentary on the incorrigible nature of the crackers. This article is an interesting example of the conflicting attitudes that dogged those liberal southern reformers who were also most intimately acquainted with the ways of the poor whites—it fluctuates between extremes of pity and accusation for their misery and the harshest kind of abusive irony and ridicule for their absurd habits. Thus the physique of the mill women provokes the following harrowing tirade:

Twenty years of vitality sapped by summer heat, eaten out by ague, stolen by dyspeptic miseries! Sickly faces, stooping shoulders, shriveled flesh, suggest that normal girlhood never existed, that youth had never rounded out the lanky figure, nor glowed the sallow cheek. A slouching gait; a drooping chest, lacking muscular power to expand; a dull, heavy eye; yellow, blotched complexion; dead-looking hair; stained lips, destitute of color and revealing broken teeth—these are the dower of girlhood in the mills.[36]

On the very next page these pathetic specimens are humorously berated for their (seemingly justifiable) tendency to complain a great deal. "The crackers are a 'whining set,' and valetudinarianism is popular. To be robust and hearty savors of bucolic vulgarity; to be 'allers gruntin' ' approaches the languid delicacy so admired in 'rich folks,' and occult maladies are a gage of respectability" (492). This curious pattern is repeated continuously throughout the article; a touching tale is told of crackers walking barefoot to church over many miles of rough ground, carrying a hard-earned pair of shoes which are lovingly donned at the church door for a grand entrance; yet these are the same people who, when provided with a reasonably decent mill house, "kicked out the panels of the doors, smashed the windows, riddled the walls, and cut up the floor for kindling wood," with the explanation that it was " 'jes ter make things sorter homelike' " (486). They work seventy-two hours a week in enervating and unhealthful conditions but are "irredeemably" lazy; they bow absolutely to the authority and judgment of the bosses yet desert their jobs randomly and irrationally. Despite the article's use of the term "proletariat," the mill worker shows little consciousness of class warfare—or indeed of anything else. "His isolation from current events is absolute, his want of general information fathomless" (493). Yet the crackers are capable of a rather surprising sensitivity, a self-consciousness about their ill appearance before others; one woman, fervently enthusiastic for the consolations of religion, admitted that she had " 'nary rig fitten ter w'ar ter meetin'. Afeerd I'll be grinned at. I'm putty tol'bly homely, but I hates ter be grinned at' " (497). Such incongruities make for lively reporting but give pause to the architects of reform. De Graffenried's final proposals for elementary education and factory legislation seem strangely anticlimactic and limited for such a dramatic and complex problem. The poor white in the mills, like his forerunners on the land, seemed to provoke literary excess readily but abjured, by his quaint loyalties and prejudices, any comparably drastic political remedy.

The peculiar fictional neglect of the southern linthead is not surprising in the immediate postwar period, when the literary emphasis tended to be rural and backward looking. However, his continued absence from novels in a later period, when muckraking and socialist writers were scouring the country for provocative subjects, is another indication of tendencies in the urbanized poor whites that precluded their assimilation for a long time into any kind of radical political tradition. When they lived in relative rural isolation, such people had little consciousness of a sense of discrimination or exploitation. There was no direct conflict with the plantation owners since they were left enough to survive, although not enough to give them any pride in improving.[37] The displacement of these people into factories would normally be expected to produce a keen heightening of such a consciousness, but in the South the essentials of paternalism were carried over from the plantation to the factory system. The mills provided housing in private villages and stores for food and clothing as well as schools, churches, teachers, parsons, and police.[38] The workers were constantly reminded by their newspapers and leaders of the unparalleled benevolence of their masters; in the churches their already profound conviction that the agonies of this world were the direct manifestation of the will of God was confirmed heartily by their preachers. The possible growth of any rebellious mentality toward the bosses was further retarded by calculated efforts to create implacable hostility between the poor whites and the only other class that shared a similar predicament and might have shared their interest, the blacks. As a result, in their desperation to cling to whatever small social advantage they had, they pushed insistently for discriminatory laws and separation: "it took a lot of ritual and Jim Crow to bolster the creed of white supremacy in the bosom of a white man working for a black man's wages."[39]

However, there were a few signs that the much-touted docility of the factory workers might not be permanent. They were acquiring class consciousness of a kind; though scarcely militant, it was a "certain suspiciousness and self-conscious sullenness,"[40] induced by their forcible isolation and contemptuous classification as lintheads, cottontails, and factory rats. They were becoming members of a closely knit community where powerful group loyalties might be formed, particularly on the strength of the close family ties in so many mill villages. Finally, there was the impact on the more apathetic lowland whites of the mountain people, driven from their homes by mining and foresting combines and attracted by mill scouts with promises of high wages. These people, who came and went seasonally from mountain home to mill, brought a frequently violent individualism into the ordered industrial routine. They were not ideal material for labor unions, since they simply would not cooperate effectively,[41] but they were unused to the reputation of an inferior caste and not readily submissive to such a system. These poor whites had scarcely yet evolved into the ideal material of a proletarian novel, but they had certainly passed beyond the literary methods of comedy and local color. A description of their physical appearance bears a startling resemblance to Ransy Sniffle—or even to Byrd's sickly skinned, ague-ridden lubbers—but having lost their squatters' or beggars' freedom, their odd habits and looks were no longer so attributable to extrasocial forces. The deformities remain grotesque and perhaps still provocative of ridicule, but no novelist appeared willing to risk the technique:

> By 1900 the cotton-mill worker was a pretty distinct physical type in the South; a type in some respects perhaps inferior to even that of the old poor white, which in general had been his to begin with. A dead-white skin, a sunken chest, and stooping shoulders were the earmarks of the breed. Chinless faces, microcephalic foreheads, rabbit teeth, goggling dead-fish eyes, rickety limbs, and stunted bodies abounded. . . . And the incidence of tuberculosis, of insanity and epilepsy, and, above all, of pellagra, the curious vitamin-deficiency disease which is nearly peculiar to the South, was increasing.[42]

That such debased specimens of humanity no longer lent themselves to treatment as clowns and villains is apparent; their local color was rather too lurid for the champions of the new industrial régime or for the defenders of the old. Thus, at the end of the nineteenth century, the southern poor white—as he had formerly been known—had virtually disappeared from fiction, although his stereotype was flourishing in historical, sociological, and journalistic writings. Only a complete change in the prevailing literary mode could revitalize this once vigorous southern tradition—a change that was already being demanded forcefully by the critics of the region.

CHAPTER II

The Image in the
Twentieth Century

The necessary stimulus for change came, between 1900 and 1930, not only from literary critics but also from political polemicists. By the turn of the century, critics were already beginning to lament the narrowness of range and archaism of southern writing and warning that its career would soon be exhausted if it did not attempt to widen its scope to include other subjects besides former plantation glory and the quaintness of provincial types. The sternest reprimands came for the willful ignoring of the facts of contemporary life in the South. "Of careful analysis of social conditions, of profound study and comprehension of the principles of human action . . . there are still few traces in the Southern literature of the present generation," wrote William Trent in the *Atlantic Monthly* in 1897. And for John Ormond, writing in the *South Atlantic Quarterly* in 1904, "the most vital criticism of the newer school of Southern fiction is that it does not represent truly the condition of Southern society since the war."[1]

One way of escaping from this trap of nostalgia was heralded by Ellen Glasgow, who declared she made a conscious effort to combat the antiintellectualism of her society and the narrowness of its literary province with a program of "blood and irony" for southern writing. Recalling the great social upheavals of her time, she wrote, ". . . the world was full of fermenting processes, of mutability and development, of decay and disintegration. The old agrarian civilization was passing, the new industrial situation was but beginning to spring up from chaos."[2] Several of Glasgow's novels are concerned with poor whites in these new circumstances, although she was more interested in examining the class barriers that were raised against them when they tried to progress in this society than in realizing the precise quality of their daily lives. In sharpening the edge of her irony against the ruling classes, she tended to ignore the very real obstacles to class mobility that were endemic in the poor whites themselves. This problem of the comic and reactionary image of the poor white would be increasingly complicated as his political partisans became more liberal and radical. In the work of many of the nineteenth-century humorists, the poor white's poverty and horror had shown an ominous tendency to protrude through the grotesque mask of villainy and folly; so for many of the poor white's literary partisans in the twentieth century, his lazy and absurd reputation would dog all efforts to make of him a wrathful and victimized hero. Ellen Glasgow did, nevertheless, initiate at the beginning of this century a serious social attitude toward the poor white and a revived degree of frankness in his treatment, which were later developed by others far beyond what she might have hoped or feared: the social criticism readily became economic propaganda, the frankness turned into the comic and horrific excesses of southern naturalism.

However, despite the primacy of Ellen Glasgow's talent, she had little recognition or appreciation from 1897, when she published her first novel, until long after the end of the First World War. The renaissance she presaged was slow in gathering strength, and with the exception of her own works, historic sentiment and local color dominated the fiction of the first two decades of the twentieth century. Then, in 1917, the self-elected scourge of the region spoke out, heralding in the words of J. Gordon Coogler a scathing attack of the aridity of southern cultural life:

> Alas, for the South! Her books have grown fewer—
> She never was much given to literature.[3]

In the essay that followed, "Sahara of the Bozart," H. L. Mencken exhibited a display of venom, bigotry, misinformation, ill-digested facts, and uncomfortable truths, which he later arrogantly considered to have been responsible for the revival of southern letters in the twenties. This revival may well have been stimulated in part by critical encouragement, for at the same time a number of literary periodicals, dedicated to publishing promising new southern writers and displaying a surprising range of young talent, were appearing. In 1921 the *Double Dealer* was established in New Orleans and the *Reviewer* in Richmond; the next year the *Fugitive* appeared in Nashville. The demands for a worthy tradition in the South were being answered, and the critics rewarded by the flowering of a large number of gifted writers around these centers. The entire scope of literary material was broadened to include many aspects of the New South hitherto untouched as well as a revival of the best of the old traditions under the leadership of Allen Tate, John Crowe Ransom, and Robert Penn Warren, who advocated the conscious archaism of an agrarian society in an industrial civilization. The local color tradition lingered, but it was now tinged with a much more meticulous concern for sociological, linguistic, and economic exactness.[4] The poor white again came into his own in this decade with a plethora of novels dealing with the new realities of his rural existence and historic psychology.

Within this tradition came two of the finest novels of poor whites in the 1920s, Edith Summers Kelley's *Weeds* in 1923 and Elizabeth Madox Roberts's *The Time of Man* in 1926. Both turned again, in the spirit of a very different age, to the figure who had so fascinated Joel Chandler Harris and James R. Gilmore—the poor white woman, denied tragic stature by her powerlessness to affect the course of her life but equally beyond sentimental pity by virtue of a naturalistic emphasis on her most alien and unattractive habits. What is most original in these novels, however, is the effort by Kelley and Roberts to explore fully the consciousness of women whose lives have been limited in every way possible—by the geography and economy of sharecropping on Kentucky tobacco farms, by a culture that encourages their marriage when they are scarcely beyond adolescence, and by their own biology, which causes Ellen Chesser in *The Time of Man* to cry, "'Out of me come people forever.'"[5] Long before the documentaries of the 1930s were to parade photographs of the blank, despairing eyes and sullen bodies of poor white women through the nation's magazines, these two novelists had asserted the fertile visions, yearnings, and resentments imprisoned within the women's apparent acquiescence to the bleakest of existences.

Judy Pippinger is the heroine of *Weeds*. Her sex, her imagination, and her love of beauty are all qualities which in her world foredoom her to failure, since that world is circumscribed by the ugly, ill-smelling sharecropper's cabin and the duties of wife and mother, in which she takes no joy and for which she has no natural aptitude. For Judy, back-breaking labor in the fields, even the harrowing experiences of trench warfare, are preferable alternatives to the stagnant routine of household life, where:

Families must be fed after some fashion or other and dishes washed three times a day, three hundred and sixty-five days in the year. Babies must be fed and washed and dressed and "changed" and rocked when they cried and watched and kept out of mischief and danger. The endless wrangles among older children must be arbitrated in some way or other, if only by cuffing the ears of both contestants . . . . Fires must be lighted and kept going as long as needed for cooking, no matter how great the heat. Cows must be milked and cream skimmed and butter churned. Hens must be fed and eggs gathered and the filth shovelled out of henhouses. Diapers must be washed, and grimy little drawers and rompers and stiff overalls and sweaty work shirts and grease-bespattered dresses and kitchen aprons and filthy, sour-smelling towels and socks stinking with the putridity of unwashed feet and all the other articles that go to make up a farm woman's family wash. Floors must be swept and scrubbed and stoves cleaned and a never ending war waged against the constant encroaches of dust, grease, stable manure, flies, spiders, rats, mice, ants, and all the other breeders of filth that are continually at work in country households.[6]

Under this regimen the lively Judy becomes at first a grim automaton, then a bitter and vicious slut. All the country folk customs that give picturesque relief to farmers' hard lives in local color fiction now appear distorted and desperate efforts to mimic a bucolic myth that had deceived them all.

On one occasion, at a dance, when the "old folks" are persuaded to take the floor, they prove to be only men and women in their thirties and forties; and yet ". . . it was a scarecrow array of bent limbs, bowed shoulders, sunken chests, twisted contortions, and jagged angularities, that formed the circle for the old folks' dance. Grotesque in their deformities, these men and women, who should have been in the full flower of their lives, were already classed among the aged. And old they were in body and spirit" (91). When one of the men, Tom Pooler, collapses on the floor under the influence of the whiskey he has been drinking to bolster his dancing, he defends himself angrily in the boastful rhetoric of the old frontiersmen, a sad comment on their latter-day humiliation: "'I tell ye, I'm a baar in the woods, I am. Nobody don't dass say nuthin to Tom Pooler that he don't wanta hear. . . . I don't take no sass from nobody no matter haow much land they got. . . . I tell ye I'm a baar in the woods'" (92). There is a similiar ironic perversion of popular folk traditions in Judy's brief affair with the itinerant preacher, which ends in neither comedy nor tragedy but in disillusion and boredom.

In this world of *Weeds*, little possibility is held out for relief from the dreary struggle of poverty. The men retreat from this awareness into the numbness of alcohol; the women, deprived even of this, exploit a narrower range of futile resistance—from Judy's withdrawal from her husband to her neighbor Hat's addiction to absurd schemes of self-improvement that she gleans from *The Farm Wife's Friend*. Beyond these temporary retreats from the monotony of endurance, *Weeds* offers no systems of either social reform or metaphysical consolation for these Kentucky poor whites. The book abounds in harsh criticism of the tobacco economy; yet it makes equally clear that material improvements would be meaningless to the heroine, for whom the security and permanence of her own home and farm would still be the antithesis of freedom. The one character in the novel who has achieved some measure of independence is Uncle Jabez Moorhouse, who has something of the anarchical freedom that comes only from absolute deprivation. With responsibilities to none but himself, he can indulge in the simple hedonism of whatever daily routine he pleases and enrich his life with small pleasures that the farm families are too busy to notice. This somewhat Thoreauvian resolution appeals to Judy, but her young life is already encumbered with commitments that make such escape impossible. "Like a dog tied by a strong chain, what had she to gain by continually pulling at the leash? What hope was there in rebellion for her or hers?" (330). Judy therefore "chooses" the only way of life left for her, a willful resignation of her lively consciousness to the numbness of endurance: "Peace was better than struggle, peace and a decent acquiescence before the things which had to be" (330). Immediately after she makes this decision, Judy hears of the death of Uncle Jabez, the living embodiment of her own restless soul. "What light and color had remained for her in life faded out before this grim fact into a vast, gray, spiritless expanse. . . . A weight like a great, cold stone settled itself upon her vitals; and as she gazed out over the darkening country it seemed to stretch endlessly, endlessly, like her future life, through a sad, dead level of unrelieved monotony" (332–33). For the critics who perversely chose to read the ending of this novel as an affirmation of family life and a triumph of the maternal will, there would be many more poor white heroines, with ever-decreasing ambivalence about their primary obligations, to follow Judy Pippinger in the next decade.

The first, in Elizabeth Madox Roberts's *The Time of Man,* 1926, was Ellen Chesser, a girl with a background identical to Judy's, if not lower on the social scale. At the beginning of the novel, Ellen's family belongs to the "road trash" perpetually moving from one piece of agricultural labor to another, camping out at night, and telling fortunes to keep from starving. While Judy suffers the indignities of bedbugs, Ellen does not even have a bed but sleeps on old quilts amid soot and rats. Yet Ellen's world is richer and more lyrical than Judy's, for her imagination makes it so by her capacity to treasure all experiences and glean their significance outside her immediate temporal realm of experience. The timelessness of Ellen's world is a strange by-product of its narrow geographical limitations; in a sphere bounded by the immediate, visible horizons and the distances a wagon can travel in one day, Ellen's mind is constantly running back and forth in time, dwelling on gravestones from the past and her own eventual death. Since she has nothing to be envied by all the other living people on earth, she compares herself constantly to those over whom she does have a unique advantage—the dead. Standing before the grave of Judge Gowan she whispers triumphantly of this "honored citizen": "'And when he was a-liven he used to ride up to town in a high buggy with a big shiny horse, a-steppen up the road and him a-sittin big, and always had a plenty to eat and a suit of clothes to wear and a nigger to shine his shoes for him of a weekday even. . . . He's Judge Gowan in court, a-sitten big, but I'm better'n he is. I'm a-liven and he's dead. I'm better. I'm Ellen Chesser and I'm a-liven and you're Judge James Bartholomew Gowan, but all the same I'm better. I'm a-liven'"(94). Since Ellen can derive triumph from this and likewise from the simple task of tobacco planting—which, moving slowly over hills, silhouetted between earth and heaven, she turns into a ceremonial procession—it is apparent that she will be an unlikely tool for propagandists out to reform the poor white's lot. Elizabeth

Madox Roberts herself asserted that the novel "'could never be an analysis of society or of a social stratum because it keeps starkly within one consciousness, and that one being not an analytical or a "conscious" consciousness.'"[7] Yet, although it is subsidiary to the author's avowed purpose, the work is a remarkable source book of poor white sociology and culture that reveals much of the typical, even when filtered through the exceptional consciousness of Ellen. The reader is bound to respond with revulsion to the filth, vermin, pain, and hunger that Ellen accepts as the normal circumstances of her life and to be aware how much of her superb energy is being sapped battling needless obstacles. When she makes her final biblical commitment to her husband, "'No, I'd go with you, Jasper, wherever you see fitten to go. . . . I'd go where you go and live where you live all my enduren life. If you need to go afore sunup, why then I need to go afore sunup too'" (379), Ellen is no longer a symbol of the resilient power of the poor over adversity. There is no logical reason in the novel for such a triumph; Ellen is credible only as the mythical being, a kind of goddess of life, whose adoring hymn is sung by her friend Luke, "'You're worth all the balance put alongside each other. . . . You're worth all the balance and to spare. You got the very honey of life in your heart'"(366). Unlike Judy Pippinger, who can tolerate living only by shackling her consciousness, Ellen Chesser intensifies her responses to the world around her and thrives on all the accidents of existence. Both women represent a remarkable advance in the characterization of poor whites by their serious philosophical treatment, not as easy agents of comedy or pathos. At the same time there is a new frankness in the exposure of the conditions in which such people live that avoids propaganda while revealing circumstances that certainly appear to justify it.

Ellen Glasgow's novel, *Barren Ground*, 1925, comes a little closer to using the fictional history of a poor white woman as a platform for advocating economic reforms in southern agriculture, although such advice is clearly subordinate in intention to the main scheme of the novel. The heroine, Dorinda Oakley, is a poor white only by her creator's insistence on the label, for she exhibits none of the material, moral, or spiritual deprivation essential to that ranking. She lives with her parents and two brothers on a thousand acres of "scrub pine, scrub oak, and broomsedge, where a single cultivated corner was like a solitary island in some chaotic sea."[8] Having neither money, equipment, nor methods to cultivate what they own, the Oakleys are "land poor"—a result of the marriage of Dorinda's middle-class mother to her poor white father. "He was a good man and a tireless labourer; but that destiny which dogs the footsteps of ineffectual spirits pursued him from the hour of his birth" (9). However, Josh Oakley has none of what Glasgow characterizes as the most typical poor white vice, that of "slighting" his work; so the failure of the farm must be attributed to other causes. These are very clearly set before the reader at the beginning:

> Thirty years ago, modern methods of farming, even methods that were modern in the benighted eighteen-nineties, had not penetrated to this thinly settled part of Virginia. The soil, impoverished by the war and the tenant system which followed the war, was still drained of its lingering fertility for the sake of the poor crops it could yield. Spring after spring, the cultivated ground appeared to shrink into the "old fields," where scrub pine or oak succeeded broomsedge and sassafras as inevitably as autumn slipped into winter. . . . Then the forlorn roads, deep in mud, and the surrounding air of failure, which was as inescapable as a drought, combined with the cutworm, the locust, and the tobacco-fly, against the human invader; and where the brief harvest had been, the perpetual broomsedge would wave. [4–5]

Two things are necessary for making this barren ground fertile— modern agricultural technology and an almost superhuman determination to succeed—both of which Dorinda acquires as a result of her betrayal by her lover. Abandoned and pregnant, she flees to New York, where she finds the strength of will to return and conquer her homeland; she also gains there, rather fortuitously, the necessary information and capital to begin the process. The kind of endurance Dorinda exhibits in building a modern, prosperous, mechanized dairy farm from acres of broomsedge is far different in quality from the forcible anesthesia of Judy Pippinger or the indomitable spirit of life that blooms in Ellen Chesser. Both of these women, in their far more straitened circumstances, derive a mysterious consolation from the landscape that is so much a part of their existence. Dorinda, however, is not sustained by the beauty or the permanence or even the provender of nature but by its incessant demands on her mind and body; it is a sublimation that she willfully forces to suffice after the failure of religion and love. The land that Dorinda labors over and gives her loyalty to rewards her richly in material terms—with lessons of fertilizers, crop rotation, and scientific methods clearly pointed. Less successful is Dorinda's personal triumph, for she has to become a fanatical and ruthless person to win the worldly accolades of her community at Pedlar's Mill, and the victory of heartlessness is not an easy one for a woman originally so ready to love. *Barren Ground* offers few insights into the psychology of the genuine poor whites, but it is rich in ideas for altering and improving the lot of people trapped in an antiquated farming system. There is certainly nothing "radical" in the economic theories of *Barren Ground*, no hints of poor whites cooperating to revitalize the land that died under the hands of a more decadent social class. Rather it displays the success of one driven woman in modernizing a farm, with no community support but that of a rich cattle breeder and a visionary storekeeper; the necessary New York capital for the project materialized out of a happy coincidence. The novel offers the experiences of one woman, far from typical of either her class or sex, who achieves exceptional results in an exceptional situation. The morals of progressive farming and women's talents are all there to be learned, but Ellen Glasgow never permits them to obtrude on the uniqueness of Dorinda's predicament and solution.

The capacity of *Barren Ground* to individualize a familiar enough tragedy and to avoid explicit economic propaganda is precisely what is lacking in Dorothy Scarborough's two novels of rural Texas poor whites, *In the Land of Cotton*, 1923, and *Can't Get a Red Bird*, 1929. Both novels—held together by slender love stories and spiced with a great deal of southern folk music and stock, festive set-scenes of dances, barbecues, and camp meetings—are polemical directives for improving agriculture in the South. The heroes in each case are poor whites, sons of sharecroppers, who dream of escaping from their hereditary bondage and of marrying women above their station. Thus, although Scarborough decries the ills of the cropping and tenant system and advocates drastic reforms in the production, distribution, and marketing of farm products, she avoids any attacks on the class system or hints that such economic changes might invade and alter the whole structure of southern society.

In the Land of Cotton deals most specifically with the evils of the single-crop system and relates in a rather dreary succession of chapters all of the natural disasters to which cotton is prone—flood, drought, the boll weevil, pink boll worms—interspersed by "conversations" among the characters analysing problems and solutions.

All misfortunes are attributed to the farmers' devotion to cotton, including the slump after the First World War and even the grisly death of a baby who falls into a gin; the excesses of this insidious plant are appropriately summed up by one man who says, "'If Job was a character today he'd be a cotton farmer, a share-cropper, I reckon.'"⁹ However, Scarborough has little sympathy for the acquiescent conservatism of the poor who bow in the face of adversity; to the complaint that cotton is cruel, her poor white hero, Ben Wilson, asserts that man is stupid and proceeds to outline a complete program for diversification, crop spraying, government loans, and long-term controls on storage, distribution, and prices. Ben, no ordinary poor white, has emerged from Baylor University a crusading idealist for reform, who dies guarding his wealthy sponsor's cotton crop and leaves his theories to be pursued by more pragmatic people with money and influence behind them. Although clearly propagandistic in purpose, *In the Land of Cotton* has no particular political ideology; many of the practical reforms it advocates were implemented later under the New Deal, but Scarborough largely avoids trifling with broader social criticism—the attitudes exhibited toward race and the war are far from the usual liberal ones and even farther from the left-wing writers who took up these issues again in the thirties.

Can't Get a Red Bird, 1929, initially gives promise of being a broader-based indictment of a society where poor whites of the high mental and moral caliber of the hero, Johnny Carr, are forced to remain in degrading poverty even while they recognize the accuracy of his claim, "'I maybe am poor myself, but we ain't pore folks.'"¹⁰ There is much greater emphasis in this book on the exploitation of croppers and tenants by landowners and on the impossibility of a poor white's breaking out of the chains of servitude. "All this talk about how any man in America could get ahead was fool talk. It was hard for a man to get a start, when he had no money, no schooling, no land of his own, no pull" (118). There are plenty of hints too of a new rebelliousness among southern women —from the middle-class Honey Barrett, who wishes to abandon her farm life for a career teaching French in the city, to the poor white Phrony Duggins, who resents her ceaseless childbearing and the pious arguments that fail to ease her misery:

"Seem to me like I ain't done nothing all my married days, but drag around havin' babies, an' weanin' 'em, an' startin' 'em to the cotton patch. Seems to me like I'd bust wide open with puore joy ef I could have one more night of gal sleep, one more care-free day!"

"Hesh, woman! 'Tain't Christian to complain o' yore lot. Looks like criticizin' the Almighty fer what He sends."

From under the slat bonnet came a flash of fire. "Mebbe there's others has a hand in it 'sides the Almighty!"

"Shet yore mouth, woman! Don't the Scripters say, 'Blessed is the meek, for they shall inherit the yearth?'"

"Tain't so! They don't inherit it, they jest *farm* it!" [76]

Nevertheless, the resolution of the novel, though rich in reforming plans, retreats into an uncritical acceptance of all the traditional values that were initially questioned. Johnny Carr does become a success through hard work: he rises at the end to a position of wealth and power without the un-American aid of family rank, money, and education. Honey sacrifices her plans for an independent career to become a farmer's wife, bear four children, and spend her few hours of leisure time reading the Bible. The rebellious Phrony's complaints are finally dismissed as the outcome of shiftlessness. The economic lessons of *Can't Get a Red Bird* are drawn in a much wider sphere than those of the earlier novel; the narrative moves outward from the first formation of an agricultural cooperative in one Texas county to the financial system of the United States and finally to the money markets of the world. Yet, in doing so, it rapidly abandons any effort to depict the quality of life among the poorest people, which would demonstrate the necessity for the reforms. Thus the novel tends to become the success story of the one poor white who transcended his origins and rose to power and wealth, albeit in the service of farmers' interests.

Jack Bethea, in his novel *Cotton*, 1928, pushes an almost identical situation one further unpalatable step by having his reforming poor white hero reap his rewards in the form of an upper-class bride and profitable returns for his employer, a northern corporation that is moving into the cotton farming business by buying up plantations in Alabama from their destitute southern owners. Larry Maynard is a poor white who has made good by spending fourteen years outside his native state, traveling and studying the world cotton markets. When he returns home, it is for the purpose of avenging the epithet "poor white trash" and bringing the methods of corporate efficiency to southern cotton growing. Since Larry immediately becomes embroiled in rivalry and opposition to Evan Shelby —the leader of the old, corrupt, inefficient system—the book easily becomes a confrontation of theories between the petty private profiteering of the past and the impersonal and amoral profiteering of the new capitalism. Bethea's, and therefore Larry's, theories are soundly based for deriving the maximum financial returns from the land, but there is less concern for the allocation of these benefits. There is little sense in *Cotton* of poor whites as a distinctive social class; the tenants and croppers on the plantation are black, and most of the whites are small-time landlords. Thus Larry's role is as prophet and hero of the new methods of farming rather than as representative of the poorest class. However, the black sharecroppers do derive some rewards from Larry's administration since his pragmatism leads him, instead of offering shares, to pay wages that are forced up by Shelby's rival efforts. As in Scarborough's books, economic and organizational reform of cotton growing and distributing is not allied in any way to broader social reforms, and there is none of that concern for revealing the intolerable dreariness and meanness of the lives of the victims of the present system that predominates in the novels of Kelley and Roberts. Food is supplied to the workers, but their welfare is always subordinate to the yield of the cotton crop; tiny children are used to help in picking with the rationale that they will make a game of it.

At the other end of the social, though not the economic, scale from the black laborers are the heroines of the book, the two Yates women who owned the plantation Larry now rules and who live in the "Big House." The house and its furnishings are perfectly preserved relics of the prewar era, where mother and daughter dine poorly but proudly off spotless but well-mended linen, by the light of gleaming old silver. Larry's modern efficiency enables him to resuscitate these ghosts of the past and, in his love affair with Mary Ruth Yates, to marry the Old South to the New. The final scenes of the novel retreat into pure antebellum fantasy, as Larry, the new master of the Big House, summons the black workers from their "quarters" on Christmas morning to distribute largesse in the best plantation fashion. They grin and caper in delight at the nuts and candy that are given out by this benevolent lord and swear to name their newborn "black mites" after him. The moral obtuseness of this novel, whereby corporate efficiency from the North helps resurrect the corpse of the *ancien régime* in the South, represents the extreme version of the novels of the 1920s that attempted to turn fiction not merely into economic propaganda but into textbooks of agricultural methodology. The closer they come to endorsing highly specific reform programs, the more their interest in the actual plight of the poor white diminishes and, ironically, the less humane they appear.

Scarborough and Bethea were both forced, by the exigencies of didacticism, to adopt stereotyped, maudlin plots in order to provide regular emotional diversion from the heavy weight of raw economic and sociological data. But, more ominously for the fictive future of the poor white, they were obliged to betray those qualities of character that had created the poor white's fascination in the first place—the combination of violence, inertia, absurdity, and cunning that had incongruously made these poor people as grotesque and contemptible as their poverty. The new poor white heroes in these novels brought to their reforming careers no evidence of the physical, moral, or spiritual deprivation of their backgrounds but only a moral fervor for improvement and a concentration on its means that were completely alien to repute. Even Kelley and Roberts, who had not disguised the numbing effects of want on intellect, energy, and conscience, had largely avoided the problem of humor, which might undermine even the most meticulous naturalism. Only one writer in these early years of the southern renaissance attempted to revive the old comic poor white and ally him to serious social criticism—T. S. Stribling, who ridiculed victims and victimizers alike with a sarcastic fury that exposed the entire South as a bastion of reactionary conservatism, bigotry, and appalling self-righteousness. Stribling added some empirical local authority to H. L. Mencken's vituperative attacks on the savage South, but his perspective was more intimate, his understanding of southern history less clogged by antebellum stereotypes of an aristocracy of genteel intellectuals,[11] and his outrageous natives subjected to serious analysis and explanation as well as comic derision.

Stribling's novels move off the land and into small towns and villages, where petty conformity represses all individualism and initiative and is enforced by lawless hypocrites. Two of his southern novels are set in Lane County, Tennessee, a remote, hill-encircled region that is an obvious forerunner of Faulkner's Yoknapatawpha, both in the balance of decayed aristocrats, Negroes, and poor whites who inhabit it and in the use of a single neighborhood to provide characters and histories that recur in slightly differing forms. His first novel, *Birthright*, 1922, is also set in this Tennessee valley region; but it deals with relationships between blacks and whites and not with poor whites as a distinct social class. However, it is an appropriate introduction to Stribling's ironic technique, which is far from subtle, and his social theories, which are devious and frequently puzzling. The irony consists largely of the juxtaposition of blatant inequities in the legal status of the two races: a black war hero arrested on a three-year-old warrant for crap shooting must wait for his trial and sentencing while the justice of the peace finishes his own gambling game of rook on his elegant lawn; Peter Siner, a Harvard-educated black, must abandon the comfortable Pullman car as his train leaves Cairo, Illinois, and move through the day coaches of the poorer whites into the noisome and noisy Jim Crow car. The ideology of the novel seems to argue strongly against the double standard of law and morality that is enforced on the two races; Peter Siner finds after reflecting on his white employer's library that all intellectual life in the South has been contaminated by this duplicity, born of the refusal to accept the humanity of blacks:

> Scarcely a department of Southern life escapes this fundamental attitude of special pleader and disingenuousness. It explains the Southern fondness for legal subtleties. All attempts at Southern poetry, belles-lettres, painting, novels, bear the stamp of the special plea, of authors whose exposition is careful.
>
> Peter perceived what every one must perceive, that when letters turn into a sort of glorified prospectus of a country, all value as literature ceases. The very breath of art and interpretation is an eager and sincere searching of the heart. This sincerity the South lacks.[12]

However, as though to avoid the label of "special pleader" for an opposing cause, Stribling somewhat paradoxically presents blacks whose sensitivity, ambition, and energy are apparently in proportion to the amount of "white" blood in their veins; whatever is lazy, dishonest, and immoral is attributed to their black heritage.[13]

Stribling's next novel, *Teeftallow*, 1926, deals with the utter poverty and monotony of the lives of poor white Tennessee hill people—a physical and spiritual dreariness punctuated only by the thrills of gambling, drinking, whoring, and fighting and by the massive orgies of purgation that follow religious revivals. Abner Teeftallow, the hero, is a prime example of Stribling's theories of environmental determinism. Brought up in the county poorhouse, robbed of his inheritance, he is buffeted entirely by fates beyond his control; he in turn performs his own share of violence, victimization, and betrayal. Ab has no moral code, no education, no resources of any kind; limited in intelligence, he is at the mercy of all the random external impulses that sway the lives of such aimless poor white youths. Like the rest of the hill people in Lane County, Ab is most suspicious of those who would help him—such as Ditmas, the northern engineer, and Shallburger, the union organizer; and his is most completely the dupe of those who conspire against him—the banker Northcutt and the magnate, Railroad Jones. Jones indeed is the hero of the whole community he has swindled and whose finances, jails, and laws he controls; since the poor whites have an absolute contempt for the law, they idolize those, like Jones, who manipulate it to their own ends, even when, perversely, those ends are directly contrary to the people's interests. The corruption of law and government by power, money, and guile has produced in these people a peculiar mixture of cynicism and dogmatic faith, though the cynicism tends to be directed toward institutions, and the faith to those, like Jones, who distort their proper working.

Most of the humor in *Teeftallow* is concerned to expose the entrenched prejudices and the corresponding profound fear of intellect that underlie the rituals and taboos of acceptable conduct in Lane County. Shallburger attempts to organize a strike against Railroad Jones by talking of "class consciousness," "unearned increment," and "plutocrats"[14] to men who believe that a Bible in their breast pocket will protect them in a gun fight. The hopelessness of bridging the chasm between organizer and poor whites, the ineffectiveness of Ditmas in bringing even a degree of common sense or honesty into local business dealings, and the suicide of the village eccentric and infidel, Belshue, offer little encouragement to revolution, reform, or even tolerance. True to the stereotype, these hill people commonly exercise hostility and violence—they are not the apathetic and exhausted poor whites of lowland tradition. Many of them are eventually persuaded by Shallburger to strike against the railroad, but their motives are highly suspect, and they desert as irrationally as they had joined. Stribling's use of northerners as the vehicles for criticism and attempted improvement infuriated many southerners, despite the fact that the reformers too are revealed as naive and foolish. It is obviously tactless of Ditmas, in the atmo-

sphere of the impending Scopes trial, to challenge parochial fundamentalism by trying to organize a Sunday baseball game, and
Shallburger's left-wing propaganda pays little heed to the personal
element that often belied the expected relationship between employer and worker in the South.

In *Bright Metal*, 1928, Stribling further explored the dilemma and
inadequacy of northern critics of the South by showing the steady
erosion of the integrity and aspirations of Agatha Pomeroy as the
Lane County environment began to work its effect on her. This
young actress comes as a bride to the South with all the unques-
tioned assumptions of Greenwich Village liberalism and very rapidly
finds her capacity for ridicule and outrage strained by the complacent guise of conservative ethics that covers all moral expediency
and antiintellectualism. Agatha's efforts to promote election reforms
through organizing the women voters misfire drastically; not only
does she aid the opposition, but she herself becomes slowly corrupted into manipulating people and institutions for her personal
ends. Her pregnancy and fear for the child's future offer the best
incentive to desert Tennessee forever, but when this rootless Cali-
fornian boards the bus to leave, she finds that the South has exerted
a stronger grip on her than she thought possible. It has given her not
only a family and home but also some understanding of the irrationality and fatalistic religiosity that sustained the hill people's
lives, as she explains to a critical "outsider" on the bus: "'You see,
order is not one of the strong points of the South. The accidental,
the . . . er . . . illogical rules down here. Really it's hopeless to ask a
people to believe in scientific law and order in the midst of social
disorder; when every day they are whirled and tossed by chance . . .
and rescued by miracles.'"[15] Such comprehension and sympathy
are completely unanticipated in the course of the novel, whose
absurd rogues and hypocrites appear to brook no such vindication;
they certainly do not prepare one for the bathetic ending when
Agatha waits weeping in the rain to return to them and a new moon
slides through a rift in the clouds. Stribling weakens his strange
brand of harsh, comic determinism with such an arbitrarily imposed
"happy" ending and his retrospective efforts to explain characters
like Napoleon Suggs, obvious heir to his shifty literary ancestor,
and Fatty Bobbs, the grotesque local constable who shoots out the
tires of speeding cars. These and many more characters, as well as
the courtroom farces, belong in a tradition of humor that antedates

Stribling's naturalism. His efforts to meld ridicule with compassion and environmental analysis remain incongruous, though they prepare the way for more effective later combinations of the same qualities in Faulkner and Caldwell.

Just as important as his efforts to revive poor white comedy was the acuteness of Stribling's recognition of the gulf that existed between the mind of the North and that of the South, epitomized in their most extreme poles in liberal reformers and poor whites. His apparent concentration on evils exclusively southern brought him some harsh criticism from Robert Penn Warren for "hick-baiting" or setting up criteria that were sophisticated, metropolitan, liberal, and northern by which to judge the inhabitants of southern rural backwaters.[16] Yet Stribling's most ambitious work, the Vaiden family trilogy, which would appear in the early 1930s, shows its author to be just as disgusted with the influx of northern urban commercialism into the South as he was with the hypocrisies of the old plantation system there. The three trilogy novels—*The Forge*, 1931; *The Store*, 1932; and *The Unfinished Cathedral*, 1934—span the years from just prior to the Civil War until 1930 and provide Stribling's historical perspective on the changing social relationships and institutions of the South. One of the prime objects of Stribling's satire in these novels is religion. In the first volume he ridicules the dogmatic fundamentalism of old Jimmy Vaiden and the pious superstitions of the slaves; but in the last volume, it is the modern, corporate institution of the church that is under attack, a situation that might well have pleased the Agrarians. Stribling's amused sympathies go in the end to the "Drownders," a visionary and unworldly sect born out of a drowning man's hallucinations—a religion, in fact, of the "hicks."

Since Stribling is interested in the complete social fabric of the South in this trilogy, poor whites tend to recede to their accepted place on the periphery of life and to their old roles of comic villains. Although no character or group in the novels wins much of the author's esteem, only the poor whites remain incorrigibly contemptible, thorns in the flesh of black and white society alike. Violent, irascible, jealous, they pursue schemes of money making and revenge that are both petty and absurd—from the horse-thieving Leatherwood gang, who pose as Confederate sympathizers in order to justify stealing mules from a Union man, to Eph Cady, the "trash" who dynamites the unfinished cathedral on top of its benefactor in erratic revenge for a minor but long-nurtured grudge. These poor whites are comic partly because the people on whom they prey are scarcely more virtuous but also because Stribling is less interested in their poverty and more in their functioning in an elaborate plot. The trilogy is generally considered the author's finest work and certainly his most famous, but it was in the novels written in the 1920s, despite the earlier incompetence of the plots and the frequently uncontrolled violence of his sarcasm, that Stribling created a vision of a grotesque and alien society that had yet a consistency in its illogicality that might be ignored by later and more utopian left-wing writers only at their peril.

By the end of the 1920s, almost every area of poor white rural experience had been explored for the fiction-reading public, while the industrialized factory worker was still totally ignored. Yet there was throughout this decade a great upsurge of interest in sociological studies of the mill worker, in such books as *The Rise of the Cotton Mills in the South*, 1921; *Darker Phases of the South*, 1924; *Cotton Mill People of the Piedmont*, 1927; *Southern Mill Hills*, 1928; and *Some Southern Cotton Mill Workers and Their Villages*, 1930. But the fiction writers' interest in the economic realities and emotional abnormalities of the lives of rural poor whites seemed to end with their migration to the towns and mills. Since the squalor and cruelty of their existence there was no longer the kind of obstacle it had been to apologists for the New South—indeed it was more likely to be a positive advantage to this generation's interests—Shields McIlwaine has proposed that the reason for their neglect was that only in the country did their "peculiar, historic psychology" operate. "The urban chapter of the Southern poor-white is being enacted in the cotton mills, where actually he is no longer a poor-white in the old country sense, but a 'lint-head,' an industrial pawn, hardly differentiated from his Northern brothers."[17] Nevertheless, by 1930 there were at last signs that the southern mill worker might have his fictional day as the hero of American literature's newest genre, the proletarian novel. This realization developed from both the literary trends and certain political events toward the end of the twenties.

The leftward swing in the allegiance of so many American writers, generally considered coincidental with the depression, had actually been given a substantial theoretical and aesthetic basis in the 1920s in the socialist and Marxist periodicals of such writers as Floyd Dell, Max Eastman, V. F. Calverton, Joseph Freeman, and

Michael Gold. While the lost generation exiles went off to Europe on the "gaudiest spree," these men stayed behind to plot the course of revolutionary art and to prepare to welcome home those disillusioned intellectuals into the literary service of the left wing. The most vigorous of these was Michael Gold, editor of the Communist *New Masses*, who, while insisting that he wanted nothing to do with "the temperamental, Bohemian left, the stale old Paris posing," was nonetheless aware of the propaganda value of attracting some of these decadent poseurs to the cause. It was partly to this end that Gold set out to explore the possibilities of finding real proletarians in America and discovered them in the unlikely southern linthead. Almost every edition of the *New Masses* after Gold's takeover of the editorship in 1928 contained articles on the political theory of the proletarian novel—how, specifically, it might be written, by whom, what material might be used, and where it might be found. Gold's attention was first drawn to the South by the completely unexpected nature of events there in 1929: the textile workers, viewed generally by the left as hopelessly inert, went on strike in Greenville, Elizabethton, Marion, and Gastonia with violent and bloody consequences.

The *New Masses* celebrated its May Day issue for 1929 with jubilant horror—the hero and location of the future revolution had been discovered—to go left meant to go South. "Who said there were no proletarians in America? Look inside a southern mill village. . . . Stirring days lie ahead in the Carolina Piedmont. . . . 'The Southerners are hot stuff. Hard to get into action, but when they're mad, they're mad clear through!'"[18] As more grisly reports of exploitation, victimization, and bloodshed began to pour in from the southern mills, a moral outrage was generated in the *New Masses* virtually rivalling that of the Sacco-Vanzetti affair but with one very important difference: these workers were "'docile, 100% Anglo-Saxon Americans. None of your damned foreigners.'"[19] And their revolt heralded more hope to the Marxists for a genuine groundswell among American workers than all the powerful rhetoric of the two foreign anarchists. The feverish pitch of the reporting in the months following suggests that the *New Masses* was determined to make the maximum propaganda possible, both in politics and literature: "The battle in the tent colony in Gastonia symbolizes the advance of a new contingent of the American proletariat—the working class of the south:"[20] ". . . liberals who continue to deplore the use of the term 'class-warfare' should go down to Gastonia and reality."[21] Events in the southern textile strikes were seen as the confirmation of Marxist theories of the inevitable class struggle in microcosm. The reactionary peasant class, dispossessed and displaced, had become the urban industrial proletariat, attuned to the ideals of revolution; repression and persecution brought renewed sympathy from other workers and solidarity in the movement. This was good general propaganda, but the details offered more material for speculation, perhaps indeed more than was necessary or desirable for the Communist cause. For the strikers, coming from the area which had moved most rapidly from feudalism to industrial capitalism, also came from the area where the past was least easily set aside; they were still poor whites and continued to think of themselves as such.[22] As a literary tradition they had been imbued with myth, mystery, humor, and horror—scarcely the most tractable substance for the unswerving logic of dialectical materialism. The inherent tension between southern tradition and Marxist metamorphosis, between reactionary poor white and revolutionary hero would become the basis for a considerable number of novels in the 1930s, six of them based directly on the Gastonia strike. Not all would endorse radical political solutions, but all of the writers had clear leftist sympathies that led them to examine the urban poor white and finally give him as much attention as the sharecropper and tenant.

Thus, at the brink of the 1930s, there was a greater interest than ever before in the southern poor white. The period began with a confluence of events and attitudes that made possible the broadest range of literary exploration: a renaissance in southern writing and the invigoration of an old tradition, a new ideological approach to literature and the historical moment most sympathetic and receptive to the poor white's predicament. T. S. Stribling had begun to revive the violent comedy of the poor white and put it in the context of a clearly deterministic pattern of history and environment; Elizabeth Madox Roberts and Ellen Glasgow had explored the consciousness of these people and had seen possibilities for remarkable endurance and perhaps even heroism there; Edith Summers Kelley had exposed the intimate and brutal details of poverty among tenants and sharecroppers; and Jack Bethea and Dorothy Scarborough had articulated possible solutions for this suffering. Sociological and journalistic surveys had begun amassing information about all aspects of southern life, and the literary left wing had placed at least its fictional hopes in the revolutionary fervor of the textile worker. In the depression decade, when the attributes of poverty were more vividly apparent to all, the poor white's allusive image would inevitably take on new and more political significance as writers developed the tendencies of this literary tradition to their extremes.

CHAPTER III

Faulkner's Celebration of the Poor White Paradox

The years that marked the sudden flowering of the proletarian novel in America coincided with the most productive period of William Faulkner's literary career and his most extensive treatment of the left wing's newly discovered fictional hero, the southern poor white. Thus while radical writers began to depict the metamorphosis of a backward peasant into a revolutionary fighter, Faulkner was reaching back into southern history, folklore, and mythology to revive both the humor and the horror of this character's tradition. Though his novels are full of the most extreme consequences of the material poverty of poor whites—the deprivation of body, mind, and spirit—Faulkner was neither politically nor aesthetically attracted to the ideals of the literary left. Indeed he strongly repudiated any kind of social tendentiousness in art:

... if one begins to write about the injustice of society, then one has stopped being primarily a novelist and has become a polemicist or a propagandist. The fiction writer is not that, he will use the injustice of society, the inhumanity of people, as a—as any other tool in telling a story, which is about people, not about the injustice or inhumanity of people but of people, with their aspirations and their struggles and the bizarre, the comic, and the tragic conditions they get themselves into simply coping with themselves and one another and environment.[1]

Yet in his treatment of poor whites and of southern society generally, Faulkner is as acutely class-conscious as any Marxist and as prone to patterns of economic sympathy and class allegiance. Such tendencies may be seen in their most extreme form in the story "Tall Men," which is a direct and highly polemical rejection of the New Deal; elsewhere in the novels there is abundant evidence of a social conservatism that displays compassionate concern for the individual but staunchly rejects the possibility of furthering it through organizations or institutions.

Faulkner's poor whites are never divorced from the worldly conditions of their existence, but these conditions are not—as in so many of the poor white novels of the twenties—the substance nor even the most influential shaper of their lives. To the sense of place that produced Stribling's narrow hill people, to the gothic naturalism of Edith Summers Kelley and the exploration of consciousness of Elizabeth Madox Roberts, Faulkner added a new sense of the historical and the mysterious. His poor whites exist in a more comprehensive setting than any of their forebears; yet they continue to defy any wholly rational explanation. His Snopeses are confidence tricksters in the tradition of Simon Suggs and all the other rogues whose only capital was their cunning ability to exploit others. In this they conform to the ethic of their society; yet such knowledge scarcely tempers the strangeness of their sudden emergence from the swamps and backwoods like a new species come to ravage humanity. Even Lena Grove, the comic, bovine goddess, and Popeye, the embodiment of sinister evil, are more than the logical products of heredity and environment, as are the Bundren family in the variety of their absurdity. Those incongruous qualities of the poor white—villainy, pathos, and comedy—so perplexing for writers who wished either to ridicule or improve them, could be fused in Faulkner's vision without danger of weakening any rigid ideological design.

Like Stribling's Lane County, Tennessee, Faulkner's Yoknapatawpha County in northern Mississippi was a literary universe; for poor whites the locale was even further restricted to the hill-cradled area around Frenchman's Bend, where "there was not one Negro landowner in the entire section. Strange Negroes would absolutely refuse to pass through it after dark."[2] The people in this area are tenants, yeomen farmers, sharecroppers, and small tradesmen with their own religious and moral codes. "They supported their own churches and schools, they married and committed infrequent adulteries and more frequent homicides among themselves and were their own courts, judges and executioners"(5). Not all of these people are strictly poor whites, but there are plenty of examples of even the most extreme form of that genre who would scarcely give cause to question William Byrd's original stereotype. There is a timeless quality about their rural life that causes their naiveté and primitivism to contrast all the more sharply with the urban backgrounds against which they are occasionally placed. This comic contrast is obviously one of the staples of the southern humorous tradition, as are the grisly tales, animal antics, and stock folk types (lecherous preachers, fabulous liars, wise idiots) that Faulkner also draws heavily on.

As I Lay Dying, 1930, deals with a family of rural poor whites who are forced by a crisis—the death and burial of the mother—out of their habitual inertia into violence, disaster, and farce. The setting is almost contemporary, though except for the few details that establish the time, it might as easily be placed a century earlier. Several critics have noted the similarities between the situation of the Bundrens in *As I Lay Dying* and the Compsons in *The Sound and the Fury*—each threatened family has a sensitive son, tending to madness (Darl/Quentin); a promiscuous daughter (Dewey Dell/Caddy); a pragmatic materialist (Cash/Jason); and an idiot younger child (Vardaman/Benjy). In each family the sins of the mother and the weakness of the father are visited on the children, but while the upper-class Compsons descend to tragedy and disgrace, the trashy Bundrens survive a grotesque parody of tragedy and in doing so provoke a kind of wry incredulity at their foolhardiness. Faulkner uses the comic stereotype of the poor white and his traditions as a base from which to explore beneath the stereotype each individual's private consciousness and beyond it the values of the society that supports the Bundrens.

Anse Bundren, the father of the family and the closest approximation to the comic villain of tradition, is a man of unbounded laziness; he hates to move so much that he detests roads because they imply the necessity. He cannot work because of a disease which, he insists, will cause him to die immediately if he ever sweats; Doc Peabody says of him, " 'Too bad the Lord made the mistake of giving trees roots and giving the Anse Bundrens He makes feet and legs. If He'd just swapped them, there wouldn't ever be a worry about this country being deforested someday.' "[3] Such a comic portrayal of sloth, combined with the selfish obsession of

Anse to achieve his personal goals when he gets the funeral moving, tend to undermine considerably the moral righteousness of some of his more "class-conscious" thoughts. Yet the implications of passages like the following from Anse cannot be wholly dismissed by the irony of their emergence from a dishonest, parasitic, and irreligious man. "Nowhere in this sinful world can a honest, hardworking man profit. It takes them that runs the stores in the towns, doing no sweating, living off of them that sweats. It aint the hardworking man, the farmer. Sometimes I wonder why we keep at it. It's because there is a reward for us above, where they cant take their autos and such. Every man will be equal there and it will be taken from them that have and give to them that have not by the Lord" (104). The Bundrens' poverty is indeed very real, and its pathos is more clearly apparent in the child Vardaman's confused dream of possessing a toy train that is beyond his reach because he is a poor country boy. "Because I am a country boy because boys in town. Bicycles. Why do flour and sugar and coffee cost so much when he is a country boy. . . . 'Why aint I a town boy, pa?' I said. God made me. I did not said to God to made me in the country" (63). Vardaman, in his childish ignorance, has not yet learned the poor white's rationale of stoical submission to the will of God. Poverty is at every point a compelling and obvious factor in the Bundrens' lives, but Faulkner does not permit it to interfere in any direct way with the kinds of moral decisions the various members of the family make; idleness, suffering, and victimization typify but do not explain or dismiss them.

Faulkner uses other aspects, too, of the comic and macabre folklore of the South as a means of classifying the Bundrens at the lowest social level and at the same time of affirming their humanity. A gruesome fascination with the rites of death exists somewhat paradoxically among these people who hold the life of the living relatively cheap. Among the poor white women, particularly, who have witnessed the rapid decay of their beauty in life, the necessity of being clad in finery for death is a compulsion. Thus the women attendants who lay out Addie Bundren are so concerned to display the fullness of her wedding-dress shroud that they place her reversed in her carefully balanced coffin, so as not to crush it; then the lavishly clad body is permitted, by the family's incompetence, to decompose and stink for seven days in oppressive summer heat. Similarly, Vardaman's efforts to assist his mother's comfort end in gothic farce: obsessed by the fear that Addie will suffocate in the coffin, her child bores holes through the lid into her face. Yet, despite their hideous outcome, these events are merely the fumbling efforts of neighbors to add a little ceremony to death and of a grief-stricken child to relieve his mother's imagined agony. They are the external manifestations of good will but limited intelligence, and as such, they are appropriate images of a central theme of the book, which demonstrates the increased sensitivity and humanity of the protagonists in direct ratio to the closeness of our perception of them. The horror can finally be understood as an incongruous result of compassion and concern.

The disaster-ridden funeral had already a notable place in southern humor from Sut Lovingood's tale, "Well: Dad's Dead," which heaped indignities upon the corpse and left the surviving spouse more concerned about loss of teeth than of partner.[4] As I Lay Dying uses similar details, but Faulkner fuses them into a broader scheme wherein the grim antics of the poor whites reflect and caricature a common human trait. The grueling journey they undertake to fulfill Addie's request to be buried in Jefferson is absurd in any objective telling of the plot. The hazards of flood, fire, starvation, injury, and ridicule are excessive by any standards, whether they be those of the binding loyalty of a death promise or the satisfaction of other irrelevant and selfish desires in the city. The nobler motive is undercut by the fact that the Bundrens do not give up when it has become apparent that their journey is a travesty of all rituals of respect; the more cynical motive too is hardly rational or plausible: false teeth for Anse, a glimpse in a toy shop window for Vardaman, even an abortion for Dewey Dell seem scarcely in proportion to the scale of danger and horror which they must surmount to get them. Only in terms of obsession—sometimes comic, occasionally tragic—does this odyssey appear credible, and it is this aspect of human conduct that the book explores from as many different levels of perception as possible.

The narrative method of the novel presents the Bundrens from at least four perspective distances: most remote is that of city strangers who know nothing about them but what they observe on this occasion and who are prone to very strong prejudices about the rural poor; a closer view is given through the eyes of neighbors and friends who know their customs better but are also swayed in judgment by their personal whims; closer still is the intimate but highly partisan vision of other members of the family; finally they are known to the reader through the private voice of their own consciousness. Thus, to MacGowan and Moseley in the city, their cortege is an outrageous object of ridicule: "like a piece of rotten cheese coming into an ant-hill, in that ramshackle wagon that Albert said folks were scared would fall all to pieces before they could get it out of town, with that home-made box. . . " (193). To the Armstids and Tulls, who know them better, the homemade box is the painstaking work of a dedicated carpenter son. However, they too allow their prejudices to attribute their own motives to the Bundrens: "They would risk the fire and the earth and the water and all just to eat a sack of bananas" (133). Tull thus assumes they are off on a perverse picnic, while to Cora, his wife, they are behaving in typically sacrilegious Bundren fashion, "flouting the will of God to do it. Refusing to let her lie in the same earth with those Bundrens" (21). In the tight sphere of family relationships, motivations are seen to be much more complex and more directly related to the pervasive influence of Addie, as Olga Vickery has pointed out.[5] Finally, inside the private worlds of the characters, we see that people who are extremely limited materially and intellectually may nevertheless be capable of great intensities of endurance, heroism, and passion. Their jealousies, sins, and obsessions are not vindicated by this evidence that the Bundrens are susceptible to all the emotions of their social superiors; but if not justified by the recognition of this fact, they are certainly granted a measure of dignity by it and thereby temporarily detached from the alien and degrading stereotype of the poor white.

This elevation is made possible not only by the multiple narrator technique but also by the language of the novel. People whose oral language is restricted to terse, formulaic, ungrammatical, and almost wholly practical utterances are permitted in their mental language a range of philosophical speculation and colorful and complex imagery that emphasizes a degree of activity and sensitivity not to be expected from their actions and conversation alone. Thus, to the drugstore clerk Dewey Dell " 'looks like a pretty hot mamma, for a country girl' " (232); to Cora Tull, a spiteful but more knowing neighbor, she is a careless and undutiful daughter; her actual spoken language (usually a single-minded preoccupation with the possibilities of obtaining an abortion) is dull and repetitive; but in the private world of her mind, the experiences of this stupid, promiscuous, and selfish girl take on a quality that is both humanly compassionate and mythic. Thus, the pregnant girl about to milk a cow becomes an image of fecundity and life, intensely aware of her secret identity with the earth: "The cow breathes upon my hips and back, her breath warm, sweet, stertorous, moaning. The sky lies flat down the slope, upon the secret clumps. Beyond the hill sheet-lightning stains upward and fades. The dead air shapes the dead earth in the dead darkness, further away than seeing shapes the dead earth. It lies dead and warm upon me, touching me naked through my clothes. . . . I feel like a wet seed wild in the hot blind earth" (61).

The stylistic innovations in *As I Lay Dying* consistently work to humanize the poor white in a way that avoids the pitfalls of pathos and sentimentality. Faulkner simultaneously undermines and reinforces the class stereotype by using it for external impressions and comedy and by exploring beneath it in the internal monologues. Poverty is important in the novel as an accepted way of life that helps to classify the Bundrens socially and shape their living habits, but it is conservatively taken and certainly not viewed with any sense of urgency or horror. No class of oppressors or exploiters exists in the book; indeed there are few glimpses of any social stratum other than the Bundrens' except for the noble and comical figure of Doc Peabody and the townsfolk of Mottson and Jefferson. The horror in the book derives less from poverty than from the uncontrollable physical elements which the Bundrens must battle and the absurd fixations that drive them on against seemingly insuperable odds. The comedy comes from their foolhardy straining of such limited material and intellectual resources. The agent of deprivation is not so much society as the villainous father Anse, who forfeits the hopes and vanities of the entire family to his selfishness. Sooner than accept the loan of a neighbor's willingly offered mule team, Anse, determined to possess a new one of his own, ravages the clothing of his wounded son Cash to steal the money he had saved for a gramophone. When this is not enough, he barters away the most precious possession of his son Jewel, his horse. He forcibly takes away Dewey Dell's abortion money to buy his false teeth and finally betrays Darl into a lunatic asylum sooner than risk a fine for his barn burning.

Insofar as the abstraction "society" plays any part in the novel, it is through the community of friends and acquaintances who constantly help the Bundrens on their way and have, from their sardonic comments, frequently been compelled in the past to help them too. Society in *As I Lay Dying* means Tull, who says of Anse, "Like most folks around here, I done holp him so much already I cant quit now" (32). It means Samson, who offers them all shelter, saying, " 'Well, would you have had me turn them away at dark, eight miles from home? What else could I do' " (108). It means Armstid: "Because be durn if there aint something about a durn fellow like Anse that seems to make a man have to help him, even when he knows he'll be wanting to kick himself next minute" (183). It means finally Peabody, "seventy years old, weighing two hundred and odd pounds, being hauled up and down a damn mountain on a rope. . . . because I must reach the fifty thousand dollar mark of dead accounts on my books before I can quit" (42). In a world where charity like this exists, the question of pervasive poverty is made irrelevant; the compassion and resilience of individuals become wonders to be marvelled at rather than symptoms of social ills. Heroism consists not in resistance but in stoicism. "I mind my mammy lived to be seventy and more. Worked every day, rain or shine; never a sick day since her last chap was born until one day she kind of looked around her and then she went and taken that lace-trimmed night gown she had had forty-five years and never wore out of the chest and put it on and laid down on the bed and pulled the covers up and shut her eyes, 'You all will have to look out for pa the best you can,' she said. 'I'm tired' " (29).

At the beginning of the novel, Coral Tull says piously, "Riches is nothing in the face of the Lord, for He can see into the heart" (7), a statement which, though weighted with some irony, might still be an epigraph for the whole process of the novel. With a God-like opportunity to see into the hearts of these poor whites, we find that indeed wealth and poverty are not to be used as moral arbiters of man and his society. The poor are certainly not blessed, but they are permitted to triumph and sin with the same range of dignity and folly as the rest of humanity.

By thus permitting his poor whites to be both heroic and humanly fallible, Faulkner necessarily deflected attention from their exploitation as a clearly defined social class. In *As I Lay Dying*, the rural setting admits scarcely any other class to be depicted by contrast; and in the other novels that are set in small towns and cities, the poor whites tend to be represented by the criminal class—the *lumpenproletariat* of gangsters, bootleggers, thieves, and prostitutes—or as the aspiring con men who remain classless but progress by preying on every class. *Sanctuary*, published in 1931, has a large population of the criminally poor, but in this novel their capacity for evil unites them to every other class, for the general subject is the pervasive moral corruption of all classes and sexes. The middle-class ethic is condemned at least as harshly as the criminal code of the destitute by those few characters who represent the last despairing vestiges of idealism and integrity. The central dramatic horror of Popeye's rape and murder carries no more moral censure than the hypocritical behavior of the "respectable" Jefferson townsfolk: the savage lust of Temple Drake and her betrayal of an innocent man, the treachery of Narcissa Benbow Sartoris, the uncharitable-ness of the women who refuse to offer shelter to Ruby Goodwin and her sick baby, and the false standards of the men who relish vicariously the details of Temple's violation and then satisfy their sadism by lynching the supposed culprit. The bitter portrayal of middle-class decadence is not balanced, as in proletarian novels, against the stalwart virtues of the working class; the poor in *Sanctuary* are as corrupt and debased in the modern world as the rich. Only the few people who look backward—either to a primitive, rural peasant existence or to an aristocratic ideal of conduct—offer any hope of moral survival.

Horace Benbow and Ruby, the only people who display any admirable moral stature, are both relics of a nobler age, and both suffer acutely for it. Horace who believes that " 'perhaps a man might do something just because he knew it was right, necessary to the harmony of things that it be done,' "[6] is finally broken of all his illusions of making a stand against injustice: he sinks back into the cynical world of his wife and stepdaughter. His stand is the last sign of moral life in the fallen nobility of the book; Gowan Stevens is of the same class, but this drunken defender of southern womanhood abandons Temple sooner than face her contempt. The cabdriver who bears Horace on his final defeated journey home was also once a member of the aristocracy. "In the old days, before the town boomed suddenly into a lumber town, he was a planter, a land-holder, son of one of the first settlers. He lost his property through greed and gullibility" (290). Now, in response to the news that Temple's rapist has been lynched, this old man voices the complete emptiness of all southern codes of honor: " 'Served him right. We got to protect our girls. Might need them ourselves' "(291).

The theme of amorality is occasionally reiterated in comic form in the novel, as in the episodes concerning the comfortable and maudlin complacency of Miss Reba, the brothel madam. Her brothel is the source of some standard comic incidents concerning poor whites in the novel, with Faulkner adding a further twist to the old story of country innocents who mistake a brothel for a hotel by having them sneak in and out of Miss Reba's establishment in order to visit a brothel. The grim humor of the incidents at Red's wake is also traditional, but neither the sexual nor the funereal comedy of *Sanctuary* serves as much mitigation of the horror of the main narrative, since they are so closely tied to its somber theme.

Although the emphasis in this book is on the loss of ethical sensitivity throughout society and the merging of all levels of moral conduct into cynicism and hypocrisy, poor white figures stand at its extreme points of good and evil (albeit strange and distorted figures of saint and devil). The moral boundaries of *Sanctuary*'s world are measured by Ruby Goodwin and Popeye, the best and worst that a debased world can produce. Throughout most of the book, Popeye represents an impenetrable evil, but in the final chapter Faulkner apparently decided to root this grotesque figure firmly in the human world by revealing some of the forces that contributed to his making. While this has some effect in assisting a comprehension of Popeye's evil, it in no way mitigates its alien character—in fact by dwelling on the horror and madness of his origins, Faulkner tends to emphasize a feeling that corruption is endemic in the universe. His father is a streetcar strikebreaker, utterly without loyalites: "'I don't care a damn who is running the car, see. I'll ride with one as soon as another'" (295). Leaving her a legacy of syphilis, he abandons Popeye's constitutionally weak mother while she is pregnant. The ailing child is reared by a mad grandmother who repeatedly tries to burn him to death; his future prospects are sexual impotence and certain death if he ever touches alcohol. If these social and psychological factors represent a satisfactorily naturalistic background to Popeye's unusually vicious disposition, we are left facing the sheltered, advantaged prosperity of Temple Drake, whose receptive capacity for evil does not appear to be fully tested, even in the horrors of this book. If the two are products of their environments, then truly there is no escape from forces so ubiquitous that class, money, sex, education, and even health cannot resist their invasion. At the end Faulkner juxtaposes the images of the two after society's judgment on them: "the slum *lumpenproletariat*, the scum of the earth,"[7] is last seen adjusting his hair before the hangman's noose, while beneath the dripping trees in Paris, Temple stares sullenly into her compact mirror. In the revenge the world takes on them, their disparate origins are apparent, but in the moral scheme of *Sanctuary*, they are members of the same class.

Ruby Goodwin and, in fact, the whole poor white society living on the old Frenchman place, without the intrusion of Popeye and Temple, represent an ironic semblance of harmonious family life and social responsibility. Although they deal in bootleg whiskey for disposal in the cities while the land lies overgrown and uncultivated, although their origins are in the lowest stratum of urban criminal society rather than in rural simplicity, there is nevertheless a kind of pastoral rhythm to their lives that compares favorably with any glimpse of city life presented. Ruby, Lee, their baby, Lee's ancient and decrepit father, and the idiot Tommy do not form a particularly attractive group, yet they display in crude fashion a sympathy and a sense of responsibility for each other. At first glance they look like a typical rural family: the woman, clad in calico and brogans, stands in the kitchen cooking meat for the supper; the men come in from outdoors in muddy overalls, and they sit down and dine together. Strangers are always asked to join their meal. While they eat, and afterwards, it becomes apparent that this unwholesome society of lawless people supports unthinkingly its own feeble and foolish, unlovely and unhealthy members. Their manners and customs are often repellent—Horace Benbow's refined sensibilities force him to look away from the table as the toothless old man sucks and nuzzles at the mixture of bread, meat, and sorghum that the woman has prepared for him—but they assume automatically duties and loyalties that those who presume to judge them violate. The best of both societies in the book confront each other in the persons of Benbow and Ruby, but her wisdom is always superior to his high purposes. Shocked at her primitive existence, he voices the bourgeois clichés of his world in an attempt to "save" her, " 'Why do you do it? You are young yet; you could go back to the cities and better yourself without lifting more than an eyelid.' " To this, the former prostitute replies only, " 'The poor, scared fool' " (16).

The stoical pity Ruby showed for Horace changes into a flood of bitter hostility in her late confrontations with Temple: sexual jealousy, class hatred, and some basic tough notions of exchange value pour out in furious confusion:

"Oh, I know your sort. . . . Honest women. Too good to have anything to do with common people. You'll slip out at night with the kids, but just let a man come along. . . . Take all you can get, and give nothing. 'I'm a pure girl; I don't do that.' You'll slip out with the kids and burn their gasoline and eat their food, but just let a man so much as look at you and you faint away because your father the judge and your four brothers might not like it. But just let you get into a jam, then who do you come crying to? to us, the ones that are not good enough to lace the judge's almighty shoes." [55]

Temple, less acute than Benbow, utterly fails to appreciate a moral scheme outside the realm of college flirting and hereditary prestige. She has none of his interest in these people, and, attempting to bribe Ruby with a secondhand fur coat, she misjudges her even more hopelessly than Horace does. This obtuseness provokes the proud response, " 'Clothes? I had three fur coats once. I gave one of them to a woman in an alley by a saloon' " (59).

Ruby, the "whore as madonna"[8] who pays dearly in physical suffering and mental anguish for her attempts to preserve loyalty and love, is the only person to emerge from *Sanctuary* with an unblemished moral character. She is in no sense a reformer or fighter—that role is left to Benbow, who is defeated and mocked for thinking he can use political institutions to ensure justice. The more the futility of legal methods is revealed, the more absurd and fantastic his notions of the moral power of the law become, until he is finally left murmuring, " 'Night is hard on old people. . . . Something should be done about it. A law' " (292). Horace's philosophy of action, " 'because . . . it was right, necessary to the harmony of things,' " is forced to take second place to Ruby's, " 'Asking nothing of anyone except to be let alone, trying to make something out of her life' " (113). Horace is fighting a world where visible and invisible evil entwine so closely that the moral crusader needs more resources than those available to one isolated and disillusioned Memphis lawyer. Since Faulkner was unimpressed by the potential of contemporary movements that were attempting to provide both a philosophy and a program of action for eradicating social evil and since he chose to imply in *Sanctuary*'s world the existence of an evil beyond human ken, the only possibility left for heroism is in the individual efforts of people like Ruby to survive with their own kind of integrity.

After *Sanctuary*, where he depicted only dehumanization and automatism in the modern world, Faulkner refused to consider the possibility of any reform emerging from its laws, government, or institutions. Beyond *Sanctuary* he moved towards an increasing admiration for independent, conservative, yeoman values and an even greater concern with the past. The excessively grim circumstances of the 1930s scarcely appear at all in his work; so after *Light in August*, published in 1932, poor whites tend to appear in historical settings for the rest of the depression decade. Faulkner reintroduced in this time a species of poor white who had long been unsuitable for the South's sentimentalist writers and who would be absolutely ignored by the Marxists—the confidence man. Bearing evil into the communities through which they move and, like their famous predecessors, exposing the innate corruption of those communities, Flem Snopes and his kin begin to appear. The works tend to concentrate more and more on the loss of an ethical center in the lives of both the poor and the landed gentry, a decay of purpose that mutually rebounds on master and servant through their intimate association with one another.

The short story "Wash" was published in *Harper's* in 1934 and incorporated, somewhat altered, in *Absalom, Absalom!* in 1936. It deals with anachronistic loyalty between poor white and landlord and explores the psychological foundations on which this loyalty is built. The relationship between Colonel Sutpen and Wash Jones is full of the paradoxes of life in a class-ridden society where rank is carefully observed; yet people live in close physical intimacy with the members of other social groups. Despised as white trash by the slaves, Wash, a squatter in a dilapidated shack on the Sutpen plantation, is at the very bottom of the social scale; yet he spends his Sunday afternoons in lazy companionship with Sutpen. "The two of them would spend whole afternoons in the scuppernong arbor, Sutpen in the hammock and Wash squatting against a post, a pail of cistern water between them, taking drink for drink from the same demijohn."[9] Wash, "gaunt" and "malaria-ridden," still retains a kind of pride in this seeming independence, although he recognizes that the slaves who taunt him are better housed, clothed, and fed than himself. His loyalty to Sutpen is not built on any kind of financial obligation to him, nor is it gratitude for the meager friendship Sutpen deigns to offer. Sutpen—or rather, the idea of Sutpen—fills a void in the desolate world of the poor white, a world that is empty spiritually and emotionally as well as physically. He offers a vision of all the high, chivalrous qualities that can only exist in a feudal world. For Wash, he becomes a kind of alter ego; he can imagine that his own dreary existence is only an illusion "and that the actual world was this one across which his own lonely apotheosis seemed to gallop on the black thoroughbred, thinking. . . , 'A fine proud man. If God himself was to come down and ride the natural earth, that's what He would aim to look like'" (538).

The story is set in the period immediately before and after the Civil War, which reduces Sutpen from an aristocratic landowner to a small storekeeper—"He dispensed kerosene and staple foodstuffs and stale gaudy candy and cheap beads and ribbons to Negroes or poor whites of Wash's own kind" (539)—but however degraded Sutpen may have become, or perhaps to whatever base level he has returned, Wash is reluctant to relinquish his idol. When Sutpen begins to court his fifteen-year-old granddaughter with ribbons and clothes, Wash affirms his certainty, amid neighboring taunts, of the nobility of character that exists in Sutpen, "'I ain't afraid. Because you air brave. . . . And I know that whatever you handle or tech, whether hit's a regiment of men or a ignorant gal or just a hound dog, that you will make hit right'" (541–42). The reaction of the two men to the birth of a girl child to the granddaughter finally exposes all the false assumptions on which the friendship had existed. Wash delightedly exclaims, "'Yes sir. Be dawg if I ain't lived to be a great-grandpaw after all'" (543). Sutpen shows himself not merely ignoble but inhumanly cruel: "'Well, Milly, too bad you're not a mare. Then I could give you a decent stall in the stable'" (535). Wash, finally forced to watch the disintegration of his ideal, at first says unbelievingly, "'I kain't have heard what I thought I heard'" (544), but when the situation is confirmed by Sutpen's slashing at him with a whip, Wash acts quickly and effectively with Sutpen's scythe to erase twenty years of falsehood. In the novel *Absalom, Absalom!* an extra dimension is added to the vengeance of Wash, for there it is revealed that Sutpen was originally a poor tenant, who, like Wash, was refused the privilege of entering a plantation house by the front door. This incident shaped all his aristocratic aspirations until they are appropriately cut down by his alter ego. His grand design of "revenge for all the redneck people"[10] fails not merely because of his inability to have a son but because he violates the proprieties of the heroic ideal that his situation supposedly demands. In the story the exposure of Sutpen leads Wash to speculate on the falsity of all the southern aristocrats, "the gallant, the proud, the brave; the acknowledged and chosen best among them all to carry courage and honor and pride" (549). In the novel Sutpen is revealed as not belonging properly to the ranks of these men but as being an obsessed pretender. Wash's life becomes worthless, *"like a dried shuck thrown onto the fire"* (549), only because Sutpen's is so hollow. There is ultimately no rejection of the *ideal* of feudal loyalty as long as the sense of *noblesse oblige* is maintained. One critic says that the story is "not a repudiation of the aristocratic concept so much as a criticism of it. . . . It is an indictment, but it is also a challenge, a challenge to those whom nature or fortune has placed above the average of mankind."[11] Thus, when the background of Sutpen as a former poor white is given, the story becomes a defense of the traditional ideal against the debasement of it by the amoral newcomer—certainly not a complete rejection of the class structure. Without this necessary information from the novel, there is still a strong suggestion in the metamorphosis of Wash at the end, from lazy shiftlessness to courageous avenging fury, that he has indeed been "teched and changed" by the virtues he believed Sutpen represented. Though the virtues are false, Wash's faith in them appears finally to have ennobled this lowly and scorned man.

That Faulkner, despite his frequent portrayals of dissolute and decadent nobility, genuinely seems to have believed that they had higher qualities than other ranks of men and certainly the capacity to inspire superior behavior among the lower classes is amply illustrated again by his story "Barn-Burning." This story, one of Faulkner's best known, has merited a good deal of critical attention. From this, there appears to be a general consensus of opinion in interpretation: Ab Snopes, the barn burner, is Faulkner's devil, disrupting the social order, destroying all sense of permanence and stability in his own family and the countryside. His younger son, Colonel Sartoris Snopes, experiences a kind of epiphany in Major DeSpain's mansion, which appeals to him as a haven of peace and dignity. This feeling, combined with a vague, supernatural osmosis of the noble qualities that must attend this given name of Sartoris, enables him to attempt to put an end to his father's terror by betraying him into the hands of DeSpain and almost inevitable death. Ab, in his contempt for tradition and order, is seen as a fitting progenitor of the Snopes family, whose attitudes "ultimately become identified with the current philosophy of materialistic progress in its brazen disdain of all conceptions of human dignity, courage, honor and love."[12] Thus the story is seen as a clear defense of the *ancien régime*, which is a stay against the chaos of the modern world—an interpretation that places Faulkner's conservatism, in the light of the details given in the story, in a very unsympathetic vein.

For the boy Sarty there is a much greater conflict going on than that between "the old fierce pull of blood" which demands loyalty to his father and the desire for respite from the outlawed life they lead. There are two moral systems at war in his mind, neither of which he completely subscribes to. The vengeful bitterness of Ab Snopes is only partially explained as the result of a foot injury, "where a Confederate provost's man's musket ball had taken him in the heel on a stolen horse thirty years ago."[13] In *The Hamlet*, Ratliff, relating Ab's story, attributes his vice to quite another cause, and in the general bewilderment about the precise reason for his souring, critics tend to ignore the fact that his hostility to the whole world of property owners is grounded in a keen understanding of his own place at the bottom of the social hierarchy. Though Ab is certainly no egalitarian activist, he goes to some trouble to expose Sarty to the inequities and exploitation of the class that lives in those elegant fortresses of stability and calm that so appeal to his son's hatred of his own involuntary disorder. Before the visit to DeSpain's mansion and the soiling of the white rug, Ab says to his son, " 'I reckon I'll have a word with the man that aims to begin tomorrow owning me body and soul for the next eight months' " (9), but this pointed reminder of allegiance does not prevent the almost magical effect the place has on the boy. "He saw the house for the first time and at that instant he forgot his father and the terror and despair both"(10). Sarty even hopes that perhaps his father will feel the spell too and be changed by it. Thus, while Ab is stamping his defiance into the rug, Sarty is "deluged as though by a warm wave by a suave turn of carpeted stair and a pendant glitter of chandeliers and a mute gleam of gold frames" (11). Though this sounds very little superior to the "brazen materialism" of the ruthless moderns, it seems paradise itself to the boy. Ab's account of it is geared to destroy any illusion. " 'Pretty and white ain't it? That's sweat. Nigger sweat. Maybe it ain't white enough yet to suit him. Maybe he wants to mix some white sweat with it' " (12). That Sarty is not deaf to his father's arguments is shown in his reaction to DeSpain's attempt to extort an unfair amount of reparation in corn from Snopes for the damage to the rug. His sense of justice assures him that his father will be right to refuse it: " 'He won't get no twenty bushels! He won't get none! We'll gather hit and hide hit! I kin watch . . . ' " (16). Thus the boy is not merely torn between Snopes blood and Sartoris spirit but between the claims of the oppressor and oppressed. He can agree with neither DeSpain's punishment nor his father's reaction to it, which, in keeping with his fiery integrity, is to burn the barn. Yet the boy, by virtue of his age and status, has no other options—he suffers "the terrible handicap of being young, the light weight of his few years, just heavy enough to prevent his soaring free of the world as it seemed to be ordered but not heavy enough to keep him footed solid in it, to resist it and try to change the course of its events" (9). In the end Sarty repudiates his father's action by warning DeSpain; thus he is forced to take one of the sides, and his desire for peace and order is a strong one. The action is a heroic one, initiating Sarty into the complicated adult world; but it is certainly no clear moral triumph, for in rejecting his father's obsessive violence, Sarty has also rejected his class and permitted himself to be used as a tool of a violence no less immoral, as the major goes after his father with a rifle. Sarty has placed himself on the side of "the element of steel or of powder" (7) against his father's more primitive element of fire "as the one weapon for the preservation of integrity" (8). If Faulkner presents DeSpain's house as a desirable symbol of order, it is certainly not the idyllic Eden of a system superior to worldliness, materialism, and violence. All his own predilection for tradition, stability, and peace does not prevent him from exposing in this story some of the unsavory foundations on which they are based.

After "Barn-Burning" in 1939, Faulkner wrote little more about the southern aristocracy. "The families of the old order—Sartorises, Compsons, Sutpens—have been abandoned, and with them, the mixture of nostalgia and moral censure they aroused in Faulkner. Now, as the Snopes clan moves toward the forefront, the main opposition to its growth comes not from the old patriciate, . . . but from several independent farmers, men of a kind only occasionally seen in earlier Faulkner novels."[14] *The Hamlet*, 1940, relates the impact on Frenchman's Bend of the arrival of the Snopeses—the barn burner and his many descendants—and the way in which they both disrupt and implement the tenor of life there. The social spectrum in Frenchman's Bend is a limited one, ranging from the affable economic tyranny of its main property owner, Will Varner, than whom "a milder-mannered man never bled a mule or stuffed a ballot-box" (5), through the frugal small landowners to the extreme level of poverty of the Labove family and many of the Snopeses. Most amazingly poor of all is the old man, Uncle Dick. "He had no kin, no ties and he antedated everyone; nobody knew how old he was—a tall thin man in a filthy frock coat and no shirt beneath it and a long, perfectly white beard reaching below his waist, who lived in a mud-daubed hut in the river bottom five or six miles from any road. He made and sold nostrums and charms, and it was said of him that he ate not only frogs and snakes but bugs as well—anything that he could catch" (349–50).

The people in the village are mercilessly exploited with a fine show of careless benevolence by the Varners, but in the context of the novel, double-dealing, duping, trickery, and blackmail of all kinds are an accepted way of life and the source of general humor and enjoyment. This comic perspective is given through the agency of V. K. Ratliff, who is a modern version of the wandering minstrel —the community's purveyor of news, earthy wisdom, and entertainment. Since the foremost characteristics of the natives of Frenchman's Bend are their individualism and their capacity to respond to challenge, they have no means or even desire for communal redress of their grievances against the Varners. They play a game whose rules are not in their favor but whose antagonist they understand perfectly—a man of rich passions and normally human failings. With the arrival of Flem Snopes, the conflict is no longer between the canny farmer and the known scoundrel but between bewildered victims and the dispassionate and inhuman calculations of a man whose soul is " 'a little kind of dried-up smear' " (151) and who arrives in hell prepared for eternity with a gross of asbestos bow ties.

Flem is not entirely a new kind of poor white. Like Sarty, his younger brother, he sees no future in the meager transient life of the sharecropper; but rather than trying to achieve the rural haven of mansion and estate that inspired both Sarty and Sutpen, Flem—preying by stealth and cunning, without even the emotional justification of a "grand design"—moves into an increasingly urban environment. Although there is a strong critical tendency to define Snopesism as though it were a consistent family characteristic (even Ratliff remarking of Mink, " 'this here seems to be a different kind of Snopes like a cotton-mouth is a different kind of snake' "), the family which filters slowly into the village shows a remarkable degree of disparate behavior and disposition. Eck is "a man who was not lazy, whose intentions were good and who was accommodating and unfailingly pleasant and even generous" (67); Ike's capacity for unselfish love, even when the object is Houston's cow, contrasts pointedly with Flem's economic bargaining for Eula; Mink's passionate nature is the opposite extreme of Flem's emotional indifference; Lump has similar Machiavellian tendencies to Flem's but lacks his scheming intelligence; I.O. is a fairly harmless buffoon. Faulkner himself may be largely responsible for this theory that the Snopes family represents a single principle of acquisitive modernism by his numerous references to it, recorded in *Faulkner in the University*, but *The Hamlet* gives little evidence of any standard Snopes conduct, unless it is simply their initial general movement from whatever backwoods and swamps they originated in to the village. Perhaps mere motion is sufficient to condemn them all since it must inevitably bring change in its wake, as they infiltrate and then permeate first village and then city life.[15]

The Hamlet returns to traditional forms of southern and frontier humor; it explores most widely the traditions of animal humor—in the conventional forms of the spotted ponies and horse-dealing episodes and also in the development of animal-human analogies. Houston's stallion is the "polygamous and bitless masculinity which he had relinquished" (218) in his marriage; the Texas ponies too become identified with the self-assertion of the men who gamble money and time on them; Eula is linguistically and thematically associated with the bovine world, and Ike Snopes's cow is called a whore. Tall stories of trickery and double-dealing abound, but there is also a darker side to the humor that develops during the novel. In the early horse- and mule-swapping episodes of Ab Snopes and Pat Stamper, Ab's carelessness with necessary money for the family results in the tables being turned by his wife, who indulges in the final farcical folly of swapping the cow for a milk separator which can only be run on borrowed milk. When a very similar incident involving the Armstids arises at the end of the novel, the humor turns suddenly tragic; here the real results of this swaggering male nonchalance with money are measured in terms of acute misery. This is one of the occasions when Faulkner reveals just how precarious the economic foundation of these people's lives is, how slender their resources, how vulnerable to pay a high price for folly. Poverty, however, is consistently shown as an accepted mode of living and is frequently treated with humor, as in the case of the poor white family of the young schoolteacher Labove, who are outfitted in University of Mississippi football boots and sweaters. Money is not permitted to become a matter of overwhelming importance in the community until the arrival of Flem Snopes, who can make even the earth goddess Eula part of a sordid financial arrangement, and of Lump, who charges money for a peep show of Ike and the cow. There is no suggestion that the inhabitants of Frenchman's Bend were in any way innocent or unworldly before, but Flem seems to act as an inevitable agent of monetary consciousness, so that even Ratliff, the one person who attempts to combat Flem, is finally duped into revealing his own greed.

Ratliff's ubiquitous presence in the novel is intended as a foil for Flem's equally pervasive influence; so he is often involved directly as a positive counterbalance to Snopes's inhumanity. Frequently, he fulfills Flem's own abrogated responsibilities—hammering up the wall of the barn to protect Ike, placing money in trust for him with Mrs. Littlejohn, compensating Houston, and looking after Mink's wife and children when he is arrested. This is all done in a perfectly private capacity, and though its effectiveness in combatting Flem's evil is obviously very limited, Faulkner insists on presenting Flem as a force that cannot be resisted any other way, by community or other organized action. The switch in heroes is a significant one from a character like Horace Benbow, a latter-day member of one of the cavalier families who was utterly defeated by evil in *Sanctuary*, to V. K. Ratliff, the sewing machine salesman with no pretensions to family, social, or educational preeminence, though descended from someone who fought in the American Revolution. In sympathies he is closer to the poor, although a friend of the rich; his worldly aspirations are appropriately contrasted to Flem's in the comparison between Ratliff's freshly laundered blue shirts and Flem's dirty, sweat-stained white ones. Ratliff's is frequently the voice of honor, tolerance, and generosity, and though in the last section of *The Hamlet* he too is shown among the poor whites as a victim of Flem, even in defeat he remains "anecdotal, humorous . . . quizzical, bemused, impenetrable" (366).

This final section, "The Peasants," although introduced by the comic episode of the Texas ponies, witnesses the pervasive destruction Flem has wreaked on the small community in terms that are close to tragic. When Flem is challenged by Ratliff about Henry Armstid's disabling injury, his reply is an interesting one: "'If a man aint got gumption enough to protect himself, it's his own lookout'" (317). This has in fact been the code of Frenchman's Bend before Flem's arrival, but the people have also been willing to volunteer help to each other when necessary. Even now, there is certainty that other neighbors will help out the Armstids as they had the Bundrens in *As I Lay Dying*, but Flem recognizes no human responsibility, either individual or communal. Thus, although Faulkner constantly insists on individual responsibility and solutions for both private and social ills, he also asserts the dependence of people on their local communities. In one of his class sessions at the University of Virginia, when discussing the possibility of organized action to defeat Snopesism, he said: "I doubt if people accomplish very much by banding together. People accomplish things by individual protest."[16] Remarks like this are placed in a context in the novels which emphasizes that individualism should not mean personal isolation or a callous disregard for the welfare of neighbors and friends. However, as soon as Faulkner perceives this concern being taken over by other agencies that are neither direct nor personal, he rejects them very bitterly, both in public speeches and fiction.

The short story "Tall Men," published in 1941, is an outspoken attack on the policies of the New Deal, especially those that were aimed at improving the situation of the rural poor in the South. The efficacy of the policies is not questioned at all (although there is some evidence that the Agricultural Adjustment Act fell largely into the hands of planters to administer and often worked against the sharecroppers and tenants), but the political theory behind welfare legislation is sharply and emotionally rebutted. This story represents the extreme crystallization of attitudes less polemically expressed in the earlier works; in its assertion of the supremacy of individual rights over those of the group, it is certainly no less propagandistic than the novels of the Communist writers who proposed a contrary philosophy. "Tall Men" is scarcely a short story at all but a scene in the life of the McCallum family—heroic, tough, independent farmers—which serves as the text for a sermon on their invincible qualities compared to the spinelessness induced by soft and risk-free living in a welfare state. Stylistically, there is no evidence to suggest that these attitudes, voiced by the old marshal, are to be modified by any other information or point of view given in the story; thus it may be assumed that they are Faulkner's own. The narrative part of the story concerns the efforts of a young federal officer to serve an arrest warrant on two of the McCallum sons for failure to register for the draft. This has nothing to do with any effort to resist war service: the patriotic and courageous history of the family is repeatedly emphasized, and when the officer attempts to issue the warrant, the boys' father says to them, " 'You just enlist wherever they want to send you, need you, and obey your sergeants and officers until you find out how to be soldiers.' "[17] Thus the family's unthinking patriotism is in no danger of being impugned. The officer is presented as a naive stranger in the district, and part of the moral superiority the marshal has over him is the fact that he had "been born and lived in the country all his life" (45). We are warned at the outset by the old man that a lesson of some sort will be learned from this visit to the McCallums, " 'And ever since we left Jefferson I been trying to tell you something for you not to forget. But I reckon it will take these McCallums to impress that on you' " (45–46).

The federal investigator is prone to assume that all southern farmers are out to dupe the government and misuse state aid, but with the first glimpse of the McCallum household, he is introduced to another tradition of rural southerners that Faulkner was coming to hold increasingly dear—plain yeoman farmers, self-sufficient, proud, clannish, and unfailingly courteous. We are told after witnessing their log house and the polite though distinctly uningratiating behavior of the first member of the family that "the investigator was a man of better than average intelligence; he was already becoming aware of something a little different here from what he had expected" (48).

Introduced finally into a room full of McCallums, we see that their tallness has nothing to do with physical stature but more with the fact that one who is lying in bed with his leg horribly mangled, says immediately," 'it was my own damn fault' " (49). Inevitably, we are confronted with a saga of heroic masculinity, from the grandfather Anse's walk to Virginia to join the Confederate Army to the amputation of Buddy's leg with no anesthetic but a jug of whiskey. While this gruesome operation goes on, the marshal sits outside telling the history of the McCallums and philosophizing on their sturdy rejection of government interference. They no longer farm cotton because of the government's attempts to regulate its production by stabilizing prices and requiring that the surplus be withheld from the market; to offers of payment for reducing their crop, the McCallums reply, " 'We'll just make the cotton like we always done; if we can't make a crop of it, that will just be our look-out and our loss, and we'll try again' " (56). They are unable to sell this cotton the first year of the new regulations, but the next year, still believing " 'in the freedom and liberty to make or break according to a man's fitness and will to work' " (56), they repeat the process. Their final decision not to accept the new regulations and to switch to cattle rearing is made on perhaps the most amazing theory of all, but one which establishes them as the final opponents of all change—" 'father would have said no' " (57). Scarcely any effort is made in the story to make this point of view particularly persuasive, except for occasional humorous jibes at the government's determination to pay them subsidies no matter what they do. The marshal's speech becomes instead a piece of emotional invective against " '. . . the rest of the world all full of pretty neon lights burning night and day both, and easy, quick money scattering itself around everywhere for any man to grab a little, and every man with a shiny new automobile already wore out and throwed away and the new one delivered before the first one was even paid for, and everywhere a fine loud grabble and snatch of AAA and WPA and a dozen other three-letter reasons for a man not to work' " (58). In the midst of this speech, the young man is asked to hold the bloody, sheet-wrapped bundle of the amputated leg, and his rather gingerly handling of it provokes a further diatribe on the modern lack of backbone. This culminates in the remarks, " 'Life's a pretty durn valuable thing. I don't mean just getting along from one WPA relief check to the next one, but honor and pride and discipline that make a man worth preserving, make him of any value' " (60). After this, the marshal stands up and proves that he too is a "tall" man.

This story illustrates the most unpleasant aspects of Faulkner's traditionalism, which causes him to create a naive and unrealistic dichotomy between the heroic McCallum supermen and the faceless, spineless, dehumanized machine-people created by federal bureaucracies. As a Jeffersonian ideal, the McCallums can only exist in an archaic rural corner which has not yet been penetrated by industrialization or even by the realities of depression agriculture. In the concreteness of the historical situation in which they are placed, they represent a wishful nostalgia for what might have been, certainly not an example that can offer much hope of dignity or honor to the kind of poor whites depicted in the WPA publications, those living on depleted soil without even the possibility of buying the most basic farm tools. To place the multiple three-letter programs of the New Deal in the context of these farmers who neither needed nor welcomed them is not to achieve a very effective condemnation of them. Faulkner's fear of innovation, embodied particularly in the fear of the encroachment of the federal government in the South, creates here a defense of tradition based on the dubious virtue of the toughness it produces in its protagonists—the ability to substitute whiskey for morphine and to refuse to consider cooperating in an organized scheme for public welfare because father would have said no. One of his critics has suggested that in "Tall Men" Faulkner "finds a usable past, a tradition among his people with which he can measure other traditions, southern or otherwise,"[18] by making them moral symbols of a golden mean between aggressiveness and passive submission, greed and inertia. However desirable such a mean may be between Anse Bundren's sloth and Flem Snopes's acquisitiveness, it is both politically naive and aesthetically disappointing. The McCallums were already a rather sentimentalized anachronism, and although Faulkner places his moral approval on their moderation, it is nevertheless the extremes of human conduct that fascinate him and produce his best writing.

Faulkner's treatment of the southern poor white leaves no doubt that his sympathies were not with mass movements that based their reform ideology on a rational analysis of man's role in an economically determined society. Though the conduct of some of his characters is clearly logical and calculated, Faulkner frequently views the sins of man as irrational and passionate, and his concentration on the discreteness of the circumstances which affect their lives works against the notion of poverty as a crucial factor. Though Faulkner makes rich use of the comic tradition and scurrilous reputation that had stamped poor whites as a class apart, their folly, absurdity, and avarice associate rather than dissociate them from the rest of humanity in his works. Their peculiar history and customs are not lost in this universalizing process but instead contribute a significant cultural factor to all the other influences at work in their lives. The implicit acceptance in Faulkner's fiction of contraries, the aesthetic use of incongruity, the play of tensions that are so "irreconcilably opposed and intermixed that only an oxymoron can express them"[19] are obviously served by the perplexing attributes of the poor white, whose very name is something of an ironic oxymoron. Faulkner did not need to forego any aspect of the poor white's accumulated image in order to serve his personal literary vision, though he completely avoids any mention of the industrialized urban workers in the South, who might well have strained his implicit political stance of self-reliance tempered by private acts of charity and an intuitive sense of communal obligation.

Caldwell's Politics
of the Grotesque

The poor whites who appear in the fiction of Erskine Caldwell, though not so clearly differentiated in terms of private history and psychology as Faulkner's, represent a broader social spectrum— from starving squatters and wily, opportunistic farmers to urban mill workers and small-town politicians. Caldwell also draws heavily on the cruel comedy and pathos of tradition but in the service of a very different social and political vision. Like Faulkner, Caldwell protested against the dangers of deducing sociological categories from what he called "the crafty dishonesty of fiction,"[1] but during the 1930s much of his major fiction and nonfiction demonstrates a clear adherence to the ideals of the literary left wing, if not to their methods.

The political ideology of Caldwell's writing has not attracted a great deal of attention, largely because interest has been diverted by either the grotesque comedy or highly publicized obscenity trials that attended his work's appearance. Nevertheless, the social history and economic victimization of poor whites play a significant role in his writing, even when they are not, as in true proletarian novels, the central issues. To mistake them for such is to be guilty of the kind of futile reductivism that led one critic to assert the literary superiority of Caldwell over Faulkner merely because he offered a practical remedy for a stagnating agriculture, while Faulkner seemed only to despair.[2] In fact, much of the pessimism in Caldwell's novels comes from the recognition that the suffering and degeneracy of his characters is virtually irremediable; each generation that survives in *Tobacco Road* is more damaged than the previous one—scarcely an encouraging situation for revolutionary change.

Caldwell's locale, like Faulkner's, is restricted—in his case to Georgia and South Carolina—and his people share similar traits: they are stubborn and randomly violent, prone to obsessive loyalties and fervent evangelical piety, both of dubious integrity; they are susceptible to disease and hunger and easily lured into fantastic money-making schemes at the expense of tedious and small-yielding labor on their land. Yet, despite similarities of setting, incident, and character, the individual details are unified into a very different creative scheme. Where Faulkner's characters finally win compassion through the fullest exploration of their humanity, Caldwell's demand justice for a humanity that is so destroyed as to be scarcely recognizable.

Caldwell's *Tobacco Road*, published in 1932, offers a number of such superficial similarities to Faulkner's *As I Lay Dying* and a radical divergence in its vital concerns. It is also a family novel about rural poor whites in a state of crisis, though in *Tobacco Road* it is absolute starvation that prods the Lester family briefly into their tragicomic action. Thus poverty is a crucial motivating force in Caldwell's novel and is directly responsible for some of the moral decisions taken by his characters, such as Jeeter's sale of his twelve-year-old daughter Pearl for seven dollars, "some quilts and nearly a gallon of cylinder oil."[3] Jeeter, like Anse Bundren, is almost a caricature of idleness, but sound reasons for his apathy are provided by Caldwell's insistence on the discouraging effects of an economic system that prevents him from taking any initiative. *Tobacco Road* has an abundance of gruesome funereal humor too, which illustrates a clearly contrary use of this favorite folk idiom. One of Jeeter Lester's more macabre preoccupations is a tale of his father's burial which is told repeatedly, with apparent relish for its grisly climax:

The following afternoon at the funeral, just as the casket was about to be lowered into the grave, the top was lifted off in order that the family and friends might take a last look at the deceased. The lid was turned back, and just as it was fully open, a large corn-crib rat jumped out and disappeared in the woods. . . . One by one the people filed past the casket, and each time it became the next person's turn to look at the body, a strange look came over his face. Some of the women giggled, and the men grinned at each other. Jeeter ran to the side of the box and saw what had happened. The rat had eaten away nearly all of the left side of his father's face and neck. [95–96]

Unlike the unfortunate efforts of the Bundren family and their neighbors to add dignity and ritual to death, there is no inner complexity of generous motivation in Caldwell's people; poverty, ignorance, and isolation set up a dehumanizing barrier between them and the reader so that we see them laughing rather than shuddering at a partially devoured corpse.

Both *Tobacco Road* and *As I Lay Dying* use the familiar comic episode of country bumpkins' exposure to the sophisticated ways of the city and their consequent economic and sexual exploitation. In *Tobacco Road* Jeeter, Dude, and Bessie predictably mistake a brothel for a hotel and add an extra degree of outrage to the comedy through the delight of the preacher, Sister Bessie, at her procurement for a night's service. In *As I Lay Dying*, Dewey Dell is taken advantage of in the same way when a slick drugstore clerk persuades her it is part of an abortion procedure. Against the horrified curiosity of city dwellers, both sets of peasants appear ludicrous: men gather to stare at Sister Bessie's noseless face, while women scatter with handkerchiefs to their noses at the stench of Addie Bundren's corpse. Yet while Faulkner uses the incidents as a comment on the callousness of the supposedly refined urban sensibility, in Caldwell they merely emphasize the freakishness of the Lesters. Even in their interpretation of poor white stoicism, the ideological tendencies of the two authors are clear, for while Cash Bundren's suffering is heroic as well as foolish, the Lester family's endurance is closer to the steady and involuntary deadening of all emotional response. They turn for relief to the only available opiate that they have: " 'When I has a sharp pain in the belly, I can take a little snuff and not feel hungry all the rest of the day. Snuff is a powerful help to keep a man living' " (31). Such examples demonstrate that the traditional image of the poor white had some considerable degree of adaptability to personal aesthetic design. However, a closer analysis of Caldwell's work shows that southern comic horror presented many more difficulties in the context of his crusading social material than in Faulkner's highly personalized universe.

From the critical reaction to Caldwell's novels, it is apparent that a vision of the poor that mixed macabre humor and social realism was liable to the worst types of misinterpretation. When he was praised it was for his "twisted comic sense,"[4] for the ability to provoke laughter at "the failure, the man left behind, the quaint person,"—in short for his direct appeal to a strain of humor which appreciates the exoticness of the freak and finds portraits of degenerate humanity amusing but which fails to connect them to any moral purpose. Finding Jeeter Lester's trip to town to sell blackjack "hilariously funny," such critics were disturbed by any serious elements Caldwell tried to introduce because they were incompatible with the comedy. They saw Caldwell's work as a twentieth century version of *Georgia Scenes* and would have preferred that he not adulterate the comedy with too profound a moral. Some were so disturbed by the candor of his treatment of the sexual diversions of the poor that, although appreciating his social purpose, they felt that he had "manured his ground too well for fibrous growth."[5] Ironically, prurient shock was the main effect of Caldwell's work on the public. Even the *New Masses*, from which he might have expected some sympathy for his efforts to make revolutionary use of southern primitivism and traditional humor, warned that "bad sociology does not improve fiction" and read him a brief lesson in proletarian anatomy: "They are all dying of pellagra and starvation, yet other organs beside their stomachs seem to plague them the most."[6] A closer examination of *Tobacco Road* may well show that the clash between techniques mars it irreconcilably, but it will also show that it has generally been found wanting in a category that was entirely inappropriate to it.

The novel is an account of the last starving days in the lives of the Lesters, dispossessed tenant farmers. Caldwell creates in them people who are so intellectually debased and emotionally brutalized that we scarcely recognize them as being of our own species. One critic has listed the few qualities of the Lester family which admit them to the human world: "They do possess language; they wear clothes; they handle implements; they can do the manual work of men; and they believe in 'God.' That is about all there is to distinguish them from other mammals."[7] In addition to their alienated sensibilities, Caldwell's people are often physically warped and hideous—Ella May Lester has a harelip which frightens off all suitors; Sister Bessie has two holes in the middle of her face, so that looking at her nose was "like looking down the end of a double-barrel shotgun" (58). Nor are these people given any opportunity such as the Bundrens are to redeem themselves through any secret and sensitive consciousness normally hidden from the world. If their grotesque behavior and appearance are a mask for any core of nobility, Caldwell refuses to divulge it. There are no interior monologues, and external language is reduced to the most mechanical and formulaic utterances which scarcely constitute a means of communication. Thus the book opens with a "conversation" between Jeeter Lester and his son-in-law Lov, in which Jeeter speaks only of his hunger for turnips while Lov pursues at cross-purposes a complaint about his twelve-year-old wife Pearl. Jeeter then switches his attention to nag his son Dude for "'chunking that durn ball against the house'" (19), but Dude replies only with fascinated comments about the sexual advances Ellie May is making to Lov: "'acting like your old hound dog used to do when he got the itch'" (23). No one is responsive or sympathetic to the predicament of anyone else. Indeed, though we wait hopefully for a single sign of humanity or kindness, Caldwell refuses to ease the burden of acceptance—the economic plight of these people has made irredeemable monsters of them. The origins of this degradation are revealed to us in interpolated passages of social history and rather uncharacteristically articulate speeches by Jeeter Lester. These heavy-handedly leave no doubt that a corrupt system of land tenure has been responsible.

The artificiality of this technique of interpolation stems from Caldwell's effort to view poverty simultaneously from two very different points of view—to comprehend the historic and economic reasons for it and secondly, to realize it in terms of the family that is suffering. Thus Caldwell must demonstrate the relationship of inertia, disease, and insensitivity to starvation, while the antics of his characters seem to belie any naturalistic explanation. His use of humor as a vehicle for the display of outrage, squalor, and injustice has much in common with the theater of the absurd, but it also has the major shortcoming attributed to that form by Martin Esslin: "it cannot provide the thoughtful attitude of detached social criticism."[8] In a novel there can be some solutions to this problem, though Caldwell's—the inclusion of explanatory sociological passages—shows some awkwardness in integrating them into the main comic-grotesque narrative. They also tend to be rather overtly sermonizing in contrast to the style of the rest of the book. For example, the following is part of a long passage about the depletion of the soil, first by tobacco, then cotton; about the decline of the Lester family, the loss of their land, and their final abandonment by their landlord, Captain John:

There was no longer any profit in raising cotton under the Captain's antiquated system, and he abandoned the farm and moved to Augusta. Rather than attempt to show his tenants how to conform to the newer and more economical methods of modern agriculture, which he thought would have been an impossible task from the start, he sold the stock and implements and moved away. An intelligent employment of his land, stocks, and implements would have enabled Jeeter, and scores of others who had become dependent upon Captain John, to raise crops for food, and crops to be sold at a profit. Co-operative and corporate farming would have saved them all. [82–83]

Such passages might have been better removed from the narrative completely and placed in separate, nonfiction interchapters as both Dos Passos and Steinbeck were to do effectively.

Where Caldwell is most successful as a social critic is in demonstrating the difficulties of creating a consciousness of oppression in a distinctly subrevolutionary class. Religion is traditionally a powerful reactionary force in radical fiction against social innovation, particularly in the rural South, and Caldwell uses it initially as the poor whites' rationale for their submissiveness. "'God is got it in good and heavy for the poor. But I ain't complaining, Lov. . . . Some of these days He'll bust loose with a heap of bounty and all us poor folks will have all we want to eat and plenty to clothe us with'" (13). However, with the advent of Sister Bessie and a closer examination of this piousness, we discover that religion to the Lesters is a form of emotional excitement which has relatively little effect on their moral behavior, either in relation to their promiscuity or, more importantly, to their acceptance of any code of endurance. A much more powerful conservative force, particularly in the men, is an attitude of mystical love and reverence for the land which prevents them from abandoning an obviously hopeless situation and moving into the cotton mills of Augusta. Jeeter's evocation of the torment of the people in the mills from "spring sickness" is a moving image of the desperate loyalty of land-loving people. "'You can't smell no sedge fire up there, and when it comes time to break the land for planting, you feel sick inside but you don't know what's ailing you. . . . But when a man stays on the land, he don't get to feeling like that this time of year, because he's right here to smell the smoke of burning broom-sedge and to feel the wind fresh off the plowed fields going down inside of his body'" (28–29). Ironically, it is this time-honored and completely pointless tradition of burning broomsedge in the spring that brings death to Jeeter and

Ada when the flames envelop and destroy their house. Thus they are both literal and symbolic sacrifices to an antiquated agricultural system.

The extent to which the members of the Lester family are aware of the real economic reasons for their plight gives Caldwell a further excellent opportunity to illustrate the problem of expecting peasants to act like proletarians. When Jeeter is confronted with city merchants refusing to give him credit and warning him that his folly will drive the whole family to the county poor farm, he replies bitterly, "'Then it will be the rich who put us there. . . . If we has to go to the poor-farm and live, it will be because the rich has got all the money that ought to be spread out among us all'" (152). Such a speech might have pleased the *New Masses* critics who had been admonishing Caldwell to go left, but Jeeter has neither the physical nor moral stamina to keep his wrath simmering. A trip to Augusta in Bessie's new car and his first meal in weeks give him a rather different perspective: "'Augusta is a fine place. All these people here is just like us. They is rich, but that don't make no difference to me. I like everybody now'" (186). Hatred and class consciousness subside rapidly on his full stomach.

The humor in *Tobacco Road* develops from satire of the incongruous activities of country innocents into a bleak parody of man's most destructive and vicious tendencies. The relatively lighthearted humor of the sexual antics is a means of establishing a comic mode that will then have to take the strain of the more macabre, absurd, and violent comedy. Caldwell steadily increases the burden of comic horror the reader has to bear until the episodes finally become intolerable and a recognition of their tragic implications is inevitable. Thus a quarrel between the Lesters and Sister Bessie starts out as childish horseplay—the participants poke each other in the ribs and hurl abuse while the old grandmother scurries across the yard to get a better vantage point for the fight. When she is halfway there, the automobile reverses over her, an accident which is merely another piece of slapstick comedy to the Lesters. The incidents climax in an attempt by Ada to hurl a stone at the car; then with the remark, "she should have known she did not have the strength to throw rocks as large as that" (214), Caldwell begins the grim process of investigating the results of this farce. "After the dust had settled on the road, Ada and Jeeter came back into the yard. Mother Lester still lay there, her face mashed on the hard white

sand" (215). The tone is detached as the injuries of the old woman
are catalogued, but such callousness now provokes a contrary emotional involvement on the part of the reader, who feels first horror
and then guilt for his laughter.

The same process of steadily impinging horror through comic
disaster is used in the account of the adventures of Dude and Bessie
in their new $800 automobile. The succession of catastrophes that
leads to its destruction is reminiscent of the progressive dismemberment of Nathanael West's hero, Lemuel Pitkin, in *A Cool Million*,
which also uses black humor to illustrate political horrors; but its
southern origin may be traced to similar tales of violent dissection
from Sut Lovingood.[9] First the front fender is smashed and the rear
spring broken, incidentally killing a man and provoking the comment, "'Niggers will get killed. Looks like there ain't no way to
stop it'" (159). This is followed by "springing the front axle,
cracking the windshield, scarring the paint on the body, tearing
holes in the upholstery, and parting with the spare tire and extra
wheel'" (199). While this expensive glory is wreaking havoc throughout the area, the rest of the family eats its final meager meal of
cornmeal and pork rinds, and the old woman continues to kindle
fires in the futile hope that there will be something to cook. The
ultimate extension of comedy for the reader is despair, though this is
never the case with the Lesters themselves. They are incorrigibly
optimistic. "Jeeter firmly believed that something would happen so
he would be able to keep his body and soul alive. He still had hope
left" (230). "'The ground sort of looks out after people who keeps
their feet on it'" (239). Such myths as these, of the survival of the
land and the people, are consistently undermined. Even the advo-
cation of collective farming scarcely seems a viable solution any
longer, though Caldwell implies that in the past it might have saved
the situation. Now the land is exhausted and the people drained of
everything but a faith which can only further their own destruction.
At the end we see the whole futile process beginning again in the
hands of an even more incompetent generation. The unfittest have
survived, and we are left with a sense, not of admiration at the endurance of humanity, but of shame at the perpetuation of such lives.

God's Little Acre, published in 1933, presents a much more appropriate and hopeful situation for the testing of Marxist ideas in literature than that of the subrevolutionary class of *Tobacco Road*. The
setting is divided between the rural farm of TyTy Walden in Georgia

and the cotton-mill town in South Carolina where his daughter and son-in-law live and work. TyTy is possessed by the notion that there is gold on his land (a theme also explored with tragicomic effects in *The Hamlet*) and neglects cultivating the earth in order to concentrate his energies and those of his family on this fruitless and obsessive search. In the urban sections of the novel, we see another world where productive work has ceased—in this case because of a strike in the mills. Here, the impetus to work is a powerful one on the side of the mill employees, who dream of turning on the power in the mill and running it themselves.

The major concern of the novel is the way in which deprived people search for satisfaction of their physical and spiritual hunger and the nature of the substitutes that they accept—a theme that led directly to an obscenity charge against it by the New York Society for the Suppression of Vice. Although it was cleared in court of pornography charges, critics continued to find fault with Caldwell for his frankness, frequently at the expense of an honest reading of the novel. W. M. Frohock says of it, "The fierce animal sexuality of some of the characters, not to mention the bloodshed, has less to do with the rest of the material than with our present novelistic conventions";[10] yet it is precisely in sexuality, the lust for gold, violence, and mystical religious faith that these people seek compensation for the hollowness of their lives, the result of generations of deprivation. Hunger becomes a basic metaphor that yokes together the various energies that supply and consume people's lives. It connects TyTy Walden's reverence for gold, the land, and the sexual power of women with Will Thompson's ritual worship of machinery, violence, and dynamic force. None of these elements could be detached from the book without destroying the complicated metaphor of interdependency and compensation.

Though it is much less gruesome than *Tobacco Road*, the method of the novel is again comic, relying almost completely for its humor on the innocence of the participants toward their own moral depravity and mental obliquity.[11] TyTy, like Jeeter Lester, is a failed farmer, but he has abandoned the growing of cotton not through lassitude but because of his fascination with gold. He diverts the labor of his family to this end and neglects to feed his two black workers, who are the only people doing any productive cultivation of the land. He is prey to all manner of superstitions, which he endorses in the name of science; he is convinced, for example, that the capture and imprisonment of an albino is a rational way to go about his search. "'We're going to get that all white man if I have to bust a gut getting there. But there's not going to be any of this conjur hocus-pocus mixed up in it. We're going about this business scientifically.'"[12] TyTy's confidence in the secret and rich abundance of the earth is directly connected to his fascination with sex and female beauty. To his daughter-in-law Griselda he says, "'The first time I saw you . . . I felt like getting right down there and then and licking something'" (44), an obeisance which in its imagery suggests a strong connection between women and nature as literal sources of sustenance. This was emphasized in an early psychoanalytic study of the oral imagery—biting, sucking, licking—of the sexual acts of the book.[13] TyTy thus views sexual activity as a token of faith in nature and a means of worship: his reaction to rumors of promiscuous behavior by his youngest daughter is "'I'm tickled to death to hear that. Darling Jill is the baby of the family and she's coming along at last'" (23). It is his delight in the beauty of Griselda that brings about the tragic conclusion of the novel, for by celebrating her beauty, he provokes a fight between his sons that results in the murder of one and the presumed suicide of the other. TyTy is left to pronounce a bitter elegy on the difficulties of fusing the godly, natural way of life, which is that of the animals, with the moral restraints imposed by man-made religions: "God put us in the bodies of animals and tried to make us act like people. . . . A man can't live feeling himself from the inside and listening to what the preachers say. . . . A man has got God in him from the start, and when he is made to live like a preacher says to live, there's going to be trouble. . . . When you try to take a woman or a man and hold him off all for yourself, there ain't going to be nothing but trouble and sorrow the rest of your days" (298–99). The old man's reverence for the spirit of procreation is distorted in a sterile, hungry world into a desire for selfish possession which leads to bloodshed and fratricide on the acre of land devoted to God.

In the factory world of the novel, machinery replaces the earth as the dynamic and sustaining power equated with sexual energy, but here it is a male rather than a female force. Consequently, it exerts a strange power over the factory girls: it makes them seem subservient to the machines they work, so that they regard both the machines and the mill with a kind of passionate awe. They can scarcely bear to leave them to return to the men at night. "When they reached the street, they ran back to the ivy-covered walls and pressed their bodies against it and touched it with their lips. The men who had been standing idly before it all day long came and dragged them home and beat them unmercifully for their infidelity" (99). This strange sexual jealousy is partially, but not wholly, explained by the economic relationships of the men and women: "the mill wished to employ girls, because girls never rebelled against the harder work, the stretching-out, the longer hours or the cutting of pay" (98–99). The connection between women as scabs and men as cuckolds lies in their attitude to the machines themselves: "The men who worked in the mill looked tired and worn, but the girls were in love with the looms and the spindles and the flying lint" (99–100). The mills in the town of Scotsville have lain idle for eighteen months during the strike, and the men dream of turning on the power again and taking control. The prospect of doing this becomes a kind of ritual chant in the conversation of the men, an end in itself, unrelated even to the production of cotton cloth: it is as though the mechanized power of the factory has come to symbolize for them all natural energy and initiative.

Will Thompson is the hero who unites both incredible sexual energy and the courage to break into the mill and turn on the power. He is the most interesting figure in the novel as a possible prototype for a visionary revolutionary leader—one of the generation of poor whites who have abandoned all hope of eking out a living from the land and have moved permanently into town to work in the mills. He is a skilled weaver who takes pride in his craft; having transferred his loyalties utterly to the town, he has no rural nostalgia: "The mill streets could not exist without him; he had to stay there and walk on them and watch the sun set on the mill at night and rise on it in the morning" (100). In the country Will is a rather comically alien figure: "The sight of bare land, cultivated and fallow, with never a factory or mill to be seen, made him a little sick in his stomach" (148). The strike in Scotsville has turned into an effort by the owners to starve the workers into submission, a course that Will resents bitterly. His impassioned drunken speeches on the owners show a keen consciousness of class injustice, which TyTy and his sons, left behind on the farm, are more immune to:

"As long as we can get a sack of flour once in a while we can hold out. And the State is giving out yeast now. Mix a cake of yeast in a glass of water and drink it, and you feel pretty good for a while. They started giving out yeast because everybody in the Valley has got pellagra these days from too much starving. The mill can't get us back until they shorten the hours, or cut the stretchout, or go back to the old pay. I'll be damned if I work nine hours a day for a dollar-ten, when those rich sons-of-bitches who own the mill ride up and down the Valley in five thousand dollar automobiles." [75]

For Will the break has been made with the land and all the traditions of the past—now he is constantly in the company of large numbers of people who share his plight and are united by their anger against the enemy. "The workers had reached an understanding among themselves that bound every man, woman, and child in the company town to a stand not to give in to the mill" (76).

The general behavior of strikers and bosses in *God's Little Acre* parallels fairly closely that of the other more specifically propagandistic novels—the mill tries to evict people from their homes, the workers harden their resolution, and there is extreme disillusion with the AFL, who, under guise of arbitration, appear to the starving workers to be merely making easy money by prolonging their plight. The impetus is, according to radical theory, to violent and cooperative action, but the motives in *God's Little Acre* are as complex as those of the men who beat the factory girls for kissing the mill walls. The machinery has appropriated more than their economic assertiveness; so when Will finally assumes the leadership of the strike, it is because his long-smoldering anger needed the catalyst of his sexual encounter with Griselda to transform it into revolutionary action. He becomes "'as strong as God Almighty Himself'" (221) and tears the fabric of Griselda's cotton clothes until they look like the shreds of lint which the workers will begin to weave again when the power is switched on. Afterwards, the population of the town surges anxiously around the mill; Will rips up his shirt and casts the pieces from one of the upper windows of the mill to where the women below fight for the fragments; then, as the roar of machinery begins, there is the sound of bullets exploding. Will Thompson has followed the revolutionary hero's path to glorious martyrdom.

However, the mill does not start; the other leaders are arrested and the people's plans thwarted. Like TyTy and his family on the land, the mill workers in the town lapse into despair. The crisis serves to unite and solidify the people of Scotsville as Will's body becomes their communal property, but Caldwell finally refuses to make any commitment to the future value of the sacrifice or to hint at any "great beginning." "The men with bloodstained lips who carried him down to his grave would someday go back to the mill to card and spin and weave and dye. Will Thompson would breathe no more lint into his lungs" (251–52). Although Caldwell's economic sympathies are clearly apparent throughout the book, he refrains from any of the polemical interpolations which so disrupted the texture of *Tobacco Road*. Instead, he creates for the first time a classic bourgeois villain who embodies the antitheses of all Will's qualities. This is TyTy's oldest son, Jim Leslie, who has disowned his family, become rich in the city as a cotton broker, and married a woman who will have nothing to do with his "linthead" relatives. Will says of him, " 'He didn't make the money he's got—he crooked it. . . . If he was my brother, I'd treat him just like I would treat a scab in Scotsville' " (108–09). Jim Leslie, in accepting dishonest and corrupt work, has also abjured the saving power and grace of sex: his wife is " 'as rich as a manure pile' " (151) with awful looks and gonorrhea. It is his frustration and selfishness that provokes the eventual murder. Even the least class-conscious members of the rural Waldens are provoked to horror at Jim Leslie's evictions of poor people from his tenement property and his attachment of their furniture: " 'I'm sorry to hear that you're selling poor people's household goods, son. That would make me ashamed of myself if I was you. I don't reckon I could bring myself to be so hard on my fellow creatures' " (178–79). These admirable sentiments from TyTy are less so in the light of his own neglect of his black sharecroppers, but the comic incongruity between his words and actions is not nearly so harmful in the context of his intimate rural community as the calculated, impersonal code of urban capitalism.

The *New Masses* was once again dissatisfied with what they now began to claim was an artificial cleavage between Caldwell's known political opinions—his support of the Communist candidate in the previous presidential election—and his aesthetic development. They found his approach to sex in *God's Little Acre* "healthy" but warned of latent "decadent possibilities."[14] They thoroughly approved the inclusion of the mill-town strike episodes but found his treatment of them "fantastic, disconnected, unbound to any semblance of reality, artificially grafted to the rest of the book." Their demand for absolute proletarian realism, for a more "thorough investigation into the causes of the southern industrial struggle," was outside the scope of Caldwell's aesthetic vision. It is perhaps the strongest indictment of the *New Masses* and those who saw art as a class weapon that they failed to appreciate or encourage a writer whose faith in art and imagination led him to experiment with symbolist and surrealist techniques as effective means of presenting material of contemporary social concern. After *God's Little Acre* Caldwell made one more attempt at reconciling his comic-grotesque technique with the poor white's ever-worsening situation—in his collection of short stories, *Kneel to the Rising Sun*, 1935. Then his work tends to separate into two streams: serious social material becomes the powerful nonfiction journalism of *Some American People* and the picture-text genre of *You Have Seen Their Faces*, while the fiction tends increasingly to sensationalism.[15]

In the volume of short stories, *Kneel to the Rising Sun*, Caldwell demonstrates the capacity of the short story to deal powerfully with social themes by creating an intense emotional effect which need never be dissipated, as in the novels, by comic diversions, unduly complex philosophy, or explanatory sociology. In the story "Daughter," a sharecropper, Jim Carlisle, is arrested for having shot his eight-year-old child Clara. Jim sits bewilderedly in the town jail, and as a crowd begins to grow outside, he can only repeat ritualistically, " 'Daughter's been hungry, though—awful hungry. . . . I just couldn't stand it no longer.' "[16] As the crowd builds, the background of the murder begins to emerge—Jim's landlord, Colonel Maxwell, has withheld his shares as payment for an old mule that died. Jim, too proud to borrow from his neighbors when he felt that he had honestly earned enough to support his family himself, was eventually driven to the desperate act of killing his starving child to alleviate her misery. The crowd is steadily growing in size now around the jail, elbowing closer to the prisoner's window, swaying rhythmically from side to side, shouting and pushing; then, "the milling crowd was moving across the street to the vacant lot. Somebody was shouting. He climbed up on an automobile and began swearing at the top of his lungs" (158). The whole situation parallels the classic arousal of a lynch mob; the sheriff deliberately leaves the jail unguarded as the crowd's fury mounts. The climax of the story comes with the realization that their fury is directed not against Jim but against the Colonel and that they are breaking into the prison to free him with the sheriff's tacit cooperation. There are no polemical speeches on class exploitation or social revolution, but miraculously, the hostile mob has been transformed into the sympathetic masses. They are neither educated proletarians nor sophisticated rhetoricians, but they do not require a high level of articulation to make their point: " 'Pry that jail door open and let Jim out. It ain't right for him to be in there' "(159).

In these stories, Caldwell still refuses to endow his poor whites with any of the qualities essential to heroism—they remain victims rather than leaders—but they are fumbling toward a sense of comradeship that is constantly exposed to destruction by their enforced peonage to another class for the basic means of subsistence. "Slow Death" is something of a classic salute to proletarian brotherhood. The story opens in a grim kind of Hooverville under a bridge by the Savannah River:

Just behind us was a family of four living in a cluster of dry-goods boxes. The boxes had been joined together by means of holes cut in the sides, like those of doghouses, and the mass of packing cases provided four or five rooms. . . . There were a dozen or more other crates under the South Carolina side of the bridge; when old men and women, starved and yellow, died in one of them, their bodies were carried down to the river and lowered into the muddy water; when babies were born, people leaned over the railings above and listened to the screams of birth and threw peanut shells over the side. [172–73]

Out of this community of despair, two unemployed friends walk through the city, where "the traffic in the streets sounded like an angry mob fighting for their lives" (174). They have no prospects of work nor any friends or organization to turn to, and when one of them is knocked down by a car, the driver insists he is faking injury in order to get money. All the hostile forces converge as the injured man dies a miserable death while his protesting friend is knocked unconscious by a policeman. However, this loss of consciousness is also a symbolic one, for on gaining his senses again, a turning point in submissiveness has been passed. Though the first friend is dead, he is now being dragged along the street by a nameless rescuer, from whose pocket the policeman's nightstick protrudes. The two are retreating as fugitives, but the fraternity of the poor, as well as the movement from passive resentment to active opposition, has been established between them. There is now a glimmer of hope that the words of the dead man may yet be fulfilled, " 'Somewhere there's people who know what to do about being down and out. If

you could find out from them, and come back, we could do it' "
(175).

This rather sentimental triumph is not typical of Caldwell's short
stories of the poor; for the most part they remain shockers where
sex and violence are the chief bargaining agents. They produce
revulsion and shame rather than the more desirable wrath of revolutionary action. The most typically horrifying is "Masses of Men,"
which plays with some irony on the favorite proletarian collective
noun, for the men here are seen as at best indifferent, at worst
positively hostile, to the world of women and children, who are at
the very bottom of the whole structure of oppression. The story
pits moral debasement, in the form of the man Johnson, against the
steady starvation of the woman Cora and her three children. Cora
goes out to prostitute herself for a little money for food, but having
been repeatedly rejected, proves more than ready to offer her nine-
year-old daughter Pearl for a quarter. The center of the story plays
cowardly lust against aggressive hunger: complaining petulantly
about the unheated room, the man hangs back for fear of being
caught in such a hideous crime; the woman urgently displays the
attractions of the child and pleads for his money. It is clear that no
moral alternative is available for Cora if she is to keep her children
alive, and the ruthless transaction, eventually completed, enables
her to buy a little food. The point is effectively made that no taboos
are sacred in a world which permits the first atrocity of starvation,
for that already constitutes a crucial debasement of any ethical
system.

The longest story in the collection, "Kneel to the Rising Sun,"
deals in greater complexity with another aspect of the question of
ethical confusion in the loyalties of the poor and with the southern
codes of behavior that obstruct a true identification of economic
interests on the part of the poor white. The setting is rural again,
among the black and white sharecroppers of Arch Gunnard; the
method is close to allegory, since every character represents a
recognizable social class or attitude, although the story is equally
effective on the immediate literal level. Arch Gunnard's tyranny
over his impotent workers is symbolically illustrated in his favorite
hobby, docking their dogs' tails. His victim in this story is Nancy,
the old hound of his white sharecropper Lonnie, a model of timid
acquiescence. Lonnie's family is starving because of short rations; he
is agonized by his dog's torture and shamed by the greater coura-

geous resistance of the black sharecropper Clem; yet he makes no objection. The pattern of the whole story is established in this early tail-cutting incident—the greater Arch's atrocities, the greater Lonnie's acceptance and the greater Clem's opposition. When Clem questions Lonnie about his endurance of such a situation, his response summarizes the anachronistic folly of the loyalty of lingering serfdom when the lord has abdicated all his responsibilities: " 'I've been loyal to Arch Gunnard for a long time now. I'd hate to haul off and leave him like that' " (223).

This horror is, of course, only a small foretaste of what is to come—Lonnie's inert loyalty will be tested much more stringently than by a suffering animal. His old father, wandering around at night in search of food, falls into Arch's pigpen and is hideously devoured by the snapping hogs—presumably the rich growing fat on the starving poor. Again, it is Clem rather than Lonnie who speaks up for justice by attacking Arch bitterly for his treatment of his tenants. The result is the formation of a lynch mob to get Clem and Lonnie's inevitable choice between black defender and white master. "He knew he could not take sides with a Negro, in the open, even if Clem had helped him, and especially after Clem had talked to Arch in the way he wished he could himself. He was a white man, and to save his life he could not stand to think of turning against Arch, no matter what happened" (233). However, Clem manages to extract the promise that at least Lonnie will not divulge his hiding place. In the crisis, Lonnie fails him: the habit of obedience to white and hatred of black is too strong, and he betrays Clem to the death of a hunted animal. The final action of the story takes place against the flaming background of the red rising sun, a powerful symbol of future bloodshed, against which the oldest southern tragedy of racial betrayal is set. This story and many of the others in the collection are among the best to come out of the proletarian art movement of the thirties, for in them Caldwell demonstrates his ability for compassionate but controlled writing with few lapses into leftist formulas, manifestos, and facile solutions that take no notice of the particular problems of the South.

In the same year as *Kneel to the Rising Sun*, Caldwell published a work of nonfiction, *Some American People*, that dealt with the contemporary plight of the poor. One of the book's three sections is devoted to anecdotes culled from a west-to-east trip across the United States, another contains some violent, muckraking journalism on conditions in the auto industry in Detroit, and the final section is on southern tenant farmers. The broader political and economic perspective on the South's problems and the contrary tone in discussing poor whites in this factual reportage is a useful indicator of how Caldwell excluded, refined, exaggerated, and concentrated this material in his fiction. Most striking in the non-fiction is the complete absence of any comic or ironic vision of the poor, who are presented solely as victims with all ridicule stripped away. Without the earthy folk humor that acts in the novels and stories as something of a counterforce to any completely naturalistic understanding of poor whites, they become mere sociological specimens, acting in accordance with clear economic laws:

Back on the hillsides the tenant families fell prey to various forms of religious excitement which served to take the place of normal entertainment. Physically, they became abject specimens of humanity. They ate what they could get, usually cornmeal and molasses. As a change many of them began eating the earth, and now communities of clay-eaters exist almost wholly on meal, molasses and clay. Clay-eaters may be identified by the color and texture of their skin, which looks and feels like putty.

In many such Georgia communities syphilis is as common as dandruff. Incest is as prevalent as marriage in these tenant regions where normal access to the outside is shut off because of the inability to travel. They are unable to travel except on foot, because there are few horses and mules, and almost no automobiles.[17]

The horror of these tenant farmers' lives is stark when unadulterated with personal folly and eccentricity, but the omission of the complex responses their degenerate antics provoke in the fiction makes it simpler for Caldwell to propose solutions to their problems. He advocates here the abolition of the landlord-tenant system and the introduction of collective farming, despite his pessimistic rejection of such measures in *Tobacco Road* as already too late to serve such people as the Lesters.

Two years later Caldwell returned again to documentary writing on the poor of the South in the picture-text book he did with photographs by Margaret Bourke-White, *You Have Seen Their Faces*, 1937. Each photograph is captioned with a quotation in which Caldwell imagines what the sentiments of the subject might be. Thus, though the longer essays in the book attempt to place the poor in a historical, geographical, sociological perspective, the emotional and aesthetic weight is largely carried by the fictional method. Once again, the South is peopled by rogues, knaves, fools, layabouts, and fanatics as well as the noble, toiling victims of an unjust economic system. There is anger in these captions, as children tell of being forced to stay away from school to work in the fields, and families describe trundling all their possessions over back roads in constant search of jobs and food—but there is also humor and inertia. One poor white grins indolently from his three-sided shack and comments, " 'I spent ten months catching planks drifting down the river to build this house, and then the flood came along and washed the side of it off. Doggone if I don't like it better the way it is now.' "[18] Though the final essay in the book concludes with a revolutionary call for change and a declaration of hope in the future, it is followed by a succession of somber portraits where the individual people negate and qualify the reformer's optimism: " 'It looks like God can't trust the people to take care of the earth any more' " (175); " 'I've done the best I knew how all my life, but it didn't amount to much in the end' " (183); " 'It ain't hardly worth the trouble to go on living' " (185). *You Have Seen Their Faces* emphasizes most clearly the dichotomy between Caldwell's fiction and nonfiction in their social values and shows how closely those values are tied to the aesthetic method he is employing. When he makes the slightest imaginative move away from reportorial sociology, even in such a small way as writing fictional dialogue for actual people whom he has interviewed, his indignation rapidly becomes transmuted into fascination with personal eccentricities and tragedies that counterpoint his hopes for masses of poor whites acting in concert to improve their lot.

Caldwell's use of grotesque comedy to further a vision of the southern poor white that is both radical and pessimistic demonstrates a certain versatility in that tradition of humor and folklore. Though he and Faulkner were often bracketed together as primitivists, decadents, or naturalists, Faulkner used the same material in a conservative and finally quite optimistic vein. Faulkner established with it a sense of community with traditions of independence and personal generosity worthy of perpetuation, while Caldwell used the same material in recording the breakdown of rural community and family life and the enforced exodus of country people to the cotton mills. The myth of the land in Faulkner had made it an affirmative, stabilizing, life-giving force to the people who remained loyal guardians of it; in Caldwell the myth is empty and destructive, since the land itself is exhausted and barren—it brings only misfortune to those who reverence it. The absurd humor of the poor whites in Faulkner was a means for revealing their basic humanity, their follies, passions, and weaknesses, while in Caldwell it is a means of emphasizing the freakish and alien qualities of people whose physical and mental depravity has inevitably encroached on their spiritual integrity. Faulkner, like Caldwell, noted the incongruous mixture of stoicism and violence in the poor whites; but while the stoicism was for him noble and the violence disruptive, in Caldwell stoicism becomes the apathy induced by needless suffering, and violence is a first step toward revolution and relief. A major difference between the two writers in their relationship to the poor white literary tradition is in their use of history. Caldwell fills in only the historical background necessary to understanding the shape of the present predicament of the poor; he recreates for the reader the regional traditions and myths that provide "truths" for his characters to live by. However, such "truths" are constantly undermined in validity for the reader, who is not encouraged to share the characters' faith in them, and hence tends to rely on them more as tools of naturalistic speculation. In Faulkner's case, these "truths" held a lingering validity even when their purveyors proved corrupt; he expended as much care on the genesis of these myths as on their decadence. He discovered the best aspects of the old southern code still embodied in the yeomen farmers and plain folk and pitted their resistance against the ravages on all established society of those people (mostly poor whites) who had abjured all ties with family, community, and history and had become faceless agents of material progress. Caldwell's vision of social exploitation is much more conventionally left-wing in terms of class warfare, for his compassion rests almost exclusively on the poor white victims of wealthy landlords and industrialists. Nevertheless, Caldwell refuses to commit his fiction to any absolute explanation of poor white degeneracy in terms of economics or his readers to any clear-cut emotional response to their activities. The idiocy, violence, religious hysteria, and promiscuity that certainly appear to stem from their material deprivation nevertheless do not constitute the features of a very wholesome advancing proletariat. Caldwell showed that the literary treatment of the poor white might produce a shocking indictment of the society that had cultivated this grotesque figure for amusement, pity, and profit. He left unresolved the question of whether that literary tradition would support the metamorphosis of its protagonist into the kind of hero the *New Masses* was demanding. The question would be answered by a mixed group of Marxist writers who made the poor white their exclusive province for some time in the decade; in the six novels based on the strike of southern mill workers at Gastonia, they would test the flexibility of the tradition to its limits.

CHAPTER V

The Gastonia Strike and Proletarian Possibilities

In both the factual and the fictional history of the poor white in the thirties, no name has acquired a richer symbolic significance than that of Gastonia. Before the events that occurred there in 1929, this North Carolina cotton-mill town was a byword among southern manufacturers for the fruits of industrial progress—reckoned not only in numbers of looms and spindles in the mills but also in the concomitant prosperity of the area's churches.[1] After the Communist-led strikes, mob violence, and bloodthirsty reprisals, Gastonia became a symbol to the rest of the country of the horrors of southern capitalism and a cynical comment on North Carolina justice. It also became the focus of a brief experiment in southern proletarian literature by providing the inspiration for at least six novels of political insurrection among poor white textile workers: *Strike!*, by Mary Heaton Vorse; *Call Home the Heart*, by Fielding Burke; *To Make My Bread*, by Grace Lumpkin; *Gathering Storm*, by Myra Page; *Beyond Desire*, by Sherwood Anderson; and *The Shadow Before*, by William Rollins. The attention of sympathetic writers was directed to Gastonia not merely by the *New Masses*, which was offering fulsome prescriptions for the proletarian novel, but also by the general tenor of the reporting in liberal periodicals such as the *Nation*, the *New Republic*, and the *Outlook and Independent*. Here, for the first time there appeared a willingness to apply the terminology of class warfare to the situation in the southern textile industry and to consider the possibility that the poor white himself might be changing.[2]

As is frequently the case when one name is used to evoke all the passionate emotions and conflicting philosophies of an era, what happened at Gastonia was neither a typical example of the efforts to unionize the southern worker (a process achieved, if at all, by the AFL rather than the Communists), nor was it even the most extreme example of the violent atrocities committed in the name of the law (strikers at nearby Marion suffered a much higher death toll). What Gastonia did offer was a histrionic confrontation of communism and capitalism, a dress rehearsal for class war, with the *Daily Worker* and the mill owners performing so zealously in their antagonistic roles that they almost upstaged the confused proletarians, who were agonizing over their choice of a battle hymn between "Solidarity Forever" and "Praise God from Whom All Blessings Flow." No revolutionary could have hoped for an enemy so blatantly prepared to pervert law and justice, so openly a friend to tactics of blackmail and terror as the officials and lawyers of the Loray mill and *Gastonia Gazette* were. No jealously paternalistic owner could have advised the Communists to more condemnatory courtroom behavior in the eyes of the South than the propaganda speeches, advocating atheism and the violent overthrow of the government, that one of their Party-instructed witnesses chose to make. Indeed, both sides seemed to cooperate in presenting to the world verification of all the suspicions it had about the mill owners' use of racial, sexual, and religious prejudices to buttress a corrupt economic system and in furthering the public's considerable misgivings about the integrity of the Communists' compassion for these workers, whom they so easily involved in strikes and so readily abandoned afterwards.

The ramifications of the Loray mill strike upon all the habits and beliefs of the tightly knit community made it a favorite research project for journalists and sociologists; there was even more tempting material for fiction writers in the romantic background of the mill workers, their close folk ties with their former mountain life, the flamboyant rhetoric of the public life of the South, the macabre courtroom incidents of the trial, the pervasive violence of the town, and the vicious assassination of the strikers' ballad maker. This was the essence of stirring left-wing journalism—or of dramatically updated local color fiction. However, the process of transmuting it into the more complex medium of the radical novel had to contend not only with the poor white as he had just revealed himself in the strike but with the *idea* of the poor white as a long-established literary personality. His propensity for the irrational—whether in regard to violence, religion, or the land—would be a major stumbling block, as would the comedy of his degenerate and unwitting behavior. His traditional conservatism toward racial and sexual roles would have to be radically reconsidered; the peasant-proletarian metamorphosis of Marxist ideology would have to be wrought simultaneously on fact and myth.

Before discussing the Gastonia novels, it will be necessary to give some account of the events on which they are based and the contemporary critical requirements of left-wing writing. This should make it possible to examine the changes and compromises that occurred in the effort to weld a new imaginative hero from doctrine, fact, and fiction. It may also help to shape some judgments on the relative artistic and political achievements of southern proletarian literature.

Most of the workers in the Loray mill in Gastonia had originally been farmers and sharecroppers attracted by the prospects of ready cash: for over fifty years they had been coming into the city from the neighboring land, quietly and sullenly accepting long work hours, low pay, and the necessary employment of all the women and children. They were slow, patient, and longsuffering, in contrast to the readily violent hill folk who were later recruited by the mills from their remote and desperate poverty. In the city, they were isolated in their own mill villages, stigmatized by the rest of the community as factory trash, and given for their leisure and consolation churches and preachers generously aided by their employers. For the segregated workers the churches provided a much-needed social center; in their later eccentric offshoots they provided a safety valve for the unleashing of pent up emotions in the frenzied manifestations of conversion; in their sermons they preached humility, hard work, sobriety, and rewards in heaven—virtues guaranteed to make malleable employees, if not good Christians. The transition from rural to urban paternalism was not a major one for the nearby sharecroppers and tenants; but for the mountain folk the move was a bitter one, from an independent existence in a society where poverty was the rule to a servile position in a society where poverty was the exception, and they could easily witness the luxury of other classes who fattened off their labor.

After the enormous profits of the First World War, the cotton industry was in slow decline in the 1920s, and managers were attempting to recoup their losses by wage cuts and greatly increased productivity for each worker. The system whereby this was achieved was the notorious "stretch-out," a name whose racklike implications were not inappropriate; workers were often required to tend two or three times the number of looms that they had formerly looked after, sometimes at reduced pay as well. If they objected, they knew they could be instantly replaced from the surplus supply of cheap labor. Southern workers, used to a certain degree of laxity, particularly hated the close supervision of the "stretch-out"; and commentators have suggested that there would have been revolts in Gastonia anyway, even without the aid of northern Communist organizers.

Into the resentment that was seething in the Loray mill in Gastonia in March 1929, Fred Beal, a seasoned Communist leader, arrived to try to organize a branch of the National Textile Workers Union. He worked secretly at first, until several of the union members were apparently betrayed by mill spies and dismissed; then a strike was called which was supported by almost the entire work force. At this point there appears to have been some dispute between Beal and the Party heads in New York over the tactics to be pursued: Beal was anxious to strive for normal union objectives in the strike and thence to play down the Communist affiliations at that time; his colleagues wished to seize the attention focused on Gastonia by the strike and proclaim their final revolutionary intentions. They differed also on the public attitudes to be taken to race, religion, and violence: Beal once again emphasizing a pragmatic viewpoint while the Party wished to be purist. Meanwhile, the mill immediately began to recruit outside workers and called in the National Guard; the strikers drifted back to work during the course of a month until by May there was only a hard core of two hundred resisters left. Although the strike was virtually broken, the mill began harsher retaliatory policies against those who refused to go back: many families, including one with a child suffering from smallpox, were evicted onto the street. The union organized a tent colony for the strikers with armed guards for protection, a necessary precaution since their headquarters had already been destroyed by a mob. This colony was invaded one night, without warrants, by the Gastonia police chief and some officers, two of whom had already been involved in a drunken display of shooting earlier in the evening. In the darkness both sides fired, and the next day the police chief Aderholt died. Mobs immediately raided the terrified tent colony, and lynch parties sought Beal and the other strike leaders.

The uncontrollable fury vented by the crowds in Gastonia was largely the result of the constant stream of vilification and counter-propaganda directed at the Communists by the *Gastonia Gazette* and the mill leaders; so when Fred Beal and fourteen others were charged with conspiracy leading to murder, it was apparent that they had little chance of a fair trial in that city. The national press, which by this time was following the affair closely, hailed the decision of the presiding judge to move the trial to Charlotte and to rule that the defendants must not be questioned on their beliefs. However, the *Daily Worker* was already determined that there would be no justice but prejudice, no outcome but martyrdom. In fact, it was more accurate in its predictions than the more liberal and optimistic northern papers, but it also contributed largely to the sacrifice with reports and editorials geared to increase the already high tension and hostility. The chief prosecutor, deprived of the most fruitful line of attack by the judge's ruling, resorted to a grisly final effort to shift the sympathies of the court, which, despite the *Daily Worker*, appeared to be not unfriendly to the prisoners. He had an exact wax replica of the murdered policeman made; clad in Aderholt's bloodstained clothes, it was wheeled into the courtroom. Aderholt's wife and daughter began to cry, but the strategy misfired, for one juror whose mental stability had been dubious throughout the trial went insane on the appearance of the gory effigy, and the judge declared a mistrial. A poll of some of the jurors showed them to have been in favor of acquittal, and this fact, along with the delayed prospects of punishment, touched off mob frenzy and violence again. Three union leaders were kidnapped and beaten up, and the most savage reprisal of all was taken on Ella May Wiggins, the writer and singer of the strike "ballets," who was murdered by mill gangsters. This killing occurred in daylight before fifty witnesses, but no conviction was ever obtained for it.

At the new trial the prosecution dropped the charges against eight of the defendants, including all the women on the pretext of chivalry, though it also appeared to make a sure conviction of the rest more likely. Unlike the first trial, it rapidly turned into a heresy inquisition after the judge permitted cross-questioning on Communist beliefs as a means of impeaching the credibility of the witnesses. All the deepest prejudices of the community were played on by the prosecutor, whose summary pictured the Communists " 'creeping like the hellish serpent into the Garden of Eden,' " " 'fiends incarnate, stripped of their hoofs and horns, bearing guns instead of pitchforks . . . sweeping like a cyclone and tornado to sink damnable fangs into the heart and lifeblood of my community.' " Gastonia was pictured as a pastoral haven of birds, flowers, and churches, reaching its rich produce of cotton yarn out into infinity. " 'Why, you could wrap it around the sun sixteen times, around the moon thirteen times, around Mercury, Venus and Saturn, stretch it from San Francisco to southernmost Africa and right back to Gastonia.' "[3] The jury, out for less than an hour, returned guilty verdicts; heavy sentences were imposed—the heaviest of all going to the northern organizers though the evidence against them was flimsiest. All of the prisoners, freed on bail while an appeal was pending, fled to Russia.

The conduct of the textile workers themselves during the strike was curiously watched by the national press, which reported on some of the incipient rebels' peculiar attitudes. "On the red clay banks of the railroad track they sit in their overalls listening to the Communist strike leader as he stands on a box in the vacant lot. They hear with blank faces phrases about international solidarity and class power. But when one of their own number stands up and shouts: 'Every striker git a scab and the strike will soon be over,' they howl with delight. They are tired, undernourished, and uneducated, but even the employers admit that they are becoming aware of their own degradation."[4] Yet their resentment focuses not on bosses or owners but on the even more desperate and degraded poor whites who act as strikebreakers. They are still attuned to the hope of immediate, limited improvement in their conditions; their long-term loyalties belong not to the Internationale but to "the Sunday school, the Star Spangled Banner, and personal friendship for the boss."[5] Communist plans for converting these loyalties clearly lay in the rational demonstration to the workers of those agencies that were operating against their own interests—a dramatic process of awakening that would presumably illuminate the southern proletarian novel.

The ideal nature of such a novel, its subject matter, ideology, and audience, was a source of incessant debate in left-wing literary circles in the early thirties, with Michael Gold in the *New Masses* leading the way in prescriptive theories. Walter Rideout, in *The Radical Novel in the United States 1900–1954*, has warned against the danger of assuming that American writers of proletarian literature were in any sense bound by these pronouncements, since there was constant dispute over what the formal "line" was and most of the writers were not official Communist party members or subject to its discipline. However, novelists sympathetic to the radical cause in the 1930s *were* obliged to a considerable extent, by the logic of that sympathy, to endorse the current methods of understanding and applying Marxism. These methods were rational, scientific, highly formal, and organized; if they anticipated a bloody millennium, they also demonstrated its absolute reasonableness. In the disintegrating, chaotic world of the depression, such certainty in interpreting history, such a clear program of action, was bound to be attractive to puzzled artists.[6]

Since many proletarian novels did have a rather formulaic inevitability in their development of plot and character, their authors were accused by hostile critics of permitting this Marxist dogma to substitute for personal insights and of writing un–American books that were more relevant to the situation in Soviet Russia.[7] The whole canon was reduced by one cynical commentator to the following summary: "The novel began with a community of workers, on factory and farm, at first divided and unaware, then opening their eyes, hesitant and afraid, being broken and at last regrouping for final combat, having learned from defeat that there are no halfway houses, that the Party is their only ally, the owning class their only enemy, and that they have a world to win."[8] That the events in Gastonia in 1929 might be molded into this pattern is obvious, but that the southern poor white textile workers might be led to these conclusions by rational argument is more doubtful in view of their fictional and factual history. Thus the writers who tackled the Gastonia strike had a considerable dilemma to contend with: they had an unprecedented opportunity to create a new kind of southern literature in the form of the proletarian novel, but the poor whites were not the best receptacles for their extremely logical materialism. Their reputation associated them with humor, gothic horror, and what one commentator called "such poverty that it was a matter of jest."[9] The difficulty of wrenching the poor whites' loyalties away from their time-honored sources makes it virtually impossible for the Gastonia novels to demonstrate "sudden conversion," and they tend rather to belong to a slightly different genre, identified by Georg Lukacs as the socialist *bildungsroman*.[10] They take up the life of the hero or heroine at a point where the conventional *bildungsroman* usually ends: with the acceptance of a traditional role in society or complete alienation from it. Then the characters are drawn into an increasing involvement with new social forces, which brings on a series of crises of consciousness. Ideally, these would culminate in a sense of harmony with the wider community and a general commitment to common ideals. In the Gastonia novels, however, a final sense of emotional unity is frequently based on the mutual suffering and tragedy of the participants, which proves a convenient mask when more basic intellectual disparities between the known character of the poor whites and their new loyalties have not been completely resolved.

Because of this difficulty in applying radical ideals to the poor whites and because of the extremely degrading conditions of their lives, some of the impetus for writing about them has been attributed not to reforming enthusiasm but to that same taste for violence and debasement that had aroused the original fascination with them—though now combined with a vindicating sense of moral fervor. Thus, Leslie Fiedler writes, "We will find two quite distinct, though linked, motivations, both operative from the very beginning. The first is a particular brand of self-righteousness, an almost pharisaical smugness in being among the excluded, which seems an inevitable concomitant of all American radicalism. . . . The second is a vision of disaster and a pleasuring in it—a masochistic wish-fear."[11] Fiedler further suggests that the reason the Gastonia events made such a popular setting for novels is "surely because their outcome was satisfactorily disastrous for labor." Proletarian writers were thus subject to quite contradictory analyses of their motives—one side saying that adherence to Marxist formulas made their works false and un-American, the other arguing that their loyalty to what are often considered peculiarly American norms (gothicism, defeat, apocalypse, millennium) far outweighed their intention of furthering Marxism. Walter Rideout has argued in his book that there was in fact a rapprochement between the two apparently antithetical sensibilities in the 1930s. "What actually happened was the adaptation of a radical ideology to what might be called the inherited literary consciousness."[12] Since the "inherited literary consciousness" of the southern poor white represented a profound challenge to the premises of that radical ideology, the Gastonia novels have an importance, beyond their admittedly limited aesthetic value, as an extreme test of the possibilities of such a consensus.

The first of the Gastonia novels to be published, Mary Heaton Vorse's *Strike!*, is a transitional work between the journalism and the fiction of Gastonia. Like several of the other novelists, the author was a reporter with a background of radical activism, fiction writing, and journalism. Her literary career had begun in 1908 with the publication of *The Breaking In of a Yachtsman's Wife*, which was followed by a regular stream of light fiction and anecdotes, notable mainly for their humor and charming characterizations. Then in 1920 came *Men and Steel*, a harrowing description of the tyranny of coal, iron, and steel over the lives of people who worked the machinery of production. The uniformly favorable reception of her work up until this time changed abruptly to the accusation of propagandizing, but Vorse's sympathy for the labor movement was unweakened by this transparent shift. She covered the Gastonia events for *Harper's* and must obviously have been working simultaneously on the novel and the reports. In fact, *Strike!* appeared so precipitately in 1930 that it outran the actual Gastonia incidents on which it was based. Thus while periodicals reviewed the noble martyrdom to which the novel brought Fred Beal and his companions, they were simultaneously reporting on their news pages the less heroic bail-jumping that concluded the factual organizer's southern career. The fictional massacre was based on events at Marion, North Carolina, rather than Gastonia, but apart from this final extra indulgence in emotional catharsis, the novel adheres closely to the events of the Loray strike and points its own honesty with rather naive naming devices. Fred Beal becomes Fer Deane; the Manville-Jenckes company, which owned the mill, becomes the Basil-Schenk company; and Violet Jones, the union traitor, becomes Violet Black. The novel's reportorial accuracy and its exclusive concentration on the strike itself as the touchstone of all activity is achieved by presenting the events through the responses of Roger Hewlett, a northern journalist on his first southern labor assignment. His business is to record and synthesize the seemingly random and capricious moods and movements of the strikers, but he is also the *bildungsroman* hero who slowly emerges from his bourgeois intellectual cocoon to find at the end his true allegiance, declassed and denationalized, with the workers of the world.

As one of the earliest proletarian novels in America, *Strike!* holds little promise of radical innovations in technique to match the ideology; the novel is heroless, or rather it has as multiple hero the entire body of strikers, but otherwise it is quite conventional in form and style. Its dramatic content derives not only from the violent historical episodes but from a fascination with mass psychology in a city divided into two hostile armed camps. The emotions of the strikers fluctuate with remarkable cohesiveness between extremes of confidence and despair; the passions of the mob ("Everyone was mob who hated the Union")[13] are more adulterated: "They were at once menacing and ridiculous. . . . They wasted their fury in futilities" (305). Both groups are shown to be extremely unstable and susceptible to the rumor and rhetoric of the moment, which the strikers hear at their frequent union "speakings" and the mob obtains from the local newspapers and Chamber of Commerce. Vorse naturally makes every effort to differentiate the quality of persuasion offered by these hostile sources—the repeated calls for nonviolence by the union leaders, the gushing benevolence and sentimentality from the bosses that thinly disguises greed and fury. The moral is that "Collectively human beings are at their best or their worst. They climb perilous heights of beauty and sacrifice together. And together they revert to the hunting pack, creatures aslaver for blood" (270).

Union versus mob represents the central struggle in *Strike!*, but the simple proletarian allegory that should emerge from the confrontation does not materialize. The amorphous mob is an effective villain, spreading violence and terror throughout the community, but the multiple hero is a curiously modern image of irony, confusion, and inner contradictions. It is first of all a union that does not know how to strike. The startling ignorance among southern workers about this means of industrial protest causes both sides to view the action as one of much greater significance than a mere method of bargaining; it is for them apocalyptic—each side believes it to be the final struggle against anti-Christ. The problems of organizing the South are suggested in the miserable comment of Fer Deane, " 'I wisht I was North. I wisht I was leading a strike of fellers I was ust to' " (14). This remark is symptomatic of an aspect of *Strike!* that made it less than satisfactory to the *New Masses*. This

was a considerable skepticism about the appropriateness of traditional Communist strike methods both for the poor whites and
other classes in the South and a sharp eye for the shortcomings,
rivalries, and animosities of the Party members who carried out the
plans. Thus, though her emotional sympathies are correct, the *New
Masses* noted the absence in Vorse's book of the "dynamic logic that
made the Carolina textile worker stand up in his proletarian dignity
with a copy of the *Daily Worker* in his hand."[14] Her workers cower
in confusion behind their leader. "The long years in the mill village,
the paternalism under which they had lived, had taken initiative
from many" (207); they put themselves in the hands of organizers
and relief workers with the same childlike confidence that they had
abandoned themselves to the mills. Those who understand that it is
their fight can scarcely be restrained from using guns. The leaders,
trapped between apathy and violence, between adoration and vilification, are "burdened with the hatred of the comfortable people and
equally burdened with the devotion of the mill workers, a load of
love and hate too heavy for their shoulders" (23). The strikers see
the union not as a rational means of organizing but as something
mystical, more akin to religion, a power that exists independently
of them: " 'It's kinda like salvation. You belong to the Union, and
somehow or other, you're saved' " (178). Indeed, they hold meetings patterned on the revivalist practice of testimonials, where mass
enthusiasm is whipped up by personal accounts of dramatic conver-
sions: " 'I heard a voice asayin' to me, "jine the Union! jine the
Union!" . . . an' one day it come to me, I just couldn't beah to yere
that voice acroakin' to me no longer, an' I started in an' with my
lame leg, I run for two miles an' I nevah stopped runnin' til' I got to
Union headquarters an' jined up' " (217). But it is not merely such
mental attitudes that portend trouble from the beginning for the
northerners—the southern poor whites are virtually unable physically to sustain a strike. They have no savings to rely on, no homes
of their own if the mill evicts them from its housing, and since
whole families must work in the mill in order to live, there are no
alternative sources of income. The union becomes instantly a charitable organization, and as the more able-bodied workers slip em-
barrassedly back to the hills and mills—" 'they ain't scabbin' in their
hearts' " (174)—it is left with the care of cripples and babies, the old
and the weak, an ironic solidarity of nonworkers.

However, when the strike finally collapses, Vorse suggests that in addition to southern obstacles, the defeat is aided by that heresy for which the Communists themselves had coined the term "male chauvinism." All the way down the chain of command from organizers to picketers, there is keen evidence of sexual jealousy and resentment. The clash is symbolized mainly in the altercations between Fer Deane, the good-humored and rather lazy union leader idolized by the workers yet dreaming of escape from the strain, and his assistant, Irma Rankin, superior perhaps in energy and orthodoxy and arrogant in anticipation of martyrdom. Irma constantly criticizes Fer's weaknesses as a leader—" 'he hasn't the caliber to organize the *South!* . . . He has no *drive!*' " (16–17)—but her hostility is clearly an affair beyond union tactics. "There was a continuous pull and strain between them of a man and woman fighting for supremacy over each other" (79). Irma and the relief worker Doris defend the militancy of southern women to a point where it begins to hurt the strike, since the southern men have a quite contrary notion of their women and will not be led by them in the picket line (114–15). When Fer orders the young mill girls to fraternize with the soldiers, Irma contends he is confusing these workers about their "natural enemies"; bitterness between them rises to a climax when Fer gains credit for the famous tent colony over which the women had labored so hard. In controversial matters of race and religion, the Communist organizers endorsed a policy that split them from the southern workers and could only be reconciled with a few; but in their theory of sexual equality, they split among themselves as well and were unable to effect their own policy without a distrust so profound that it almost ruined the strike. There is a final irony too in this struggle, for it is Fer who becomes the reluctant martyr of the whole affair, while Irma and Doris live on to organize again.

Perhaps to try to counteract the negative effect of this male-female rivalry, Vorse introduces two love stories which in their excruciating sentimentality destroy some of the journalistic integrity of *Strike!* without adding any compensatory fictional quality. One affair, between a local girl Lissa and Fer Deane, is largely a reward for Lissa for finding a field for the tents. The other is between a local organizer and the ballad singer Ella May Wiggins, here known as Mamie Lewes. These two lovers are brought together by their passion for the union and held apart by their dedication to it: " 'We got too much to do to get mixed up this away' " (294). One lover from each couple is sacrificed to the guns of the mob, but the romances gain melodrama rather than dignity from their historic setting, and the composite hero of the novel becomes fragmented by this sudden emphasis on the private lives of characters we knew only in public.

The trial incidents are used effectively to add to the sense of southern grotesquerie of the whole affair by depicting it as a parody of courtliness, "a stately ritual, an eighteenth century affair. . . . A bloodless duel with feints and parries. An elaborate structure built of courtesy and culture, something between a duel and a minuet" (282). The result of this elegant game is the bloody effigy of the murdered man wobbling slowly in on wheels. It is like the mob singing hymns as they destroy food and supplies for the children—horrifying but also incongruously ridiculous. In her anatomy of the strike, this ironic sense of the contradictory emotions it encompasses is the most successful aspect of the novel. The whole movement of the strike, as well as the mob action, seems to be pervaded by chaos, hesitation, and whim, and there is little effort to idealize the general progress of union principles or distort the attitudes of opponents. However, this is scarcely a vindication of the New Masses's judgment that the book lacks dynamic logic: the objective ideology of the strikers does advance, albeit unevenly, against the subjective limitations of the individuals involved. The author is clearly partisan, but in dissecting the strike she manages to give both external journalistic accuracy and a sympathetic portrayal of the inner tensions without resorting to propagandizing and deception. If the purely aesthetic successes of Strike! are very limited indeed, it nevertheless achieves through the form of the novel a sense of the local, irrational, very human aspects of Gastonia that the fine journalism could not so effectively explore.

CHAPTER VI

Poor Whites, Feminists, and Marxists

Two years after *Strike!* four more Gastonia novels appeared, three of which treated the events from the point of view of poor white mountain girls who had recently come from the hills to the mill villages. Walter Rideout describes these three—by Burke, Lumpkin, and Page—as being "in effect local-color fiction performed with a radical purpose,"[1] but the differences in the books are as important as the similarities. *Gathering Storm*, by Myra Page, is quite clearly a piece of Communist propaganda; not wholly without literary merits, it is tendentious, arbitrary, and fallacious in its handling of southern problems and shows every sign of adherence to the contemporary Party line of hostility to socialists, intellectuals, liberals, and trade unionists; so it was already curiously dated in a few years by comparison with the later proletarian novels of the United Front. Grace Lumpkin's novel, *To Make My Bread*, is closest to Rideout's stereotype—most of the novel takes place before the strike, and much of it is set in the mountains, where it explores the background and customs of the poor whites before they go into the mill towns. Fielding Burke's novel, *Call Home the Heart*, also has the rural-urban antithesis, but in this novel—by far the best of those on Gastonia—the particularities of the immediate situation are transcended, and the problems, though rising out of this economic clash, are of a universal nature.

However, one important aspect that the three books have in

common with each other and with *Strike!* is their authorship by women. All of them use the historical circumstances of Gastonia not merely to explore the growth and embitterment of the southern industrial proletariat but particularly to examine the role of women in a period of great social crisis—why they changed from the most docile workers to the most recalcitrant strikers, what place was available for them in the organization of unions and in Communist leadership, and most insistently, how they were to reconcile their traditional pride as the bearers of large families with the increasing poverty, squalor, and disease that seemed to attend each new child's birth in a mill village. This latter question was generally the foundation for the others; and the repeated guarded attempts to discuss birth control, the open portrayal of the anguish of each pregnancy, and the grisly tales of amateur abortion efforts sometimes suggest that Margaret Sanger rather than Marx might have been the hero they sought.

The concentration in these novels on heroic female protagonists, often traced back through several generations to pioneer ancestors, was not a new feature in southern literature: in the previous decade both Edith Summers Kelley and Elizabeth Madox Roberts had written of the poor white heroine who was driven by the intolerable circumstances of her life into various forms of private rebellion. McIlwaine, in his history, points out that these rebellions ended invariably in defeat or compromise,[2] not merely because the women were isolated from any sympathetic group who might give moral sanction to their rebellion but because they themselves felt finally compelled to admit that their duties lay with home and family. The lonely revolt of these peasant women seems far removed from the popular image of the 1920s feminist, but there was a connection in the many important organizations established by women's movements in the South to make the most effective use of the newly won franchise. They immediately began detailed enquiries into the plight of the poor and were consistently behind improved welfare legislation for sharecroppers, tenants, and cotton-mill workers. Indeed, the North Carolina League of Women Voters argued in retrospect that the Gastonia events might never have occurred had their precise plans for the textile industry been followed.[3] For a few brief years in the thirties, it seemed possible that communism might bridge the gulf between the feminists' assertions of sexual and intellectual equality and the female reformers' zeal for radical social change, as well as bring the poor white woman into an active political role for the first time. Thus the women novelists of the Gastonia strike concentrate almost as much on the egalitarian and fraternal aspects of communism for women as on the class war and proletarian advance. Their heroines need no longer feel that a retreat from family life is eccentric or selfish, for they can now play an equal role in the betterment of all families. The romantic image of the "rebel girl," the young adventurous battler for bread and roses immortalized in Joe Hill's ballad after the Lawrence strike, was buried with the utopian dreams of the Wobblies. The poor white heroine of the thirties was usually older—often the veteran of a ruined marriage and the mother of several children—and prominent in the less dramatic aspects of unions and welfare rather than in confrontations with police and troops. Nevertheless, there is still a tension in these novels between the traditional personal loyalties of the heroines and their newfound ideological commitments; Page and Lumpkin try to avoid it by constructing fortunate deaths and desertions of children and husbands to release the women from these responsibilities, but Burke, with more intellectual courage, forces the issue to a confrontation and tries to work out her own uneasy synthesis.

Before the depression era and the advent of the proletarian novel, Fielding Burke had already established a considerable literary reputation under her real name, Olive Tilford Dargan. Unlike Mary Heaton Vorse, who had come to the Gastonia events from outside the southern literary tradition, she had personal roots in the South and had written of the North Carolina mountain people in both poetry and fiction. In 1925 she had published *Highland Annals*, a series of sketches of mountain life, embellished with tall tales, songs, and rapt descriptions of scenery, that conform closely to the stereotypes of this genre of local color writing—characterizations of people who are humorous, hospitable, violent, avowedly religious, improvident with their narrow material resources. However, Olive Tilford Dargan had also had a good deal of experience with radical writing even earlier in her career, albeit of a much more curious nature than any of her Gastonia contemporaries. Her lyric poetry was a vehicle for contemporary social criticism and for what the *New York Times* disapprovingly called "bathetic struggles with insoluble questions." But her taste for the philosophical and ideological in literature had found its strangest form in a series of esoteric blank verse dramas, whose archaic language and remote settings (Assaria, Goldusan) made an incongruous background to the toll of modern industry on the working class. Thus in *The Mortal Gods*, 1912, Prince Chartrien, coached by the revolutionary Rejan Le Val, calls the roll of capitalism's horrors to the tyrant king Hudibrand of Assaria in a remarkable speech:

> As many lives tramped out in hunger's scramble,
> As many factories where driven wives
> Forget the altar dream of babes and home.
> As many sweating traps where flames may feed
> On flesh of maidens, leaving still, charred bones
> Whose only fortune is to ache no more.
> As many brazen mills that noise their thrift
> Above the ceaseless shuttle of small feet,
> While you, the great arch-master, thinks, none hears
> That drownèd pattering. As many marts
> Where in law's shadow, girl-eyed slaves are sold
> To blows and lust. As many cripples thrown
> Upon the dump-heap of a soulless Peace,
> Each season piled to meaning wreck more high
> Than ever War made in its darkest year.
> As many holes where life must lie with death
> For privilege of sleep. Oh, I could give
> Black instances till yonder sun be set
> Nor end your loathsome list![4]

Undeterred by critical ridicule, Olive Tilford Dargan collaborated in 1922 with Frederick Preston on a series of one-act plays which continued to give dramatic form to revolutionary sentiments about the Japanese oligarchy in China, the place of scientific visionaries in the modern world, and the evils of child labor. The reiterated themes in these plays do not perhaps constitute a very precise social philosophy, but they are not at odds with the author's later Marxism in their pleas for justice for the masses and in their admiration for science. One other significant motif in them is the danger presented to the advancement of any social or scientific cause by individual love between a man and a woman, which constantly threatens their loyalty and concentration. This becomes central to her first proletarian novel, *Call Home the Heart*, 1932, written under the pen name

Fielding Burke, in which the author's radical sympathies are united to her intimate knowledge of the North Carolina mountain people.

Call Home the Heart is about the predicament of a woman morally and intellectually committed to communism but drawn by a powerful emotional urge to an idyllic and independent agrarian life that embodies the best of Jeffersonian and native American traditions. Rationality, duty, and principle point for Ishma to a life of service to the Marxist world revolution, to involvement with the industrial proletariat in the mill towns and a grim dedication to a utopian future not to be realized in her lifetime. Irrationality, passion, and nostalgia summon the heroine always back from the dreary mill towns to a life of wildness and freedom in the North Carolina mountains, to a beloved husband and a tradition of family service and personal rewards. In this conflict between head and heart, the heart is finally triumphant: Ishma, having deserted her family and mountain farm for the cotton mills of Winbury, where she experiences the awakening of her mind and conscience through the grueling ordeal of the strike, in a moment of impulse flees home again. She is drawn there by her love for her husband but equally driven by revulsion from her new duties. The emotional climax of the book is thus the desertion of principle for love and the rejection of a profound sacrifice in return for conventional fulfillment. But both Fielding Burke and her heroine are clearly undeceived by the joyous reunion on the mountain top—the paths of morality and joy have diverged so sharply in the novel that there can be no wholly satisfactory reconciliation. The dilemma is only finally resolved in a sequel written three years later, in which the Emersonian triumph of principle finally brings Ishma peace, though at the highest price possible.

Ishma, clearly in the heroic tradition of poor white women, matures in a fatherless, matriarchal family, where she is profoundly influenced by the powerful personality of her pioneer great-grandmother, Sarah Starkweather. This formidable old woman passes on to Ishma not merely her extreme competence in housewifery and motherhood, but a daring skepticism in all matters of traditional authority, from medicine to religion. She is revered among the hill folk for her dedicated rearing of seventeen children but also (more subtly for the direction of the book) because she only brought into this food-hungry world one child of her own flesh. This freedom from childbearing is pointedly juxtaposed to Ishma's slovenly and exhausted sister Bainie, who, in her early twenties, is "the wearily incompetent mother of four small children."[5] The notion that life "oughtn't to be all work and dirt and younguns" (49) determines Ishma to resist marriage and its inevitable breeding and to grasp at what straws of education are available to an adolescent mountain girl, who, "before she was seven . . . had joined the class of burden-bearers" (1). Her first reading is done from the Bible under the watchful eye of Granny Starkweather, who affirms that " 'a body has to know how to pick over it' " (66) and censors with calm assurance, " 'Mark that fer skippin', darter. We'll not read that twict' " (65). Ishma's mind thus learns early to sift the limited material available to her; she rejects *Pilgrim's Progress* as stupid but revels in a history of England and a daringly romantic novel. A young schoolmaster, impressed by the fourteen-year-old's enthusiasm, attempts to direct it more suitably, away from her current infatuation with Jeremy Taylor, by giving her a subscription to *Woman at Home*. This opens up to her a world of fantasy far beyond the splendors of the novel. " 'He has prepared me a table in the midst of mine enemies' " (11), she quotes, with a very appropriate disregard for context.

However, the victimization she was trying so hard to avoid finally claims Ishma in carefully acquisitive metaphors. "Radburn Bailey was looking at her with greed and longing in his pleasant blue eyes; but Britton Hensley looked at her with the thrill of ownership" (14–15). Her marriage to Britt is an impulsive and impassioned decision, and though the two strive bravely to overcome the disadvantages of depleted soil and parasitic relatives that sap their vitality, after three years they are beaten by poverty, illness, and misfortune into the same dreary pattern she had watched in her sister. Ishma, pregnant with her fourth child, having already buried two, accedes in despair to the pleadings of her former suitor and escapes to the mill town with him. The mountains, which have consistently represented her safety valve, the source of nourishment for all spiritual exhaustion, have now become a prison. The panacea of nature is now the taunting setting of all her failed dreams; so her flight must be down the mountains to Winbury, "a town of many mills in the mildly billowing Piedmont region between mountains and lowland" (178).

It is at this point in the novel that the critics who reviewed it decided almost unanimously that the transition from art to propaganda occurred, only to be redeemed into art by the final return to the mountains. Undoubtedly the rural poverty is more picturesque than its urban counterpart; the first part of the narrative is colored with Indian myths, ballad-making contests, and a richly humorous folk tradition, while life on the mill hill is a monotonous and sterile struggle whose gaudy, installment-bought consumer goods seem small compensation for the loss of the communal friendship and sympathy of the countryside. However, it is only possible to sense a break in the style here by ignoring the whole pattern of feminist discontent that has been established in the first part. The personal sexual rebellion is complete long before the Marxist philosophy of the NTWU provides a rationale for it; Burke has meticulously anticipated the dialectical pattern of the novel by clearly placing peace, harmony, and natural beauty in opposition to her heroine's worldly education. "Ishma didn't know that, to the mind born for questing, somewhere on its burning road, love and beauty must become hardly more than little nests for the comfort of the senses" (150). The urban interlude will provide the intellectual antithesis to the tranquil opiate of nature; the ideological orientation that Ishma develops there is in no way incompatible with what we have learned of the great-grandchild of Sarah Starkweather, whose large character had also demanded a wider sphere than the individual family to exercise her unusual talent.

Although the eventual outcome of Ishma's few years in Winbury is an education in class consciousness and an active sympathy for the proletariat, the whole subject of mill-town horrors and social inequities is handled rather obliquely through symbolism and tends to remain for a long time on the periphery of her personal life. The question of the tragic waste of powerful potential is treated thoroughly in the relationship of Ishma to her little daughter. Vennie, born prematurely, is a fragile and sickly child who harnesses Ishma like "a war-horse pulling a toy sled" (198); the mother, though loving the child deeply, is conscious of an obligation so heavy that it must inevitably destroy all her aspirations. The issue is handled delicately, and it is not until much later in the novel, when the strikers' course is blocked by ignorance and hostility, that the full personal and political implications of the following images are apparent to Ishma:

She thought of a time when, as a girl of ten years, she had gone for a long climb up a mountain trying to reach a grey spur from which she knew she could see the far world. . . . Near her goal, she found herself between a cliff and a jutting boulder. Climbing up between them, she sat down with her eyes shut. She hadn't looked back for the last mile of her climb, saving her emotion for what she could see from the top. Safely on her ledge, she turned and opened her eyes. There in front of her, growing out of the cliff, was a stunted loblolly. . . . She could do nothing but look into the branches of that poor little pine that hid the far valleys, the sunlit peaks, the long, dreamy ridges, and the pale path of rivers. [231]

The urban sections of the novel provide a complete antithesis to the rural parts, largely through the symbolic personality of Derry Unthank, a radical bourgeois doctor who represents all the qualities of mind and disposition that are diametrically opposed to those of Ishma's husband, Britt. Derry is an urbane, educated, professional man, who has rationally considered the possibilities of remolding the world to a better state and thence committed himself to a direct personal involvement in communism. He is in every way opposite to the whimsical, fun-loving farmer, whose virtue is instinctive and who will always seek peace through Christianity rather than attempt to temper the world's justice himself. Through Derry, Ishma begins her education, practically, by working with mill employees, and theoretically, by starting with a reading of Henry George and H. G. Wells and progressing to Marx and Bebel.

With Ishma's growing activism, she begins to discover the intense pleasure of humanitarian service: "she was upheld by that supreme ecstasy, the consciousness of transmuting daily life into an ideal" (306), but the problem of developing her political sophistication in proportion to her everyday material awareness of Marxist rationale demands more than the patient reading of books. For this purpose, Fielding Burke introduces many lengthy speeches and debates from union leaders, management, leftist intellectuals, liberals, socialists, and aesthetes, which tread an uneasy line between didactic partisanship and propaganda.[6] What saves them from the latter is the author's refusal to distort the main capitalist and bourgeois figures into caricatures of grasping self-interest and cruelty and also the frank nature of the discussions on sensitive issues such as genetic control and "racial individualism." It must be admitted that the exploiters and all who gain by capitalism are treated with rather more compassion than the contentious, intellectual fellow travelers who seem to have reached the nadir of rejection in the novels of this period. Nor is the book entirely free from rather naive, manipulative literary devices which are in danger of having a contrary effect on the reader's sympathies. These include the juxtaposition of lovable workers and vindictive authority—" 'I could live on one potato a day an' never miss the picket line,' said Grandma Swithin, fifty years old and eyes in a fiery dance. She was the first to be bayonetted" (312); asides on the mistreatment of foreign immigrants in Pittsburgh that have no valid connection with Ishma's personal story; and some remarkable passages of apostolic exhortation:

"We saw, reaching out and around us, the soft hands of charity. . . . Not only could we see misery around us, we began to pierce to its cause. Before that time we had accepted sorrow and given it beauty. We made songs of shadows and suffering. Over ugliness and defeat, we threw the sheen of art, the pale holiness of resignation. We guarded our griefs jealously. We hugged them as from God. We went about our jails and almshouses with the shining stolidity of virtue. But intelligence has won. The new instrument has not failed us. We see full circle. . . . We have work ahead. We have to unclog the gate of evolution. We have to sweep out the clutter of unseeing ages. We have to release even spirit through the door of intelligence." [326]

This speech from Derry Unthank voices the highest aspirations of the human mind, the rational antithesis for Ishma of the passion that draws her always back to the mountains. But her final retreat from the strike is spurred not only by love but by hate—the consequence of a scene that shows the agonizing struggle that must occur within these North Carolina poor whites before they can accept emotionally the racial equality that they logically must concur in.

Earlier, in a discussion of race relationships, assimilation, and intermarriage, Ishma had referred to blacks as "earth-currents" and Derry too had asserted, " 'I'd like to see a black race keeping to its own lines of life, intuitive, rhythmic with nature" (355). Ishma had come away with a determination to defeat her prejudice for the sake of solidarity, and she gets a fine opportunity for heroic action when Butch Wells, one of the black union leaders, is kidnapped by a lynch mob. In a tense drama (which the *New Masses* condemned for its unethical display of individualism) Ishma rescues the bleeding Butch, and entering triumphantly into his home, she revels sentimentally in the anticipated gratitude of his wife and friends: "She loved those black and bronze women with their big, tender eyes" (382). Her complacent fantasy is shattered by the embrace of Butch's wife, a huge, odorous woman who pays the glorious compliment, " 'We'll all be in heaben togeddah! Sistah! Sistah!' " (383), and fills Ishma with uncontrollable revulsion. "The fat bosom shook against her own. The sickening smell of disturbed animal sweat rose and fell with the black body" (383). Ishma strikes out viciously at the thankful wife, beats her to the ground, and then runs in furious horror. Dreaming only of escape to the "high, clean rock on Cloudy Knob, half-covered with sweet moss and red-tipped galax," she makes her way back to the mountains, the "relapse into art"[7] that is not Burke's rejection of collectivist ideals but a tragic falling-off in the heroine from strength to primitive weakness.

The book ends in the heady inebriation of nature and passion. "Ideals, theories, the struggle of a world for breath, had thinned to nothing on the edge of her absorbing desire to feel mountains under her feet and Britt's head on her breast" (386–87). The novel that fought so hard against the irrational restraints placed on women culminates in a partial betrayal by the heroine of the intellectual integrity for which she had sacrificed so much. This rather pessimistic outcome of the dialectical scheme of the book is anticipated much earlier by the character of Ella Ramsey—a kind of alter ego for Ishma—a middle-aged woman whose entire life is dedicated to the service of the union. "Personal matters were small matters to Ella Ramsey, unless they were related to her consuming purpose—a livable wage and endurable hours for the workers" (227). Ishma is not capable of this ascetic, self-denying choice; so the novel ends in a joyous celebration of mountain and marriage from which, however, the pristine enthusiasm has been distilled by the act of rejecting humanity for one human being. The events and impressions of Winbury are not to be erased merely by ignoring them, and there can be no retreat possible for the urban masses into a Jeffersonian idyll. The emotional satisfaction of the reconciliation does not resolve the moral dilemma, a task left for the sequel. The Gastonia events in *Call Home the Heart* are the backdrop for a universal moral drama of a warring head and heart, a testing ground for setting the supreme rationality of communism against the archaic forces of unreason.

In *A Stone Came Rolling*, a less eloquent sequel to *Call Home the Heart*, the struggle for consciousness has been calmly won and there is no danger of any further lapses on the part of the heroine into primitive and emotional forms of reaction. Set in the North Carolina mill town of Dunmow, this second novel is again ostensibly about the tension between contrary principles, no longer a private war between head and heart for Ishma but a collective battle for the entire community between the rational utopia promised by communism and the supernatural heaven promised by Christianity. Ishma is the inspired prophet of the former, though she displays a remarkable tendency to preach in the imagery of the latter, with beatific visions of the fulfillment of man's potential in the post-apocalyptic world of "meadows of inconceivable release."⁸ Like Ishma, most of the other characters have assumed predictable roles and merely appear to act out like puppets their predestined course in an inevitable movement toward upheaval, destruction, and rebirth. True to this formula are Bly Emberson, a distraught and noble mill owner for whom there can be no resolution but suicide; Verna, his fundamentalist southern belle wife whose villainy is heinous and merciless; Unthank, the radical pessimist, and Schermerhorn, the radical optimist; Kik, the compromising union leader, and Hickman, his ominous exploiter; Amy Bigrose, the bored intellectual dilettante with no moral commitments—"she enjoyed playing with fireworks when convinced that the surrounding vacuum insured safety" (88). There are also a number of spokesmen for varieties of religious idealism and expediency; at times the novel seems close to allegory in its alignment of spokesmen and ideologies in confrontations whose outcome is never in doubt.

The subject of most of the debates is religion or eschatology. As a background to them, Burke spends a chapter tracing the long history of the establishment of Christian institutions in Dunmow, which admits to some of the same nostalgia for the anachronistic church that the first novel did for the whole personal code of Britt Hensley. Britt still represents the best traditions of the Christian world, but even in its purest form that world can offer no higher principle than love, and that is no longer enough: " 'There are signs that it [love] has fulfilled its destiny in evolution' " (268). If Christianity can offer no solutions to the suffering of the world, there is still the hope or danger that it may offer consolation for them, and the author is prepared to give some uncynical consideration to the power of spiritual sustenance, even for those who share the new economic consciousness of the future. A single thread of despair runs through the novel in the person of Job Waygood, one of the earliest converts to the Communist cause, now a miserable, skinny beggar, blacklisted everywhere. His attempts to act jauntily about his fate strike Ishma as "only intolerably pathetic" (233); "he was a derelict on the shore of her own logic" (232). Job's predicament taunts Ishma with the fear that intelligence, like love, may not be enough to combat evil, a fear further aggravated by Britt's murder, which throws Ishma herself into the position of Job: "What had she done? What darkness! What savagery! Had her great light led to this?" (342–43). At the climax of this second novel, Ishma's pursuit of rational, altruistic goals seems to have led her to an even greater horror than the irrational selfishness whereby she had failed in the first. Now, with Britt gone, there is no retreat into the mountains away from the future, though she does consider the suicide of the most hopeless.

The final sections of *A Stone Came Rolling* unite Ishma's private agony and rebirth with the most turbulent phase of class war that Fielding Burke had described; the upheaval that has been looming throughout the novel finally erupts. Ishma's active participation in the revolution comes as a result of a rebaptism into reality through a final testing in nature, in which she makes a triumphant resistance to the transcendental mysticism and inertia inspired by natural beauty. Hoping to find contact with Britt's essence, she returns briefly to the mountains—"Down among their foundations, . . . she would come into eternal touch with him" (363)—and she finds that they exert all their old power over her. They overwhelm her with a sense of her own puniness and finitude: "she was swept insubstantial by invading space, whose sun-systems that would never be counted were wheeling and weaving to destinies that would never be sighted" (367). Ishma clings to all the forces of reason to resist the mockery of eternity against the youthful strivings of the "collective human spirit," fashioned into "an instrument of mind" (368). After her ordeal of resistance to these enervating cosmic visions, Ishma falls into a slumber "too deep for sight, sound, or dream" (368). When she awakens in the cold twilight, all the surging energy that was numbed by the suffering of Job and Britt has returned. Instead of being " 'cured . . . of the disease of time' " (369) by the stars, rocks, and rivers, Ishma has discovered a new imperative for urgency and vital action in her own temporal life. The meaning of her own name—waste—only now achieves full significance beyond the narrow sphere of her background as a poor southern woman, in the broadest possible historical and geographic perspective.

Thus, although the last scenes of the novel are back in the midst of the bloody industrial warfare in Dunmow, it is not this lesson of economic inevitability that these two *bildungsromans* combine to tell. The revolution is not characterized by violent hordes bent on destruction, though that may be the momentary manifestation; the mental upheaval is much more cataclysmic than any mere physical sign of it: the final assumption by man of the full powers of his intellect and the rational understanding of the meaning of history.

By contrast with the broad philosophic scope of Fielding Burke's novels, Grace Lumpkin's *To Make My Bread* appears to be on a rather minor scale, though of all the Gastonia novels it received the most uniformly favorable reviews. It is closest to Rideout's stereotype of "local-color fiction done with a radical purpose," and as such, appears to have offended few with its ideology and touched many with its compassion for bewildered peasants, uprooted from their centuries-old mountain life and thrust into monstrous factories that grind them down to make bread for the wealthy. Both the successes and failures of this novel can be traced directly to the conventions of its genre: it is most effective in using the traditional gulf between rural expectations and urban reality to produce a fine sense of moral irony, but this tends to be exploited for pity rather than as a prelude to rational action. Pity, though a fine literary emotion, is not a constructive tool of communism, and the *New Masses* was quick to point out the novel's neglected opportunities for revolutionary optimism, sardonic class portraiture, and a broader perspective on the local struggle that might view it as part of an international movement.[9]

Grace Lumpkin, like Fielding Burke, was a native southerner who found in her own region plenty of stimulation for both her literary and political inclinations. She had spent several of her girlhood summers among the North Carolina mill people; she later mixed in left-wing literary circles in New York and published her first story in the *New Masses*. If less theoretically ambitious than *Call Home the Heart*, *To Make My Bread* is nevertheless a thorough investigation of the cultural heritage of the southern poor that helps to explain their later behavior in the mill towns—that strange vacillation between pious passivity and startling violence—that so confounded capitalist owners and Communist union leaders alike.

The most significant shaping force of their contradictory characteristics offered in this novel is religion, particularly the emotional melodrama of the Baptist church, which preaches humility, meekness, and suffering but at the same time offers physical rituals of a highly cathartic nature. Scantily clad adolescents are immersed in a chilly, fast-flowing mountain stream as the community sings:

> There is a fountain filled with blood,
> Drawn from Immanuel's veins,
> And sinners plunged beneath its flood,
> Lose all their guilty stains.
>
> Savior wash me in the blood,
> In the blood, in the blood of the Lamb.[10]

Later in their lives, when these young people listen to mill preachers draw cunning parallels between Christian humility and economic suffering, they reluctantly accept them; but the urban churches can offer no comparable equivalent to the symbolic cults of exorcism of their more primitive hill life. Thus the periodic bouts of violence by striking workers and town opponents are noted by several Gastonia novelists as temporarily purging the angry community and bringing briefly that religious sense of calm release. The fiction of Gastonia occasionally suggests that an alliance might have been forged between the more radical churches and the union, but the facts deny this, demonstrating a bitter intransigence on the Party's side. "Inability of the Communist leaders to use this religious heritage convincingly and to conceal their own attitudes toward religion was a serious handicap to retaining the loyalty of the workers. . . . the antireligious tendencies of the Communists did more than any other single factor to divorce them from continued leadership of the workers."[11] Grace Lumpkin, gifted with the hindsight the real organizers could not have, steers an uneasy course between attacking the hypocrisy and biased worldliness of the church and at the same time refraining from condemning, as Burke does, the irrationality of its fundamental appeal.

The McClure family, which provides both heroes and villains for the novel, is shown early to be capable, like Ishma, of picking over the most satisfactory beliefs offered by the Bible and rejecting many of the preacher's recommendations. Grandpap, a talented fiddler, marches out of the mountain church when the preacher condemns music and dancing, and, in a moment of prophetic solidarity, the entire McClure clan leaves with him. Later the younger children, John and Bonnie, moved by the Bible story of Abraham and Isaac, decide they will sacrifice their beloved puppy in a similar show of submission to God's will. However, at the crucial moment, they doubt the punctuality of God's intervention and decide to save the dog for themselves. To their surprise, and significant warning for the future, there are no supernatural repercussions for this delinquency, and the children come away with an increased sense of their own power.

In the mill villages, Lumpkin attacks greed, collaboration, and self-interest among churches and preachers fairly conventionally, but this attack on the latter-day perversions of Christianity might as easily have been made by good Christians and indeed was constantly reiterated in the pages of the *Christian Century* throughout this period. Lumpkin is more reluctant to apply herself in this novel to the question of whether religion is inherently the enemy of communism. The falsity of the assumption that there is a benevolent power in the universe is raised twice in the novel, once by focusing on a congenitally crippled child and a second time by presenting the brutal flogging of a convict on a chain gang. Both scenes are presented to John and Bonnie by their friend Robert, the brother of the deformed child, who is convinced that no hell could be worse than this earth and no God could be love who permits such atrocities. However, Robert's stand in the novel as the only clear enemy of a divine ideal tends to be weakened by his movement from youthful skepticism to adult cynicism: " 'And I tell you there is no plan and no guidance. There is no order, no law, no purpose, no progress for the human race. History repeats itself over and over, and here we are, the human race in all its ugliness, just the same as ever. It's for a man to get out and while there's a life to be lived, grab just as much as he can and to hell with everybody else' " (292). The contrary response to these situations of John, who will later be the main union leader, is rebellious but not outside the church's tradition. "A sickness had come on him. Like Job of old he wanted to curse God and die" (250). John's final conversion to the union cause is even given biblical sanction, when, moved by the story of Sacco and Vanzetti, he discovers a passage in the Bible betokening God's condemnation of the rich and the fury that will be visited on them, "'Go to now, ye rich, weep and howl for your miseries that are coming upon you'" (325). Thus, in this novel it is the cynic who defies God, while the pragmatic unionist adapts what is useful—a method which, according to the strike's main analyst, might have been more effective than the purist line that was actually taken.

Although *To Make My Bread* has dual heroes in the persons of John and Bonnie McClure, it is, like Burke's novels, particularly interested in the plight of poor white women, though Lumpkin, more traditional in her solutions, refrains from presenting even the most revolutionary women with the unpalatable choice between loyalties that Ishma had to make. The major burden for the women is once again childbearing, which strains their exhausted energy, removes them from the work force, and provides each year a greater drain on the family's meager financial resources. However, preferring to see in the economic advantages of unionism a sufficient panacea for their problems, Grace Lumpkin avoids the subject of birth control or of any radical new role for women. The women are well aware that a change in their attitudes has taken place—from their passive peasant suffering and even pride in their most extreme trials to their angry stand in the forefront of industrial agitation. They explain it by saying that the factories forced them out of their preferred position in home and child-caring, but their constancy to the strike cause stems from a more fundamental emotional reason. While separated from their own sick and hungry children, they first become aware of the pampered and luxurious offspring of the mill owners and executives, who prosper from their labor while their own families suffer.

The traditional sensitivity of these women to all the manifestations of social superiority and their ready mixture of jealousy and humility toward the symbols of material comfort provide a fine scene in the novel where class consciousness is realized with no unnecessary Marxist homilies to point the moral. Emma and Ora, two newly arrived mill employees, pay their first visit ever to a downtown ice cream parlor, where, dreading that they may be asked to leave at any minute, they hover nervously at one of the most secluded tables. "They waited a long time, and both were strained, waiting. They could not talk at ease. A boy in a white jacket went to other tables, bringing ice cream and drinks in high glasses. Emma wanted to call him or go up to him but she did not dare before the other people. She wanted to talk so she might keep Ora from noticing, but there was nothing to say" (225). Eventually, the two friends leave without being served and assure each other that the waiter must not have seen them. But Emma has heard one woman remark, " 'They're mill hands,' " and before they enter any more stores that day, they check first to make sure that their occupants are as poorly dressed as themselves.

These two women belong in the novel to a transitional generation that still has its roots in the mountains and dreams of returning there. Their expectations of urban life are shaped by a rural consciousness that they never fully lose. They are first attracted to the mills by news brought to the mountains by a hunchbacked peddler, like a messenger from a fairy tale, promising them riches and rewards if they are prepared to make the journey to the city. To Emma, the prospect of employment in a spinning factory conjures up visions of a prosperous, more organized version of their cozy community life, where women will sit together quietly working to the gentle movement of spinning wheels and talking in a neighborly way, like one of their joint quilting sessions. When they face the reality, Emma finds herself unable to comprehend it, except in terms of the fairy-tale dream turned into nightmare; she sees the factory as a fiendish ogre whose machines murmur, " 'I'll grind your bones to make my bread' " (219). Her naiveté and that of the other first-generation immigrants to the city gives life to the truths that their children will preach; they help particularly to demonstrate the entrenched belief in inequity that these people themselves hold. Emma and Ora, newly acquainted with the theory of holding stock in the mill, discuss their former ridiculous conceptions of the term. " 'Ye know,' Emma said, laughing at herself, 'at first I thought stock was us. You know how Hal Swain used t'say he owned twenty head of stock or thirty. I though hit meant we was the stock and they owned us.' 'That was right foolish.' 'I know. Hit made me mad, thinking of being owned, till Grandpap set me right' " (223). Thus they turn their misplaced irony on themselves at their anger for thinking they were considered mere animals—to be possessed and driven by the mill; they are quite happy to discover " 'hit means ye get money without working' " (223).

The only section of To Make My Bread that consciously handles radical political activity is the final fifty pages, where the events parallel the Gastonia strike closely with only a few minor changes.

Bonnie discovers an unusual talent for composing and singing songs and becomes this novel's version of the strikers' ballad singer, Ella May Wiggins; she is shot in due course and laid out on the union table. Events are slightly reordered here so that her murder takes place before that of the police chief, but the funeral comes afterwards. Here Lumpkin uses her final artistic license to make over Bonnie's grave the stirring funeral oration that was lacking in the factual events. The cadences of it are biblical, but the message is to remember in bitterness the evil that must be purged from the face of the earth. The emotional note of the ending is thus quite correct—future-oriented anger and hope—though there is nothing in the desperate circumstances in which the strikers are left to give much rational justification for optimism or even to predict the next logical step forward. This vacuum points to one of the problems in Lumpkin's technique of entering completely into the perspective of the uneducated poor; it is moving and effective in eliciting the maximum compassion for them, but it also leaves the novel without a figure, either fictional or real (in the persona of the author), who can articulate the Marxist solution. There are no informed debates between wrongheaded liberals and militant Communists, no decadent bourgeois theoreticians to open up the complicated fields of dialectical materialism. Such answers as there are to southern poverty in this novel must be inferred by the reader without much guidance, for the ignorant perfection of the workers never evolves much beyond their emotional education in revolutionary attitudes and scarcely at all beyond the threshold of intellectual consciousness.

Grace Lumpkin's next novel, *A Sign for Cain*, 1935, reportedly written under Communist party coercion,[12] makes a considerable effort to correct the imbalance of feeling and thought in the first by having as its hero a middle-class radical newspaper editor. However, in spite of the preponderance of philosophical viewpoints represented, the novel still permits personality and emotion, instead of ideology, to shape its political responses. All the characters line up in attractiveness according to their political stances, and there is no attempt in the central debate between the lovers Bill Duncan and Caroline Gault to create the tension that existed in the clash between Ishma and Britt. Bill, a committed Communist from the outset, never falters in his allegiance but matures in every crisis and emerges braver and more dedicated; Caroline, also something of a rebel, but with a quaint code of individualism, proves utterly dishonest—she retreats behind the barriers of race and class at the first challenge to her family. The love affair proves completely hollow as soon as the nature of the lovers' loyalties is revealed to each other.

The central contrast in *A Sign for Cain* is between the decaying aristocracy of the South and the vigorous new alliance being forged at the opposite end of the social scale by black and white share-croppers. This is effected by concentrating on the Gault family and their black servants. The family is a symbol of the latter-day corruption of values that once were tinged with nobility. At its head is the Colonel, a Civil War veteran with a reputation as a silver-tongued orator, now dying painfully of throat cancer. He is a benevolent, paternalistic employer, scrupulous and high-minded, but also a stubborn old man whose consciousness is fixed in the 1860s on a code of honor that is vain, selfish, and complacent, though not hypocritical. His three children contribute to, rather than diminish, his distaste for the contemporary world. The oldest Charles is a clergyman with High Church leanings, who has con-quered his scruples in order to live at peace with his environment; Caroline is a novelist, twice divorced, who attempts to demonstrate the power of individual over collective action by forming intimate friendships with poor girls whom she finds personally repulsive; Jim, the youngest, is a wastrel and drunkard, the epitome of self-loathing and disgust, who murders his wealthy aunt, permits two blacks to be arrested for raping her, and then murders them in a drunken imitation of revenge.

As in all the novels that offer a contrast between the diseased values of the collapsing middle class and the healthy activity of the workers for the future, the moribund villain seems to demand much more attention than the emerging hero. Lumpkin concen-trates heavily on the southern code of white gentility and illustrates its evils with many gory episodes concerning the rape mentality, the gothic terror of attempted lynchings, and the pervasive brutality toward blacks. Relying wholly on their sensationalism to produce the correct responses, she handles them with a good deal of descrip-tive relish but not much effort at analysis. The economic plight of the poor receives almost no emphasis compared with the first novel, although religion is shown as an even more powerful reactionary force; this time it is in the black community, where there is a spontaneous revolt against the preacher during a sermon on the text, "My punishment is greater than I can bear." The *bildungsroman* elements are not neglected but tend to be confined to Bill Duncan, who is finally transformed through the grueling loss of his black friends and the betrayal of his white lover from a benevolent, open-minded young radical to a mature, hardened fighter. The metamorphosis has striking physical manifestations: " . . . while Bill sat before his desk, a change began to take place in him. The change was not apparent at once, but even then it began to show on his face. The soft contours of adolescence sloughed off and the more determined and manly planes sharpened at his cheek-bones and jaw. Four horizontal lines on his forehead deepened and became permanent."[13] Similar dramatic images embody the final moral contrast of the novel—in the humble cabin where the workers meet to organize, the light from a single lantern magnifies their shadows to heroic proportions on the ceiling and walls and appears to multiply their numbers, while in the great mansion, the orator with the diseased mouth feels the wintry touch of death in the air. The waxing and waning powers of the South seem controlled, in spite of the presence of many erudite Party members who might have explained it otherwise, by dark mysterious forces that have no clearly logical connection with the rational, human, revolutionary activity. The atmosphere of hatred and bloodthirstiness, the predestined array of attractive and repulsive personalities on opposing sides, and the highly emotive incidents and images of oppression combine to provoke wrath rather than the pity of the first novel. It is a more militant response, yet one that is the obvious result of literary contrivance rather than intellectual conviction.

The reaction of reviewers to *A Sign for Cain* was remarkably consistent: they hailed it as fine propaganda but noted its weaknesses as a novel.[14] Their assumption that it is effective propaganda appears to derive from the obvious manipulation of sympathy for the Communist heroes and against the capitalist villains and from the shocking nature of the atrocities of the plot. But there is a certain condescension in expecting the novel's audience to be swayed by such transparent devices. It would be dangerous to accuse Grace Lumpkin of dishonesty in her handling of these extremes, particularly since, as Louis Kronenburger pointed out in his *Nation* review, the southern press can easily verify the most horrible incidents, and "fantastic, undernourished caricatures" of people can easily be produced as witnesses to this kind of social realism. Yet there is a distortion, a ripping out of context in this kind of selective portrayal of southern horror—a disorientation that refuses to admit the aesthetic rules of the gothic but nevertheless wishes to capitalize on its terrifying effects. Flannery O'Connor has noted the dangers of this kind of writing, " 'Any fiction that comes out of the South is going to be called grotesque by northern readers—unless it is really grotesque. Then—it is going to be called photographic realism.' "[15] That the grotesque mode of fiction does not adapt easily to political purposes was clearly seen in Erskine Caldwell's difficulties in reconciling the absurdity of his vision of man with his melioristic hopes for society. Grace Lumpkin's lurid South in *A Sign for Cain* tends to give some credibility to Leslie Fiedler's theory that the one thing literary radicals feared in the thirties was the failure of fear itself; so they cherished horror as a counterthreat to the official optimism and limited reforms of the New Deal.

Certainly Myra Page, who came to fiction writing from a background of reporting for the *Daily Worker*, relished the literary prospects of terror. Like Fielding Burke and Grace Lumpkin, she was a native southerner who, having published in 1929 *Southern Cotton Mills and Labor*, a Communist-oriented study of the textile industry, was also familiar with the ways of the poor white factory workers. Her 1932 Gastonia novel *Gathering Storm* is a book so ideologically "correct" that it was almost wholly ignored by reviewers to the right of the *New Masses*, who were presumably less delighted than that magazine that someone had finally treated the strike events with the proper social understanding of "one who has studied Marxism and Leninism."[16] It is a *bildungsroman* only in a very limited sense, for there are no reactionary peasants to be converted here but rather a highly class-conscious urban proletariat from the outset. The Crenshaw family, having produced three generations of mill workers, has gradually come to forget the freedom and beauty of a former mountain life and has learned in the mill towns to substitute renewed religious fervor for the other ecstasy that has been abandoned. They are firmly fixed in urban ways, and though they lead a nomadic existence, constantly on the move from one mill hill to the next, they no longer contemplate a life away from the textile factories.

The seeds of revolution are already strong in the family in the person of Old Marge, a formidable matriarch reminiscent of Ishma's Granny Starkweather, who has arrived independently at conclusions that will later be part of the union program. The relationship between Old Marge and young Marge, the heroine, is almost exactly parallel to that in Burke's novel: this old woman too cites scripture for her own purpose and educates her granddaughter in highly antitraditional attitudes to race, poverty, and war. The acuteness of her analysis of the calculated hatred between black and poor white, her untutored intuition that Hearst was responsible for the Spanish War, and her lyrical indictment of the owners—" 'The bossmen'll feed them machines the gold outta your hair, the shine outta your eye, the quickness outta your fingers' "[17]—ring rather false in their articulate comprehensiveness. In her dying seconds she castigates the " 'stinkin' mills . . . took all, give nuthin' " (100) and extracts from Marge a promise that she will fight for her rights. Thus, from the beginning Marge has no ambivalence about her allegiances—the purpose of the remainder of the novel will be to heap coals on the fires of indignation that her grandmother has set alight, by exposing in fact and theory the full arena of oppression, suffering, and brutality to which workers are subjected throughout the world.

Since Marge is already committed to the ideals of revolution, some of the horrors are bound to seem, as in Lumpkin, more gratuitous than persuasive to the reader. Marge's first introduction to socialist literature is *The Jungle*, but lest this hint is not sufficient for the reader, we are given two violent, nausea-inducing episodes to remind us. The first is in a fish cannery where "the floor was covered with water and slime, smells of dead and rotting fish assaulted their nostrils, and the salt bit into the open sores in their hands, cut and bleeding from the sharp edges of the shells" (77). If we have any revulsion to spare, it is tapped by the slaughterhouse incident. "So George stood all day, his hands dripping with animal blood, his apron and face spattered, a small stream of red fluid gushing over his straddled feet. His job was to slash the throats of hogs as they swung by him, suspended head downward, their feet tied to a moving chain. For ten hours he plunged his knife until his head reeled from the stench of stale blood and the sight of that never-ending line of squealing, lurching animals moving toward him" (204). More of the same comes with the violent rape and murder of a young black girl; when her fiancé attempts revenge, the reprisals taken on the black community are described minutely in all their savage variety. There is a horrifying catalogue of amateur abortion methods practiced by poor southern women who will willingly risk agonizing deaths sooner than produce another child; and lest the indictment may seem exclusively American, we are not spared the European trenches of the First World War. Without rejecting Page's thesis that this is the world capitalism has wrought, one has nevertheless some difficulty in garnering sufficient optimism after this atrocity show to place much hope in any schemes for improving that world. A surfeit of evil can endanger the propaganda value of this novel, for there is little to counter that vision but the repeated slogans of Solidarity Forever and The Internationale, which eventually come to seem as much a drugged substitute for reality as the Sunday night hymns around the wheezy organ, whose "harmonies stirred their souls with a mysterious beauty far beyond their humdrum lives" (42).

That Page's purpose is propaganda is further apparent from the didactic tone of the narrative, which never fails to spell out the morals clearly implicit in the incidents, e.g., "Everyday, while their elders were at work in the mill, unknown to them, two tow heads and two kinky ones would spend happy hours along the creek's bank, floating boats on its muddied waters or sliding down its inviting slopes" (69). This description makes its point, albeit rather sentimentally, but Page adds, "For children, like nature, know no color line. Humans are humans to them. Of race and caste they know nothing and care less, until their elders, out of their worldly wisdom, take them in hand" (69). When the inevitable separation of the friendship comes, she adds to its pathos. "Something ugly and mean, dimly comprehended but deeply emotional, entered their souls and tainted their breath" (71). When Tom finds a job in New York, his companion says, "'We're fellow-workers'n friends, Tom, shovin' freight'n organizin' th'working class, side by side'" (87). Apart from this fairly obvious device of making Party slogans appear as though they occur spontaneously in conversation and a most unconvincing habit of the workers of referring to themselves as Po Whites, there are a number of other kinds of overpropagandizing. These include heavy and unsubtle sarcasm, ". . . in a businesslike manner [they] proceeded to beat the two handcuffed men to the floor, . . . hurling curses at the devils who dared defy this great government of law and order" (159); the informed aside that undercuts all opposition arguments, "*The Chicago Tribune, Herald-Examiner* and the Negro paper, the *Defender* (all backed by packing and financial interests), . . ." (211); and the mystical power of solidarity that transcends all rational causation, "As the dirt street sounded with the thud of marching feet Marge felt a new life rising in herself, in those around her, uniting them in one tremendous mass" (285). There are conventional attacks on the AFL, socialists, liberal intellectuals, and all the "darn pinks" (312) as well as a fairly severe reprimand of the northern union leader for his readiness to compromise principles in order to win strike objectives and for his university elitism. " 'You claim to read Lenin a lot," he is chastised by the southern workers, "Wal, that's one point he allays made— not to use high fallutin' phrases' " (307). The novel suffers from the lack of humanizing details that prevented Grace Lumpkin's mill workers from turning into mere proletarian abstractions. There are one or two incidents that might have served this purpose—the trip of Sal and Gertie to the five-and-ten store for a pair of glasses or Aunt Polly's illiterate efforts to figure out possible news copy from looking at the photographs—but their humorous development is invariably cut short by the unnecessary reminder that poor whites cannot pay for a real eye doctor or the page of the newspaper being turned to reveal a picture of "a dark form, hanging limp from a tree, at which flames licked greedily while white-hooded figures crowded around" (121).

Even the heroine Marge is little more than a mouthpiece for all the generalized problems of the poor white woman and an unquestioning receptacle for the teachings of Sinclair, Marx, and Bellamy. In many ways she invites comparison with Fielding Burke's Ishma— determining like her to resist marriage and childbearing but being early trapped by a man not unlike Britt; ultimately she is freed again of husband and all her children by their deaths in mill-related tragedies. Marge's marriage is depicted not so much as the triumph of emotion or desire over reason (as Ishma's is) but rather as an event wholly determined by the circumstances of her life. Books and education have been denied her; so there is no possibility of an intellectual life. The hypocrisy, greed, and lust of the church ministers have destroyed any hopes of spiritual escape; so for her the prospect of a little joy in sex is represented as the sole relief from her bleak routine, in spite of her clear vision of the pursuant terror of littl'uns. Although she is certain that the rich must know how to avoid getting children, Marge "gets caught" immediately, as the mill women spitefully taunt her, and for a desperate period of uncertainty, her faith returns enough for her to pray, "'God, doan let it happen'" (174). Her daughter is born while her husband is away in the war in Europe, and this interlude in the novel when the men are away and the women are running the mills and supporting families alone is emphasized by Page as a period of sharpened bitterness. Determination rises among the women to organize better conditions for themselves. The death of Marge's mother of typhoid and her baby of malnutrition make her determined to try to find union help, though there is resentment among the remaining men and many of the women toward female leadership. However, eventually the workers come to accept the new role of women as they listen to Ella May's songs and Marge's speeches. In this South they rapidly learn to reject the church and accept racial equality, although there is something of a concession here to "racial individualism" as Page tells us, "It was a good chance that Soviet America would include a Negro Toilers' Socialist Republic" (328).

In contrast to the unfavorable emphasis on southern horrors and the favorable distortion of the flexibility of the southern workers, the historical incidents of the Gastonia strike seem to be treated with a good deal of accuracy—the union leaders' squabbles over policy, evictions, tent colony, death of Aderholt, and subsequent riots. Page attempts to balance the vitriolic attacks of the *Gastonia Gazette* by incorporating in the text letters from the strikers to the *Daily Worker*, though she never permits a character to present any arguments hostile to her cause, no matter in what ludicrous or repellent guise. The friendly sheriff who helps Tom, the union leader, escape lynching is the one misfit in the class morality system, "overlooked so far by the clumsy machine of North Carolina politics" (355). One major surprise is that so little is made of the trial incidents, considering their high drama and capacity to reveal a system weighted hopelessly against the strikers. Page breaks off the factual narrative immediately after the mistrial and the revelation that the jury were for acquittal. This avoids some of the best propaganda material, but it also enables the less-principled bail jumping to be ignored. Even more important, Page does not have to end her novel on the note of embattled local catastrophe, which the other Gastonia novels tend to have, with only a glimmer of hope for the future in the solidarity of desperate people. Instead she transports the defendants to a massive Communist party conference in Cleveland, where the implication of their own parochial southern affair can be translated into greater political significance; the price paid for the minor gains in Gastonia seems worthwhile when the textile delegation proudly takes its place amid the miners, auto workers, metal workers, and sailors. There is a sense at this conference that the triumph of the workers is imminent; Marge catches it while staring at the great skyscrapers and traffic of the city, " 'Gee, Tom, it'll be somethin' to take over'n run places like this!' " (367). Speeches, songs, and informal fraternizing by the various union delegates establish a further sense of emotional excitement; so the gathering storm of the title begins to take shape in the prose. Sentences break into fragments of apocalyptic dreams as each speaker interrupts another with his vision of the future; hard times and disaster are foreseen, but now the ultimate goal seems within reach.

A final chorus of the Internationale, some Russian tea, and ecstatic rhetoric complete the tendencies of this novel—not from rural peasant to urban worker or even from ignorant to educated proletarian but rather from historical model to programmed formula. The book is a display of virtuosity in including all the proper Party doctrines and giving them life in a wishful vision of the South, but it demands the sacrifice of both the reader's credulity and his right to confront the material with some measure of independence. Thus it remains deservedly the most neglected of a group of little-read books.

Among these women writers the relative emphasis on feminism and communism varies widely, though all see the two as inevitably linked. Vorse is skeptical not only of the Communists' tactics among the southern poor whites but also of their own ability to adhere to their ideals of sexual equality, while Page, at the other extreme, creates a poor white proletariat free from any trace of racial or sexual jealousy. Lumpkin assumes that the problems of women will be automatically solved in a Communist state, while Burke warns that there will never be any Communist state without a prior radical revision of the relations between men and women, including the remarkable recognition that personal love between the two sexes is obsolete or has " 'fulfilled its destiny in evolution.' " Just as the general poor white stereotype had to be altered to fit the demands of a left-wing image, so had the fictional poor white woman to be revised, not merely in her social behavior but, more problematically, in her relations to the poor white man. The more dramatic way in which this was done by the three southern writers

—Burke, Lumpkin, and Page—reflects perhaps the strength of the literary precedents rather than any contemporary example that was being offered by the Communist party. Besides the example of the lonely rebels of the 1920s literary revival—Ellen Chesser, Judy Pippinger, and Dorinda Oakley— they had also the tragic heroism of Harris's Emma Jane Stucky, the avenging fury of Mrs. Feratia Bivins, and the value orientation of Mrs. Bony Mulock who sold her white trash husband for $100. This last case is an interesting one, since it elevates the poor white woman at the expense and degradation of the poor white man, reversing rather than equalizing sexual roles. The comic moral value of this is unquestionable, but the similar tendency that may be noted in the Marxist novels poses a threat to their philosophy of solidarity. Thus Burke's heroine Ishma, Lumpkin's Bonnie, and Page's Marge all marry men who are good-looking, charming, and frivolous while the women are much more serious-minded revolutionaries. All three writers make compensatory gestures by giving the heroines loyal and embittered brothers, whose fraternal love is sympathetic to their sisters' endeavors but untinged by any other personal claims on them.

However, beyond these efforts to revise the social assertiveness of the poor white woman and the heavy campaigning for birth-control information, there is relatively little interest in the novels of these women writers in sexuality as an aspect of feminist revolt. Although all of them admit an unusual attraction between their heroines and the powerful new excitement of the factory world, preferring to concentrate on the disillusioning experiences of industrial conditions, they never develop it into the strange sexual adoration that Erskine Caldwell explores. The more sophisticated psychological problems of alienation and reification which came to have a central importance in the novels of the last two Gastonia writers, Sherwood Anderson and William Rollins, could too readily prove a distraction from the feminist aspects of egalitarianism. Thus, when sexuality is discussed at all, it is viewed as yet another threat—like religious ecstasy or the consoling beauty of the physical world—to communal goals of organization and class struggle.

CHAPTER VII

Sex and Class Consciousness among the Poor Whites

The reticence of left-wing feminist writers to deal with questions of sexual as well as social and economic liberation for women is only partially explained by their avoidance of the irrational aspects of poor white conduct. The Communist party line in the thirties showed relatively little enthusiasm for the issue, which they felt smacked of "Village Bohemianism,"[1] and there was positive hostility to Freud in Marxist circles at this time, since he was viewed not as a fellow scientist but as a prophet of hedonism, a metaphysician, and an idealist. Thus though Freudians and Marxists alike were engaged in the investigation of contemporary alienation from different bases, Marxists were reluctant, at least until the end of the decade, to extend their materialist logic into any methodical study of sexuality. Yet it is obvious that some of those American writers who veered leftward in the thirties had had a good deal of acquaintance with the literary Freudianism of the previous decade—indeed Frederick Hoffman suggests in *Freudianism and the Literary Mind* that the sexual rebels of the postwar period were very often the economic radicals of the depression.[2] Although none of the women writers on Gastonia came to Marxism by way of the new psychology, the most eminent novelist who did, Sherwood Anderson, had a reputation as the "American Freudian."[3] Whether such an assertion of influence was justified or not, Anderson's fiction before the 1930s certainly exhibited trends that were then considered rather inimical to Marxism—an interest in individual frustration, repression, and the bourgeois disease of *angst* that traced its causes to something more intangible and mysterious than the symptoms of class war. D. H. Lawrence was partly the inspiration for Anderson's attempts to portray the desperate gropings for fulfillment of an effete generation that had lost touch with the wellsprings of its vitality; beyond that there was the echo, if not the influence, of Freud in Anderson's concern with sexual inhibitions, dream symbolism, and psychoanalytic methods that "encouraged hostility to the social sources of repression."[4] In addition to these somewhat anticollectivist trends, a style that used elements of modernism and naturalism combined to produce a reputation that was almost an antithetical stereotype of the ideal proletarian novelist of leftist prescriptions.

Anderson first acknowledged a public commitment to communism in 1932 when he participated in a *New Masses* symposium on "How I Came to Communism." Glorifying in this endorsement from such an auspicious literary figure, the magazine refrained from making any qualifying comment on Anderson's stated credo: "I believe and am bound to believe that those of you who are revolutionists will get the most help out of such men as myself not by trying to utilize such talents as we have directly as writers of propaganda but in leaving us as free as possible to strike, by our stories out of American life, into the deeper facts."[5] Since 1932 was a relatively late point in Anderson's career, it is possible to seek in his earlier work precedents of this political commitment, although they do not always augur well for the nature of Anderson's radicalism.

Windy McPherson's Son, 1916, Anderson's first published novel, touches only tangentially on industrial conditions and the labor movement as they impinge on the life of the sharp-dealing businessman hero, Sam McPherson. Sam is no real friend to the cause of labor, although he is willing to experiment in strike tactics as he also dabbles in marriage, religion, sex, and dissipation to achieve some essence that is missing in his successful career. This empiricism, which was to characterize so many of Anderson's heroes, was also an accurate forecast of Anderson's own later attitude toward communism. His hero's rejection of socialism in this first novel is based on his disgust with the limited aims of the workers—a ten percent raise in wages instead of a new vision of society. Anderson was searching for a more profound ideal that would not yield to petty compromises or be intimidated by power, although at the same time he condemns socialist leaders for their insistence on principle at the expense of pragmatic success. Despite the confusion this novel reveals about Anderson's understanding of socialism, it does display a highly class-conscious writer with great compassion for the dreary lives of the workers. Perhaps more ominously, this compassion is tinged with a good deal of skepticism about their integrity and worthiness, while his admiration tends to be reserved for the kind of ruthless individuals who would participate in a mass movement only as leaders.

In this latter vein is Beaut McGregor, the hero of *Marching Men*, 1917; this book, dedicated to "American Workingmen," traces the rise of McGregor—a charismatic leader who organizes armies of men to march and drill in unison, apparently in anticipation of some apocalyptic goal that is never clearly specified in political or social terms. McGregor is fascinated with the potential power of the mass organism he creates and with its capacity to bring order into a chaotic world; since Anderson never dissociates his own views from his hero's, he presumably endorses McGregor's contempt for democratic socialism and his faith in "something" more mystical, totalitarian, and antiintellectual. The cohesiveness of the marching men is at one point threatened by individualism, which McGregor punishes brutally, and by family life, which he rejects utterly; but in the end the movement collapses because McGregor attempts to articulate its meaning, and "'talk kills dreams.'"[6] Despite the fact that the *New Republic* hailed the work as a proletarian novel and it received warm praise from other radical critics, it is obvious that it has little in common with the genre that flourished in the depression. *Marching Men* is not only devoid of theory and goal, but it is also largely uninterested in the plight of the workers or in opposition to their capitalist exploiters. Anderson himself later drew the parallel between the ideology of his book and the Fascist movements that were to sweep Europe, saying, "When I saw the dream I had put into action I grew afraid of my dream."[7]

Anderson's literary reputation crested with the publication of *Winesburg, Ohio* in 1919, and during the next decade he made the obligatory trips to Paris to meet Gertrude Stein and James Joyce and lived in both New York and New Orleans. The fiction of this period continues to present bewildered heroes searching for fulfillment, but the emphasis is now more strongly on sexual problems than on economic or political ones. Then in 1925 Anderson decided to live permanently in Virginia, and he discovered a new interest in the lives of small southern communities and particularly in the southern textile factories, which he began to visit methodically in 1930. His interest in southern labor conditions combined with a newfound fascination with the dynamic energy of industrial machinery to produce in 1931 a collection of prose poems and essays, *Perhaps Women*, in which Anderson attempted to suggest links between technology, sexuality, and economic exploitation. In this early and perhaps unwitting exploration of some areas where Marxism and Freudianism confront each other, Anderson deals with alienation and despair in terms very close to Marxist theories of reification.[8] People in factories are shown to have become mere adjuncts of things, tools in the production process—but Anderson does not follow through by articulating any logical economic solution. He tends to dwell instead on romantic, anarchic cures that may be effected on the individual psyche and ignores the scientific, problem-solving aspects of Marxism that were most highly prized by its adherents in the thirties.

The prose essays and poems of *Perhaps Women* oscillate between Whitmanesque celebrations of the beauty and power of machinery and dark warnings of the humiliation and perhaps castration of modern man by the machine. A vague hope exists for the salvation of the race through women, who have secret inner reserves that technology cannot tap. Anderson sees that in factories men have lost touch, literally, with the materials of their labor and have become separated from its end product. However, instead of seeing the Marxist necessity to abolish the capitalist system, Anderson would like to substitute the reactionary mystique of a return to nature to find the secret springs of man's pride once again: "men will have to go back to nature more. They will have to go to the fields and the rivers. There will have to be a new religion, more pagan, something more closely connected with fields and rivers."[9] Such a retreat from the economic implications of exploitation and the careful distinctions made in the responses of the two sexes to factory work is scarcely tractable material for the forming of revolutionary consciousness. The general attitude to women, seeing them as the voracious consumers who benefit most from mechanization and are least dehumanized by it, is both hostile and envious. Their ascendancy increases with the impotence of the men before the machines; Anderson describes an incident in a factory where the lighting fails, and in the darkness the women taunt the men maliciously for their emasculation.

Coexistent with these attitudes in this book is a rather different set of sympathies, which show in a more conventionally socialist fashion the depths of Anderson's pity for the weariness and meanness of the lives of southern mill workers whose villages he tours and his extreme bitterness against the debasement of human dignity in a system that values production above everything else. Two of the most powerful sections of the book, "Lift Up Thine Eyes" and "Loom Dance," depict the efforts of factories to automate people as efficiently as machines. The first is a savage satire on a "scientific" assembly plant, where all activity is subordinate to the manufacture of the Bodel car: "Let the notion grow and grow that there is something superhuman at the core of all this" (24); "The belt is God. God has rejected me. You're fired" (26). The second is the frenzied aping of the dance of the looms in a mill where a weaver has rebelled against the tyranny of a "minute-man." "He hopped up and down in an absurd, jerky way. Cries, queer and seemingly meaningless cries, came from his throat" (36). He symbolizes all the pent-up fury of oppression, and soon the whole room whirls into the resentful activity:

> Lights danced in the room.
> The looms kept dancing.
> A weaver was dancing on a minute-man's watch.
> A weaver was dancing on a minute-man's glasses.
> Other weavers kept coming.
> They came running. Men and women came from the spinning-room.
> There were more cries.
> There was music in the mill. [37]

A major problem in *Perhaps Women* is a discrepancy between the tenor of its ideological arguments—against modern woman and for a return to earthy life and religion—and the metaphorical vehicle that should convey them, the vivid episodes from factory life. These episodes seem to suggest that the problems of all the workers are the result of a calculated and heartless profit motivation and therefore point to communism or syndicalism as the answer. The abstract theorizing, however, seems to search for something more irrational, indeterminate—essentially beyond the scope of social revolution.

Between the publication of *Perhaps Women* in 1931 and his Gastonia novel *Beyond Desire* in 1932, Anderson made his public commitment to communism. It was at best a tentative commitment, at worst an example of considerable intellectual irresponsibility. Writing to Dreiser, he was skeptical of the saving qualities of the new creed he was endorsing, " 'It may be the answer, and then it may only be a new sort of Puritanism, more deadly than the old.' "[10] He was also almost completely ignorant of Communist theory: he gave Edmund Wilson permission to use his name on any Party document Wilson thought might benefit from it and told him, with a fine disregard for consequences, " 'Where you are willing to go I'll go.' "[11] Out of his declining talents and this medley of contradictory attitudes, Anderson produced *Beyond Desire*, a novel using much of the background of the Gastonia events, which reveals both his hopes and doubts about the effectiveness of communism to cure the contemporary malaise as well as his reservations about its methods of operation. It was pronounced, not surprisingly, "a work of incoherence. Its structure is a chaos. . . . Its prose is in an advanced stage of decomposition. . . . And its theme. . . soon becomes a sad botch."[12] Almost unanimously condemned by critics who readily admitted to sharing the infectious bewilderment of both Anderson and his adolescent hero, Red Oliver, it was generally viewed as a failure even in the genre of the proletarian novel. Oscar Cargill wrote of it, "Anderson really was too much absorbed by sex and too willing to hide in his naiveté to write a proletarian novel,"[13] and Reinhold Niebuhr remarked rather primly, "there is more about fornication than about the class struggle in this book."[14] However, it is precisely this relationship between sex and political activism that interests Anderson—not in the opposition of passion and intellect or of one beloved individual and the masses, as in Fielding Burke's treatment of the subject, but in the capacity of sexual, social, or indeed religious commitment to fill the internal void of his tortured characters. Anderson's attitude toward communism is therefore rather calculatedly empirical, and his hero's final martyrdom for the cause extremely sardonic. Red's sacrifice is neither noble nor effective but a piece of foolish bravado and a self-inflicted penalty for his own guilt.

The novel is constructed of four disparate sections that touch tangentially but never finally merge into a unified whole. The first section deals with the formative influences in the life of Red Oliver, a middle-class, college-educated southern youth who sweeps floors in a Georgia cotton mill while trying to assess his priorities in life. Red's highest aspirations are measured by his envy of a radical college friend who is having an affair with a liberated schoolteacher in Kansas: "She had become a sincere Red [Communist]. She thought there was something beyond desire, but that you had to satisfy desire and understand and appreciate the wonders of desire first."[15] Red's friend endorsed this point of view heartily and argued that "the revolution was coming. When it came it was going to demand strong and quiet people willing to work, not just noisy ill-prepared people. He thought that every woman ought to begin by finding her man" (9). Red hungers for an experience like this, but in the Georgia mill town his only experience of sex is the vicarious misery of his parents' marriage, his only contact with prospective revolutionaries the vague curiosity and deference of the mill workers to someone who is obviously in a class apart from them; they finally give him a hesitant invitation to play on their baseball team.

As a background to Red's story, Anderson provides a rapid survey of southern history, customs, and institutions; he investigates the role of southern churches in promoting industrialism and the sexual relationships between southern blacks and whites. These two samples of explanatory sociology demonstrate once again Anderson's ambivalence toward conventional left-wing interpretations of the origins of class war. The indictment of the alliance between mill owners and churches is perfectly orthodox, but the primitivist emphasis on the healthy immunity of blacks to neurosis while the whites are tortured by frustration and guilt is (like the separate classification of women in *Perhaps Women*) obviously contrary to a desirable solidarity. Such a division by race implies that the maladjustment of the whites is not economically derived, since the happy blacks are undoubtedly at the lowest level of material welfare. It also complicates the "beyond desire" theory articulated by Neil; according to it, blacks should be in the vanguard of revolution, while Anderson places them completely outside it in this novel.

The next two sections of the book, being in the first case a study of the inner life of a group of mill girls and in the second a psychic biography of Ethel Long, help to expand and perhaps further confuse Anderson's attitude to the problems of southern whites. Ethel is a modern bourgeois woman, educated in the North, who is paralyzed, paradoxically, by her liberated consciousness, since there is no way in the archaic traditions of the South for her to fulfill her newfound notions of freedom. Differences in class and social position seem to account here for significant differences in sexual behavior and mental adjustment in these women. The ease and warmth the factory girls feel toward each other and their guiltless enjoyment of physical contact is opposed to the lack of spontaneity in Ethel's world. When Doris massages Grace's aching body, Grace compliments her on her "good rubbing hands" and drifts happily into a reverie of her mountain life before she entered the mills. When a similar occasion of close physical contact arises between Ethel and her youthful stepmother Blanche, Ethel remains rigid and cold to Blanche's first pathetic advances and finally, when Blanche becomes desperate, beats her with all her strength, drags her hair, and thinks, " 'Never. Never that.' . . . Here was something she would never want any man to know" (223–24). There appears, in the candor of the mill girls' affection and the fearful deceit of the two middle-class women, to be a comment on bourgeois repression and selfishness, but one is always reluctant in this book to risk such generalizations, since the situations are so particularized. Even if there is a truth here about white women, it is unlikely to be transferable to either men or blacks.

The "Mill Girls" episode does demonstrate, however, Anderson's keen sympathies with the plight of the lintheads; his compassion for them is neither manipulative nor condescending, nor does he make them artificially heroic. The mill world with its infuriating injustices is also depicted as an exciting and often beautiful place. "It wasn't ugly. It was big and light. It was wonderful. Their life was in a little narrow hallway inside a big room. The walls of the hallway were machines. Light came from above. A fine soft spray of water, really mist, came from above. That was to keep the flying thread soft and flexible for the machines" (94). Red Oliver even notices an affinity between the girls and their machines—they are like little mothers looking after their own children. But these child-charges are ominous, for they produce the fine lint floating in the air that the mill people believe is the source of their frequent tuberculosis. Thus the workers do not share the romantic and sometimes grotesque view of the machinery that comes to the reader, modified by the perspective of Red, who sees it in highly unnatural images. When a strange woman comes to town with plans for establishing a union, the enthusiasm of the workers for this practical solution to their problems must be balanced against the impenetrable mystique with which Red surrounds the technology of the mill. Anderson refuses to weaken the implications of the human pragmatic or the inhuman—almost demonic—points of view by holding them in equal prominence throughout the book.

Even Red's final turn to communism seems less motivated by his observations of mill life than by a seemingly inevitable train of events, begun when he has a disappointing sexual encounter with Ethel. As town librarian she has been ordering Marx especially for him. When Ethel leaves home after the lesbian advances of Blanche, Red mistakenly assumes that his affair with her is responsible; he immediately packs and sets out on the road that will eventually lead him to death for the cause. Thus the first step toward his final commitment is a foolish error about his personal significance to Ethel. From this point on, a series of involuntary incidents precipitates Red into the final crisis.

He awakens some indeterminate time after he has left his home in Georgia to discover that he has been asleep in the tent colony at Birchfield, a striking mill town in North Carolina where the ballad singer has just been shot. Anderson has his hero contemplate "by what a queer chain of circumstances he had got there" (247); the final link of this chain was his mistaken identity as a Communist union leader. This produced an offer of shelter from a woman in the camp, and Red was too embarrassed to inform her of the truth. Before this fateful accident, Red had been involved in some incidents on the road that helped shape both this decision not to reveal himself and his final sacrifice. One of the incidents, which has obvious symbolic connections with his final action, occurred when he was bumming with a group of tramps; Red had seven dollars hidden in his shoe, and when one of the tramps befriended him in search of food, he denied that he had any money at all. The man left him and begged fifteen cents, which he spent on food for both of them—food that was naturally embittered by Red's guilt. This combines with his feelings of inadequacy about Ethel and his shame for not having stuck by the mill workers in Georgia to create his need to do penance.

While Red is approaching his final crisis, the Communists are pushing ahead with their plans to organize the South; their disciplined activities are developed parallel to Red's aimless journey. Again, quoting from all shades of favorable and hostile opinion but endorsing none himself, Anderson demonstrates a multiplicity of attitudes toward them. One accusation that he does appear to support seriously is their callous readiness to sacrifice workers for propaganda, but he modifies even this with his admiration for their ruthless energy. "There was something in them harder, more unscrupulous, more determined . . . they were something quite different from the old leaders of labor in America" (270). Red himself never gets beyond the stage of finding the whole movement "queer and puzzling"; but having found that religion and sex are not competent to fill his hunger, he feels that communism may be worth a try. The dramatic nature of the experiment is forced by his mistaken identity. In the front ranks of a march of strikers from the tent colony, Red finds himself confronting the local militia, led by Ned Sawyer, a young man of almost identical background to Red's. The two young men face each other in a nervous showdown, marked by the keen embarrassment of each at his foolish, mock-heroic prominence. Thinking, "'I'm a silly ass,'" Ned issues a challenge that anyone who advances will be shot. Thinking, "'I'm a silly ass,'" Red steps forward to accept it (356). He is shot instantly. The strikers stage a short riot; a week later the factory is running as usual. The novel ends by emphasizing neither the defeat of the strike nor even the possible future activity of the workers but with Ethel—distraught at Red's end though she cared little for him while he lived—driving frantically through a lashing thunder storm.

It is difficult to see how this "striking into the deeper facts" that Anderson had proposed in the *New Masses* could have been of much benefit to proletarian literature. Not only does it lack the authoritative solutions common to this school of writing, but it lacks the capacity to pursue any ideas beyond their mere proposal. Granville Hicks tried valiantly to find significant hints in the novel of the stirrings of the poor—"the awakening of a people may be foreshadowed in this awakening of a writer who has always been close to them"[16]—but he clearly evaded the main problems of the book. What value it has must finally rest on Anderson's willingness to investigate questions which he was in no way equipped to answer: important interrelationships among sexual, racial, and class notions of personal fulfillment; the primacy of acquired philosophy or fatal circumstances in shaping momentous decisions; the ethics of revolutionary violence; and the role of communism in effecting a cure for the psychic as well as physical deficiencies of American life.

Anderson must also be credited with some innovations in the treatment of poor white characters, especially women, in *Beyond Desire*. Those qualities in Anderson's writing that prevent him from assuming an authorial omniscience over the bewilderment of his fictional people are the same qualitites that preclude the possibility of any condescension on his part to poor white "types." Though he has thoroughly assimilated the mountain history, folklore, and sociology of his mill people, they are still presented as utterly individual personalities. The mill women share a monotonous routine at work, they live in identical mill-built houses, they sense instinctively when each other's feet begin to ache from running and tending to the machinery, they sing in unison trite songs about the Milky Ways and Cokes that relieve their exhaustion, but behind the common external facade Anderson explores utterly discrete kinds of consciousness. Such people prove very willing to support unions, preferably "the worst kind" (as one of them refers to the Communists), but Anderson refrains from establishing a connection between this limited kind of class consciousness and the essence of their dreams of a different existence.

The last of the Gastonia novels to be written, William Rollins, Jr.'s *The Shadow Before*, 1934, takes up precisely this latter question of the relationship of communism to the sick and deprived soul with a more penetrating survey of middle- and working-class maladjustment, perversion, and fantasy. The setting is a strike in an East Coast textile town, with the Gastonia events transposed from the South in order to use a large immigrant population as a foil to basic ideals of Americanism. Consequently race is eliminated and religion greatly reduced as issues for the townspeople and strike organizers; instead the independent upward mobility of native tradition and immigrant dreams clashes with united action by the permanently trapped laboring classes. The novel is similar to Mary Heaton Vorse's *Strike!* in handling community psychology, although Rollins works through powerful individual characters rather than attempting, as she did, to chart mass emotions. A tightly organized plot brings together a representative group of characters from a variety of classes and backgrounds, all of whom appear to be abnormal emotionally—although only one, the mill owner's son, is criminally insane.

The license Rollins takes in moving the Gastonia events to New England obviously makes theories on the treatment of southern poor whites largely irrelevant; although the contrasting treatment of immigrants with no laudable revolutionary antecedents or lingering Jeffersonian ideals excludes the likelihood of any nostalgic bias. There can be none of the southern writers' rather maternalistic approval of properly rebellious attitudes in their newfangled proletarians. Rollins's strikers appeal to no national sentiments, nor are they particularly engaging personally: led by Larry Marvin (a neurotic version of Fred Beal) they are noteworthy for their prominent drunkenness, promiscuity, homosexuality, and violent cruelty. Rideout finds that Rollins "labored so hard not to idealize his workers in *The Shadow Before* that they appear to be as morally irresponsible and emotionally unstable as their antagonists."[17] In spite of this, a significant distinction is made between their predilections, which are in a sense positive and actively pursued, and the vices of the middle class, which are characterized by their frustration, stultification, and impotence. Of the workers Micky, the tough Irish girl, is unrepentant in the pursuit of her casual love affairs; Doucet, the Frenchman, drinks to excess; and Olsen, the Swedish bobbin boy, takes a savage beating because of his frank homosexual love for Doucet. In contrast to these are the discreet and guilt-ridden manias of the Thayer family, Judge Simonski, and Harry Baumann, the representatives of the middle class. Mrs. Thayer, middle-aged and sexually desperate, is a secret drinker whose genteel hypocrisy prevents her from even the enjoyment of her indulgence; her daughter Marjorie is an aspiring actress, so paranoid that she does not dare venture outside her own home, much less to her dreamed-of drama school in New York; Judge Simonski derives a gleeful vicarious excitement in the courtroom when he orders the father of a nineteen-year-old girl striker to publicly spank his daughter. Harry Baumann, the Jewish son of the mill owner, is the only member of this class to dare to act out his repressed fantasies of rape, murder, theft, and arson (all considerably more ominous in execution than any of the workers' vices) until finally only suicide is left to complete the destructive chain. Harry, like Red, toys with the idea that radical commitment may fill the "lonely void" within him but is too intelligent and honest to continue long in naive self-deception about his motives for setting up a farm home for the strike children and finally trying to burn down his father's mill.

Perhaps because of the complexities of intrigue and guilt that accompany it, the bourgeois decadence of *The Shadow Before* proves a more fascinating literary topic than the more wholesome vices of the strikers—a comment those skeptical about the motives of proletarian writers were to make frequently. Yet sensationalism is obviously not one of Rollins's techniques; in accordance with his shift from the real-life southern setting, he also removes from the plot the more lurid and grotesque incidents which tend to have a grimly comic, disorienting effect on the serious, rational tone. The Committee of One Hundred here do not sing hymns as they destroy cans of dried milk for babies, and although a large part of the novel is dominated by fictional transcripts of the trial, the waxwork stunt is minimized. Rollins's milieu is not a distorting, deviant one but is presented as normal, a random choice of setting, which the South never purports to be.

As Rollins refuses to make revolution palatable by placing it in an American tradition that reminisces about Debs, the Wobblies, and Bellamy, he also presents Americanism as a selfish grasping creed that can be fulfilled only by narrowing one's horizons and warping one's personality. Its chief proponent is Benjamin Franklin Thayer, a mill superintendent whose name suggests, as well as the great apologist for private enterprise, the hated judge in the Sacco-Vanzetti case. Thayer takes on the task of educating his immigrant Portuguese protegé, Ramon Vieira, in his personal ideology of success, which is to be achieved by " 'hard work, getting to know things. Ignorance is—dirty. If you play clean games in the company's gym, read clean books—.' "[18] By these means the young man is to combat godlessness and bolshevism; only on the subject of the more rebellious employees does this icy man become alive. " 'Give them their rope . . . in regular life, and down at the mill . . . and then—' he turned to Ramon; the thin smile vanished; '—tighten it in!' " (130). Thayer chants repeatedly his formula of "hard work, brains and loyalty," but it is his obsession with moral hygiene that creates in him vigilante fantasies in which he will " 'clean up the town as a whole, clean it of lawlessness, subversive elements, clean it of the immorality running rampant, *clean the whores and bastards out*' " (328). When the trial jury appears to have begun the process of eliminating the " 'nests of vipers,' " Thayer proposes to visit the lovers' cave where they allegedly propagate their species and prevent them from ever breeding again. When only a few curious adolescents offer their assistance, he thinks, "So with a ragged faithful remnant, Washington crossed the Delaware" (376). In the cave they find only the suicide corpse of Harry Baumann, son of the biggest stockholder in Fullerton mills, renowned product of hard work, brains, and loyalty.

Thus victory for the workers does not seem altogether remote in this novel, in view of the rapid disintegration of their opposition. The strike fails miserably in *The Shadow Before*, and the prospects for the future seem slim, in spite of Micky's valiant final decision to fight to the end and name her expected child after Lenin; but the seeds of self-destruction seem so firmly implanted in the bourgeoisie themselves that the "final conflict" of which the strikers sing in inch-high block capitals may scarcely even require their aid. Their bosses and owners are already succumbing through their dissipated intellects, emasculated volition, and fanatical lack of purpose.

In style, Walter Rideout selects *The Shadow Before*—a novel that reviewers generally agreed owed a good deal to both Joyce and Dos Passos—as the "classic example of proletarian experimentalism."[19] The narrative shifts constantly through different levels of consciousness—from thought to its verbalization to imagined response and actual response—a technique particularly well suited to exploring the schizoid and guilt-ridden characters like Mrs. Thayer, Marjorie, and Harry Baumann. Familiar Dos Passos methods of introducing songs, newspaper headlines, fragments of speeches, court transcripts, play scenes, and Party slogans are skilfully integrated into the main body of the text—not set apart as in *U.S.A.* under Newsreel and Camera Eye headings. Visually, the book tries to create an impact with superlarge, multilingual printings of lines from the *Communist Manifesto*—the single slogan, "Workers of the World Unite" repeated in English, French, Portuguese, and Polish, each time dominating a full page, is an attempt to introduce a visual echo of picket banners and posters into the text. More effective in conveying the ambience of the factory world is Rollins's sensitive ear for the multiplicity of noises that assaults the workers constantly and the mechanical rhythms that dominate their lives. Doucet's ears are subjected to a barrage of scolding and song in two languages when he reaches his tenement home, but the incessant sound of the machines still controls him: " '. . . *pour écrire un*—' She sidled to the window, craned her neck to look sideways, down—'Jeanne,

JEANNE!—alors,' she whirled to the baby in her arms; 'veus-tu te taire une petite moment—JEANNE! you slap Marguerite and I give you something on the behind—*donnez-moi ta plume, pour écrire un mot . . .*' Doucet bit into a burning hunk of potato. '*Merde!*' he muttered. *THUMP*   THROB; *THUMP*   THROB" (51). In the mill itself all the action and conversation of the workers is subservient to the machines: they become mere accessories to them, their function utterly superseded by the equipment they handle. The reader's comprehension of what is going on is filtered through the jerky movements and noiseless speech that emerge from the roaring dominance of the machine's activity. "Clamp them on; snap them off. Young Olsen, the bobbin-boy, was in the aisle beside her. They moved their lips in talk, and now she shook her head and clamped one on, and suddenly their mouths were opened wide with noiseless laughter. UP; down. UP; down. Olsen was speaking, peering through his thickened glasses at the girl, and while she snapped a thread and watched, his softwhite, sleeveless arms gesticulated, sluggish, through the roar, up and down. UP; down" (92).

Sometimes Rollins's innovations seem less controlled and logical than these—he tends to favor run-on words like "ofcourse" and "neverendingly" and "farprojecting" that gain little in significance from the typographical novelty; extra heavy capitals appear at times to be used arbitrarily, as when Harry Baumann orders "ONE CHICKEN PIE AND POTATO SALAD" (193). Such emphasis might be understandable in a starving worker who rarely has the capacity to make such an order, but for a wealthy man who has displayed no special interest in food it seems pointless. The trial is reported with considerable contempt for the court procedure, but it is nevertheless startling to be confronted suddenly by a young woman reporter named Alice, for whom things get "curiouser and curiouser," since Rollins generally plays down the more fantastic aspects of the original in order to concentrate on the specious legal arguments. In reporting the prosecuting lawyer's histrionic peroration, Rollins uses all the resources of his irony and then suddenly seems to relinquish the effort to make literary techniques work for his point. " 'Do you believe in the flag of this great country, singing the song of emancipated minds? Do you believe in its roads that you ride along, hearing the birds sing and seeing its lovely flowers and trees? . . . Take the coat of this unstained Christian, riddled with bullets, and keep it with you as an emblem of justice. I grieve for you! I grieve for our community! I'm full of compassion for that bereaved lady, I'm full of sorrow for her children, . . . *I'm full of anguish, I'm full of shit*—' " (356). The conclusion indicates a kind of despair about the efficacy of any art form to express his profound outrage, a problem that James Agee later confronts in *Let Us Now Praise Famous Men.*

In spite of this authorial reservation, *The Shadow Before* is generally conceded to be one of the finer proletarian novels of the thirties. It succeeded with much the same subject matter as that with which Anderson had failed, though the success is partially due to a simplification of the problems. Rollins's workers are in no way idealized as attractive or moral people, but unlike Anderson's lintheads they do possess a clear vision of justice and are opposed by a bourgeoisie that is slowly destroying itself and for which there is no way out. Neither Anderson's workers nor his middle-class hero and heroine have the confidence of such certainty; his novel is pervaded by doubts and bewilderment to which the author is party and over which he appears to have little control. Rollins thus comes much closer than Anderson to endorsing the theory that communism is spiritual as well as material health, but it is significant that this conclusion emerges from the only Gastonia novel deliberately removed in setting to a background freed of the gruesomely violent and comic aspects of southern culture and the mystical and Dionysiac elements of the southern church.

The six Gastonia novels and their two sequels stand centrally in the school of American proletarian literature that Walter Rideout defines from a much wider range of books; they share almost all the motifs he painstakingly catalogues, and in technique they represent a perfect proportional microcosm of the broader range. Four are realistic (Burke, Vorse, Page, and Lumpkin), one is highly experimental (Rollins), and one hybrid (Anderson).[20] Wide narrative license with the factual events of Gastonia is taken in almost all of them, and the thematic and philosophical emphasis is strongly individual. Such a heterogeneous group of novels obviously allays widespread fears of uniformity among American radical writers.

However, there is one common area of debate that emerges in various forms in all the novels and rises directly out of the special relationship of poor whites to communism, although it is also a significant topic for the broadest literary study of human character.

This is the recurrent conflict between the Apollonian and Dionysiac aspects of man's nature: between reason and faith, mind and instinct, science and the supernatural, and—in the Gastonia context—political innovation and tradition. It is symbolized in these novels by the opposition of Marxist rationalism and Christian ecstasy; community responsibility and family loyalties; racial equality and inherited hate; the "healthy" group member and the alienated, neurotic individual; the blight of property ownership and mystical devotion to the land. The extent to which such contrary themes were accommodated in poor white proletarian literature is often a measure of the dogma rather than the literary skill of the authors. Yet there were a number of aspects of the poor white's literary tradition that the Gastonia writers found ripe for assimilation into Marxist-oriented industrial novels—notably the heroic mother figure and the newly rebellious poor white wife. The angry exposés of melioristic naturalism and the ironic humor of the newly urbanized peasant were also adaptable, though the emphasis in the latter had to be shifted from satirizing rural expectations and naive behavior to condemning more explicitly the mill-town reality (a difference most apparent between Caldwell's *Tobacco Road* and Lumpkin's *To Make My Bread*). More difficult to reconcile with left-wing optimism was the use of comic absurdity and grotesque horror: the former had already proved exceedingly complicated for Erskine Caldwell to handle in combination with a serious program of social reform, and the latter, although used freely by both Lumpkin and Page, tends to endanger the acceptance of the solutions offered by raising the ominous suggestion that evil is a stronger and more impenetrable power in the universe than the mere humans who practice it.

Most difficult of all, however, for the Communists to reconcile, both aesthetically and ideologically, was the power of religion and their own necessary worldliness. Since the actual organizers of the Gastonia strike had found religion the prime obstacle to winning the support of the southern poor, the novelists are less ready than the ideologues to condemn it as pie-in-the-sky without admitting its attractions. Their inquiries into its institutional origins inevitably turn up corrupt alliances between the churches and capitalism, but the more thoughtful authors pursue the influence of mystery and otherworldliness and acknowledge the need for such consolation in an imperfect world. Nevertheless, as heralds of a perfect world, they must insist on its rejection. The aesthetic difficulty becomes apparent from the language in which this rejection is made and the rational utopia of communism anticipated. The rhetoric is imbued with the borrowed apocalyptic imagery of the Christian millennium. The disparity between the logical human goal and the passionately supernal orations suggests that there is a sound literary bonus to be gained from the creation of extrarational myths, even for the most reasonable social movements. Several critics have argued that Marxism demonstrates a remarkable capacity for this mythologizing process; it displays, according to one commentator, ". . . all the earmarks of organized religion. It is a faith, emotional and mystical. It has its dogma, creed, and scripture; its theology and apologetics; its orthodoxies, schisms, and heresies; its mythology, hagiography, and cult. It serves all the vital social and psychological functions of religion."[21] This analogy, no matter how useful to the Communist writers of the thirties, would have been absolutely rejected by them. Their opposition to its emphasis on superstition, faith, and authority finds its best expression in Fielding Burke's rather delirious panegyric to the rational human mind and the conquering power of intellect, " 'We have to release even spirit through the door of intelligence.' "[22] Even the novels of Anderson and Rollins, which have less concern with organized religion, come from a rather different angle to a similar conclusion—the regenerative powers of communism become a means of sublimation for other, more irrational aspirations, which are most successful only when the Gastonia events are removed from the southern context.

All the novelists share the dilemma that religion, mythology—all the apparatus of the mind with its logical faculties in suspension— were outside the pale of their philosophy; yet their subject seemed to be best served by these methods. Reason had to be their way of conquering the primitive instincts of violence, prejudice, and faith, which the southern poor whites brought to their industrial life and which were used to buttress their acquiescent misery. Thus, in its most crucial area, their adaptation of a radical ideology to the inherited literary consciousness had to be an inverse and surreptitious one: the Gastonia writers showed an omnivorous and unconfessed tendency to appropriate the practices of the cults they were bent on destroying—a pragmatic course of action that might, in the nonfictional situation, have prevented its disastrous conclusion.

CHAPTER VIII

Agee's Aesthetic of an Unimagined Existence

By the latter half of the 1930s, the possibility of any writer's approaching poor whites with a mind and sensibility erased of preconceptions about them was a very remote one. The Communist writers, no less than Faulkner and Caldwell, had a carefully fore-ordained schema in which the poor white had his appointed role. In the work of all these novelists, he was the product of an artistic vision that stamped him into the pattern of a grander design—whether moral, sociological, or political. Despite Erskine Caldwell's protestations against the "crafty dishonesty of fiction" and the distortions of the reality of poverty into the service of a traditional stereotype, he draws as richly as Faulkner on the comic lore and folk mythology of the poor. These are tested in his personal dialectical aesthetic—not against the observed facts of reality but against a highly personal vision of the tragic waste of life and land. The pattern of the Gastonia novels, though a more original one for southern literature, was equally harnessed to a preconceived artistic vision of class war, and if aspects of southern life seemed to jar with this vision, the resulting inconsistencies were as carefully masked as possible. No writer was prepared to forego completely the har-mony of his vision and the clarity of its illumination by focusing with undue conscientiousness on the complexities and disparities of its real-life inspiration. Such comments may seem like mere literary truisms, arguing the inevitability of bias and selectivity in any work of art, but they are necessary as a prelude to the work of James Agee, who strove to reject them. In his experimental treatment of three Alabama poor white tenant families, Agee determined to deal with their situation "not as journalists, sociologists, politicians, entertainers, humanitarians, priests or artists, but seriously."[1]

What "seriously" means for Agee is defined in his own bipartite projection of the purpose of *Let Us Now Praise Famous Men*. "The effort is to recognize the stature of a portion of unimagined existence, and to contrive techniques proper to its recording, communication, analysis, and defense" (xiv). The book will thus seek to convey a substance that is new (unimagined, since all previous efforts have been warped by the imagination) and will attempt to find a form that will give the broadest license possible to the transmitter to avoid creating a unified work of art, satisfactorily digestible to a public greedy for moral outrage. This antiaesthetic stance of Agee's seems less petulant when viewed against the plethora of "serious" investigations and artistic experiments with southern rural poverty that were giving the poor white's squalid misery and quaint customs a fashionable prominence by the latter part of the decade. In the early thirties the Communist Gastonia novels had been read by only a minute audience of leftward-leaning intellectuals, and sociological and journalistic analyses had been largely confined to liberal and academic periodicals. However, with the documentary programs being undertaken by the Farm Security Administration and the Federal Writers' Project, a new and more popular form of recorded suffering began to emerge in the picture-text genre. Erskine Caldwell and Margaret Bourke-White's *You Have Seen Their Faces* appeared in 1937 and was a combination of photographs, fictional captions, and essays that described ecstatic women "coming through" in religious conversion as well as the chilling horror of chain-gang slavery—the whole displaying, as usual, a keen eye for the grotesquerie of withered limbs and the bulbous swelling of diseased bodies. In 1938 Archibald MacLeish produced *Land of the Free*, a combination of government-sponsored photographs and his own verse, and in the following year Dorothea Lange and Paul Taylor published *An American Exodus*, a pictorial and verbal study of "human erosion in the thirties." Many "human" studies of the poor appeared in the form of reported intimate conversations, personal reminiscences, and testimonials: Caldwell's *Some American People*, 1935; Harry Kroll's autobiographical novel, *I*

Was a Sharecropper, 1936; Margaret Hagood's *Mothers of the South* and the Federal Writers' Project's *These Are Our Lives*, both in 1939; and Arthur Raper's illustrated study, *Sharecroppers All* in 1941.[2] In the field of periodical publishing, fascination with the poor white's predicament shifted gradually from the *Nation* and the *New Republic* to the more popular monthlies and illustrated weeklies; so by the end of the decade, his plight was duly and frequently exposed in the *Saturday Evening Post*, the *American Mercury*, the *Atlantic*, *Colliers*, *Scribners*, and finally *Newsweek* and *Time*. Thus southern poverty was in the process of becoming a journalistic institution that catered to the prurient and the shamed alike, with ample atrocities for their curiosity and plentiful indignation for their guilt.

In keeping with the newfound concern for the wretched of the South, *Fortune*, the magazine for businessmen, commissioned James Agee and Walker Evans in 1936 to do a feature study that would encompass the life of a southern sharecropper family, farm economics in the South, and government and state efforts to improve the situation. Spending six weeks in Alabama in July and August, they lived with three tenant families and participated in their normal activities. Their experiences excited and moved the two men beyond all their expectations, and neither proved able to confine his reactions to the sort of social report *Fortune* was demanding. After their material was rejected by the magazine, they worked on a greatly expanded version of it against the literary background already described. In 1941, this was finally published as the full-length book, *Let Us Now Praise Famous Men*. Evans's photography was unanimously acclaimed, but Agee's innovative "coequal" text provoked considerable dissension, presumably a not unsatisfactory response for someone who so dreaded "the emasculation of acceptance."

The discovery of an appropriate form and style for the verbal part of *Let Us Now Praise Famous Men* was a particularly crucial problem for Agee. He was more than usually tormented by the capacity of a complacent and heterogeneous society to institutionalize its dissent and assimilate its most scourging and defiant art:

Wiser and more capable men than I shall ever be have put their findings before you, findings so rich and so full of anger, serenity, murder, healing, truth, and love that it seems incredible the world were not destroyed and fulfilled in the instant, but you are too much for them . . . ; and one by one, you have absorbed and have captured and dishonored, and have distilled of your deliverers the most ruinous of all your poisons; people hear Beethoven in concert halls, or over a bridge game . . . ; Blake is in the Modern Library. [14]

Thus Agee's first and most constant stylistic assault must be on the liberal-minded reader, eager to cooperate in any of the author's vagaries in order to absorb and pay smiling tribute to his great fury. Agee defies him to classify this work in any familiar context of thought or categorize it in any recognizable literary tradition by a calculated program of insult and cajolery and the planned confusion of seeming logical and chronological chaos.

From the outset there is a perversity about the layout of the book: sixty-two untitled photographs are followed by a preface that the "serious" reader is advised to ignore but that contains important statements of purpose as well as condescending advice about how to read the book (aloud and continuously). Then quotations from *King Lear* and the *Communist Manifesto* are accompanied by a foot-note explaining that they are there to "mislead those who will be misled by them" (xviii). Slightly disoriented, and not a little alien-ated from the author, the willing reader is finally given a table of contents high in dadaist value and a list of dramatis personae ranging from the tenant families to Celine, Blake, Christ, and Freud. Next the reader—castigated for not being serious enough and reprimanded if he seeks more evidence than Agee is prepared to grant—is himself cast in the text as ignorant, snobbish, sentimental, frivolous, and insincere. He is at the mercy of Agee's disjointed chronology—"I am going to shift ahead of where I am writing, to a thing which is to happen, or which happened, the next morning (you mustn't be puzzled by this, I'm writing in a continuum)" (62)—and of his capricious experiments with punctuation:

(?:)
((?)   )   :). [81]

Subjected to a deluge of repellant excretory imagery, he is also expected to accept the extravagantly overwritten prose passages, which made one despairing reader wish to curse Agee for "an Ezra Pound in Wolfe's clothing . . . a belligerent mystic posing with a purple pencil on the Left Bank of *Fortune*."[3] Agee writes thus of the Gudgers' farm: ". . . it is the wrung breast of one human family's need and of an owner's taking, yielding blood and serum in its thin blue milk, and the house, the concentration of living and taking, is the cracked nipple: and of such breasts, the planet is thickly and desperately paved as the enfabled front of a goddess of east india" (129). There is no respite from the consciously antagonizing onslaughts even at the conclusion of the book, which provides appendices of motley literary references, newspaper articles, and a diatribe against language, which includes a two-page list of several hundred "anglosaxon monosyllables" that are neither Anglo-Saxon nor monosyllabic.

Yet despite all these contrivances to shatter the edifice of documentary aesthetics and avoid the "kiss of Judas" of official acceptability, Agee must offer his audience some common ground on which to try to convey "the stature of a portion of unimagined existence" and give the results of his inquiry into "certain normal predicaments of human divinity" (xiv). He is required therefore to have sympathy if his task of reproduction and communication is to be an effective and honest one, and to this end he is obliged to plead humbly for the reader's cooperation: ". . . if these things seem lists and inventories merely, things dead unto themselves, devoid of mutual magnetisms, and if they sink, lose impetus, meter, intension, then bear in mind at least my wish, and perceive in them and restore them what strength you can of yourself" (111). Not all directives about how to read the book are as facetious as those in the preface; he repeats several times the attempt to achieve a thematic arrangement similar to music and also lists what he considers to be the four separate levels at which the different prose styles of the book exist. These four planes are methods of conveying truth of various kinds; they consist of first, the contemplative, almost mystical strain that occurs in the three separate sections entitled "On the Porch," when Agee allows his mind to roam freely in the darkness of night and receive impressions where it will; second, the straight narrative "as it happened" record; third, a method of recall where memory and imagination play dual roles; and finally some consideration of the immediate problems of recording the experience as he writes it (243). This classification is performed for the reader so that he may judge Agee's relative degrees of accuracy in representing his experiences among the tenant families. Since the author is seeking the purest form of truth humanly possible, he takes the rather drastic step of placing himself most fully in the book, not merely as the sensitive receiver of impressions but as a complex human being whose responses are likely to be distorted in any situation by all his accumulated history and personal experiences. Thus, not only does Agee confront us again and again with an accumulation of episodes celebrating the misery of his own white, middle-class guilt (for interrupting the black foreman's Sunday party, for terrifying a young couple on the road, for disturbing the Gudgers from their beds late at night, and for rifling, voyeurlike, through their most intimate possessions), he also discourses at considerable length on his adolescence, the impending breakup of his marriage, his desire for a prostitute, and the possibility of his ever writing good movies. Some reviewers wryly attributed this immodest intrusion of self into every aspect of the lives of the ostensible subjects of the book to Agee's newfound freedom from the enforced anonymity of the Luce magazine,[4] but it is clearly an invitation to the reader to make the adjustments of bias that Agee himself could not. We are given the opportunity to calculate the probable personal impact and subtract, if we will, Agee's known whims and prejudices from the whole.

Agee had thus found ways to negate the stultifying effects of institutional acquisitiveness for art, the smugness of readers, and the warping personality of the author, but he still had the more positive problem of finding techniques to convey the exact quality of the daily lives of the Gudgers, Rickettses, and Woodses. His ideal method would have nothing to do with language at all, since Agee felt it could at best only describe, never embody: "It would be photographs; the rest would be fragments of cloth, bits of cotton, lumps of earth, records of speech, pieces of wood and iron, phials of odors, plates of food and excrement" (13). Since such tangible physical emblems are obviously both incommunicable and perishable, the alternative is to provide as wide a variety of media, structures, and approaches as possible. These include Evans's photographs; quotations from Shakespeare, Marx, Blake, and the Bible; poetry; descriptive and analytical essays on the work, clothing, shelter, money, and education of the families; catalogues and inventories of the exact contents of their shelves, drawers, and closets; a lengthy extract from a *Partisan Review* symposium; and all the levels of speculative and narrative prose that Agee had outlined for his four planes of truth. The resulting book disturbed some critics by its

haphazard unwieldiness, and one suggested that the general awkwardness and diffuseness of the book was simply due to Agee's
failure to find an adequate symbol for the expression of his ideas.[5]
Yet to do this would, for Agee, have been a submission to traditional
aesthetics; he preferred that acceptance remain painful.

The success of these techniques varies widely, even among the
similarly structured essays: that on "Cotton" is superbly written,
that on overalls is almost a comic self-parody—their texture and
color are described merging, with age, ". . . into realms of fine
softness and marvel of draping and velvet plays of light which
chamois and silk can only suggest, not touch; and into a region and
scale of blues, subtle, delicious, and deft beyond what I have ever
seen elsewhere approached except in rare skies, the smoky light
some days are filmed with, and some of the blues of Cézanne"
(267). The essay on education—the most unsatisfactory—is an
attempt at savage satire whose wrath is dissipated by being spread
too thinly over too wide a range of causes, from fractious quibbling
with the title of Louise Gudger's school poetry book, *Trips to Take*,
to utter despair at a worldwide theory of education that is causing
the "unconscious murder" of the potentiality of the human race.
Agee's apprehensions are always most stirring when they are most
sensuous and immediate; hence the odors of the Gudgers' house—
of "pork, lard, corn, woodsmoke, pine and ammonia . . . of bed-
ding and . . . of all the dirt"; the touch of the soft, soiled baby
clothes stored in drawers; the "feathery, sickening" taste of the
Woodses' water; and the vivid visual assault of the Rickettses'
fireplace wall are all more effective in convincing the reader of the
intrinsic quality of their existence than the more artificial attempt
to hallow their lives by introducing them within the framework of
religious motifs. These motifs are used in the presentation of the
Gudger house: coining for it terminology from church architecture,
Agee progresses through setting, facade, and entrance to the fireplace altar and tabernacle, which is a table drawer. Similarly, parts of
the Catholic church service—inductions, gradual, testament, and
recession—parallel the ceremonies of visiting and meeting the families; but their sanctity is less established by these labels than by
Agee's exhaustive respect for the minutiae of their lives, witnessed
in many records like the following, an inventory of the objects on
the Gudgers' mantel:

A small round cardboard box:
(on its front:)

Cashmere Bouquet Face Powder
Light Rachel

(on its back:)

The Aristocrat of Face Powders.
Same quality as 50c size.

Inside the box, a small puff. The bottom of the box and the bottom face of the puff carry a light dust of fragrant softly tinted powder.

A jar of menthol salve, smallest size, two thirds gone.

A small spool of number 50 white cotton thread, about half gone and half unwound.

A cracked roseflowered china shaving mug, broken along the edge. A much worn, inchwide varnish brush stands in it. Also in the mug are eleven rusty nails, one blue composition button, one pearl headed pin (imitation), three dirty kitchen matches, a lump of toilet soap.

A pink crescent celluloid comb: twenty-seven teeth, of which three are missing; sixteen imitation diamonds.

A nailfile.

A small bright mirror in a wire stand.

Hung from a nail at the side of the fireplace: a poker bent out of an auto part.

Hung from another nail, by one corner: a square pincushion. Stuck into it, several common pins, two large safety-pins, three or four pins with heads of white or colored glass; a small brooch of green glass in gilded tin; a needle trailing eighteen inches of coarse white thread. [172–73]

Agee strongly disavows any intention to see the universe in a grain of sand, and although such extravagant lists of trivial possessions do frequently lead him into the widest realms of speculation about human experience, their main purpose is to impart to the reader some idea of the significance of these tawdry items for the families; to revere equally the ugliness of life, which is as precious as its beauty.

He emphasizes from the outset that the value of what he records is intrinsic to its mere existence. It is not to be the tool of any school of reform, journalistic curiosity, or artistic revelation but "should be accepted and recorded for its own sake" (467). Yet Agee is not so foolish as to imagine that his consciousness can respond to these tenant lives in a moral or philosophical vacuum, any more than it can in a sensual or emotional one. Thus, while abjuring any thesis or single point of view, the book is nevertheless highly and often contradictorily opinionated. Any attempt to synthesize these contradictions is both futile and offensive to Agee's conscious heterodoxy, but some of the more consistent and prominent attitudes demand attention. From its opening determination to inquire into "certain normal predicaments of human divinity," the book uses many of the methods of naturalism to support a super- or antinaturalist position: everything that is, is holy. Agee's ruthless violation of the homes and most intimate possessions of the poor can provoke shame, anger, and guilt; but overwhelmingly, it demands humility, for the dignity, beauty, and love of these families are no less important than their squalor and brutality. Their existence "shines quietly forth such grandeur, such sorrowful holiness of its exactitudes . . . as no human consciousness shall ever rightly perceive" (134), a point made very effectively in the graveyard episode, where we are led to reverence the dead through the gaudy, cheap, and absurd symbols with which the poor decorate their graves: blown-out electric light bulbs, glass butter dishes, children's toys, and colored buttons.

The desire to be humble before the divine mystery of these tenant families and to pay tribute to the daily quality of their physical lives leads Agee into some rather perverse stances. He contends, for example, that their houses "approximate, or at times by chance achieve, an extraordinary 'beauty'" (202) and that "the partition wall of the Gudgers' front bedroom IS importantly, among other things, a great tragic poem" (204). He argues of the homes that "their esthetic success seems to me even more important than their functional failure" (202)—this in contrast to Mrs. Gudger's despairing comment, "'Oh, I do *hate* this house *so bad*! Seems like they ain't nothing in the whole world I can do to make it pretty'" (210). If, as readers, we share Agee's appreciation of the beauty of the houses, we are chastised for sharing a privileged and class-biased education; if we sympathize with Mrs. Gudger's misery, we are sternly informed that the culpability for it is our own. If we dare to think in terms of "Improving the Sharecropper," we are warned we will undoubtedly defile their simple holiness and probably make their lives less tolerable than at present. We are sunk in original sin, with no mortal salvation in sight, while the Gudgers, Rickettses, and Woodses have no crimes to answer for. This unnatural innocence of the poor appeared to Lionel Trilling to be a major moral flaw in Agee's conception of them. "He writes of his people as if there were no human unregenerateness in them, no flicker of malice or meanness, no darkness or wildness of feeling."[6] Trilling attributes this falsification to guilt, but it is also possible to see this seeming moral discrepancy between the tenants and the readers in terms of Christian pride. The families, for a variety of reasons, have anesthetized themselves and have submitted meekly to what seems to them the will of God; it is the arrogance of armchair reformers who would tamper carelessly with the great "weight, mystery and dignity" of human life that must be sharply castigated.

This emphasis on the most socially reactionary of religious values —submission of the human will to a divine order—may seem at odds with Agee's affirmation, "I am a Communist by sympathy and conviction" (249). In fact, he deliberately focuses on the inconsistency by quoting the most militant lines of the *Communist Manifesto* —"Workers of the world, unite and fight. You have nothing to lose but your chains and a world to win."—and the Beatitudes, normally a favorite target for Communists critical of Christian acquiescence and otherworldliness. This acknowledged communism of Agee's seems very remote from the ideology that the Gastonia writers subscribed to; he professes it almost as a religion that will be fulfilled perhaps in some ideal world but which has no immediate relation to any program of action to be undertaken among the southern poor. There is no evidence in the text that Agee ever discussed social and political reforms with the three families or that he heard any revolutionary rumblings from them; indeed, he finds their ignorance of their own ills more unfortunate, if possible, than consciousness would be, since it provides the rationalization for the middle-class southerner that "they are 'used' to it" (210). Much of the book is imbued with a profound pessimism and even a fatalistic sense that escape is impossible. Agee uses the questions "How were we caught? In what way were we trapped? Why is it things always seem to go against us?" in various forms to give a kind of choral effect to the first introduction of the families; he answers them with the grim response *"Ruin, ruin is in our hopes: nor hope, help, any healing"* (148), scarcely an encouragement for the radical left.

Part of Agee's despair of improvement lies in his profound contempt for the nature of the reformers themselves; part of it lies in his ontological approach to these tenants, which demands that he explore primarily above or below the social level—on that of the individual or the universal. The venom directed against the advocates of various improvement schemes is the bitterest in the book; they are depicted as appallingly ignorant, both of the real conditions of the tenant farmers' lives and of the particular psychology of the southern poor; so their imported plans are likely to destroy what is most valuable in these lives: "I go blind to think of what crimes others might commit upon them, and instil into them." Even more damningly, they are depicted as hypocritical dilettantes, dabbling in fashionable causes—"rapid marchers in the human vanguard . . . wearing Enna Jettick and W. L. Douglas shoes by day . . . and Russian Gift Shop Peasant Pantoufles by night" (215). Such hostility to fellow radicals, who seemed by their compromising, limited, and stopgap measures to betray the heart of the revolution, is not unfamiliar in proletarian literature, but Agee's condemnation of them is based not, as is usual, on their frivolous or expedient political treason but on their limited consciousness of the human divinity and potentiality of the poor. This leads him to the somewhat ambiguously stated but very important belief that the nature of change must be twofold: "I know there is cure, even now available . . . in science and in the fear and joy of God" (307). Looking to science and human ingenuity alone cannot be enough. Yet in spite of his many strictures on the dangers of activist complacency—the comfortable delusion that a problem has been solved when it has barely been uncovered—Agee does not wholly resign himself to the pessimistic inertia of the cynic. Though he scorns those who attribute the ills of the southern poor to the tenant system, he is nevertheless acutely aware of the iniquities of it, as the essay "Cotton" explains. "It is the one crop and labor which is in no possible way useful as it stands to the tenant's living; it is among all these the one which must and can be turned into money; it is among all these the one in which the landowner is most interested; and it is among all these the one of which the tenant can hope for least, and can be surest that he is being cheated, and is always to be cheated" (326). Similarly, while admitting that there can be no meaningful change in the educational system without a worldwide revolution of consciousness, Agee is at pains to point out the most trivial kinds of faults in the schoolchildren's texts and to object strongly to segregation and the misuse of school funds.

This capacity to oscillate between cosmic grief and the more conventional muckraking anger is an indulgence that only the eclectic format of *Let Us Now Praise Famous Men* could permit. It is a luxury denied to the more conventional Communist writers and indeed foresworn by some who were tempted toward the kind of universal and eternal speculations on the mystery of life that Agee declares to be a necessary part of his account. He wishes to escape at all costs the kind of labelling of the poor that was most meaningful to the Gastonia novelists—"how am I to speak of you as 'tenant' 'farmers,' as 'representatives' of your 'class,' as social integers in a criminal economy" (100)—and instead he sees each human life as "a child of the substance and bowels of the stars and of all space . . . created forth of an aberration special to one speck and germ and pollen fleck this planet, this young planet, on that broadblown field" (101). This was precisely the kind of tantalizing speculation that Fielding Burke's heroine had to resist as she sat on the mountain top between the eternal rocks and stars; she had to force herself to flee from this deathly cure for the disease of time and infinity back into the temporal and social world. While Agee berates man because we "cannot bear, for any length of time, to carry in our minds in any literalness the fact of our small size and our youth" (247), because we pridefully assume our fleeting life to be more important than any other forms of cosmic existence, Burke's heroine Ishma is drawn back by "clinging reason" to reject the demeaning effect of distant suns and heavens. "How meaningless to be out there, at one with those globes of cohering atoms, just as mechanically driven, just as unfeeling, unknowing?"[7] The disruption of categories in a universe where everything is holy puts an intolerable burden on the rational reformer, who would prefer not to see, as Agee does, the bloated little belly of Ellen Woods as a thing "so strong, so valiant, so unvanquishable . . . [that] I know it shall at length outshine the sun" (442). The Gastonia novelists knew the danger of entering into an uncontrolled and unlimited exploration of consciousness that was not tied to "race," "class," or "sexual" exploitation, but for Agee complete abandonment to all the currents of human experience— natural and supernatural—was the revolutionary act that must precede and create change. Communism was for him a conceivable means toward the end of the full release of "consciousness, action and possibility," but he would not tolerate any concession to means if they seemed to put the end in danger of death. This seemed to him the case in Soviet Russia, with its programs of high pay and social eminence for its artists, an ominous sign for any society. "A good artist is a deadly enemy of society; and the most dangerous thing that can happen to an enemy, no matter how cynical, is to become a beneficiary. No society, no matter how good, could be mature enough to support a real artist without mortal danger to that artist" (355).

Thus, in spite of all his furious attacks on the contemporary role of artists in society and his initial plea for his book, "in God's name don't think of it as Art," Agee is finally making a profound statement of faith in the power of art. Certainly it can be corrupted, institutionalized, and made to serve the needs of a complacent age, but it is also in the end the best, as well as the most potentially misleading, key to truth. "It seems very possibly true that art's superiority over science and over all other forms of human activity, and its inferiority to them, reside in the identical fact that art accepts the most dangerous and impossible of bargains and makes the best of it, becoming, as a result, both nearer the truth and farther from it than those things which, like science and scientific art, merely describe, and those things which, like human beings and their creations and the entire state of nature, merely are, the truth" (238). *Let Us Now Praise Famous Men* is a definition by example of the true "revolutionary" role of art as opposed to the art that is merely willing to serve a particular revolution. Rejected by all but a few critics in its own time, the book is now ironically worthy of enshrinement in the institutional dialectic between "hard" and "soft" left. One critic distinguishes the "romantic anarchist" soft left from the "rational" hard left by noting the former's most typical ideological and stylistic directions: it is characterized by religion, mysticism, subjectivism, personalism, a belief in liberation through "art and aesthetic education," and a technique that is "gnomic, testamental and confessional."[8] That these traits fairly accurately characterize Agee's book is evident; that he should have so feared such characterization now seems irrelevant and even a trifle naive; it can neither touch nor contaminate the essence of the book. Agee's contribution to the literature of the southern poor whites was to make them witness to the squalor and joy, the shame and dignity of all human life and to restore to them qualities conveniently lost in the crusades to improve their condition. It was also a rejection of what society wanted or expected from the artist and a reaffirmation of his role as mystic and revealer of the more complicated and less palatable truths of human existence.

Agee's revulsion from the literary exploitation of poor whites had led him to suspect artistic reformers of the basest possible motives. "The comfortable have always been able to lick their chops over the hunger of others if that hunger is presented with the right sort of humorous or pathetic charm; if certain Christian or

Marxian glands are tactfully enough stimulated, they will drool as well."[9] In his extreme concern to give no satisfaction to this unseemly appetite, Agee had therefore avoided exploring in any detail the actual attitudes of the tenant families themselves toward social and political change, even though, by 1936, they must have had some response, at least to the New Deal programs if not to more radical proposals. Certainly the poor whites who told their stories in *These Are Our Lives* to the members of the Federal Writers' Project seemed delighted to expound in detail on their politics, although one must allow for some partisanship on the part of the WPA reporters. Nevertheless, the discourses of an illiterate farm laborer, humbler in status than even the Gudgers, Rickettses, and Woodses, indicate the degree to which the insulation of the southern poor white had been invaded by the end of the 1930s: "'I'm a Democrat; I stand for the New Deal and Roosevelt. I am for the WPA, the NYA, the NRA, the AAA, the FHA, and crop control. I'm going to vote for control in December.'"[10] Such glib parroting of what Faulkner had called in disgust "three letter reasons for a man not to work" is certainly no indication of any advance toward the kind of political consciousness that liberal and left-wing writers hoped might be born out of the unusual suffering of the depression. Rather, the readiness with which the poor rewarded these piecemeal enticements with their allegiance was ammunition for conservative writers like Faulkner and, more emphatically, his brother John, whose two novels, *Men Working*, 1941, and *Dollar Cotton*, 1942, are harsh satires on government bribery and poor white gullibility.[11] Such ease in transferring loyalty was virtually ignored by Marxists, who needed heroes and victims unsullied by such pettiness; any sacrifice of ideological integrity for desperately needed material gains was too disillusioning for these writers to countenance. Even Agee, despite his massive effort to take the poor whites "seriously," permitted this solemnity to disguise not so much what Trilling had called their "human unregenerateness" but qualities less dignifiable—petty greed, roguery, selfishness, meanness—that intrude neither in the text nor in Evans's "frank," "staring" photographs.

Thus a strange dichotomy was perpetuated in depression literature between those worthy and victimized poor whites who, somehow, deserved revolutionary change and those cunning and servile poor whites who, somehow, deserved to go on living in poverty, contempt, and neglect. At the very end of the decade, Carson

McCullers came close to observing this tendency in her 1940 novel, *The Heart Is a Lonely Hunter*. Here the author's sympathy for both the black and white poor of a southern mill town does not distort a devastating and despairing portrait of the traditional vices and shortcomings generally associated with the two groups. The blacks have a model leader and hero in Dr. Benedict Copeland, who attempts to instill in them pride of race, personal dignity, and a sense of justice; they respond with abject acquiescence in their mistreatment and look only to heaven for relief, where "'straightway us will be white as cotton.'" The poor white mill workers are even harsher and more hostile in their response to Jake Blount, a self-appointed apostle of revolution reared in Gastonia, who "sometimes . . . talked like a linthead and sometimes like a professor." The factory workers greet Blount's efforts to arouse their righteous anger with such a display of inertia and crude ridicule that he too is driven to hurling at them the abusive epithets with which his own enemies have demeaned them, "'You pasty-faced, shrunk-gutted, ricket-ridden little rats!'"[12] McCullers presents a bleak future for political and social radicals in the South: they are so utterly estranged from their community's mores that they become like the grotesque characters in Sherwood Anderson's Winesburg—the truths to which they are committed distort their possessors because they must be so fanatically preserved in an alien environment. Though both Copeland and Blount refuse to capitulate and admit the futility of their aims, one is last seen broken in strength, preaching to a nonexistent audience, while the other is retreating from the tormenting evidence of yet another failure in a seemingly endless succession. If McCullers's novel does not absolutely close out hope for reform in the South, it certainly appears to be a bitter and accurate recognition of the pitfalls before any idealist with a scheme for saving or radicalizing the poor there. No other chronicler of the poor whites in the thirties maintained a revolutionary social and economic vision that was combined at the same time with the kind of abrasive irony that Brecht used on the German proletariat or O'Casey on the poor of Dublin; for these latter writers "deservingness" depended less on any prior moral disposition than on poverty itself. The traditional disabilities and disinclinations of the southern poor white certainly provided a stern test for any writer inclined to argue their moral worthiness, and only Erskine Caldwell came close to supporting the alternative. Caldwell's poor are certainly in no sense "deserving," and he contrives to make them offend middle-class sensibilities as grossly as possible while maintaining fervently the necessity for fair treatment of such manifestly inferior types. Yet the moral force of Caldwell's fury was dissipated by Caldwell's own obvious fear that his subjects might already be beyond redemption and fit only for ironic and recriminating display.

The possibility of any writer's creating out of southern poor white material characters who were fictionally credible and potentially revolutionary seemed close to hopeless as the decade of their most public agony drew to a close. Young southern writers with leftist sympathies, like Agee and McCullers, were dramatizing the dangers and obstacles in any major effort to reorder the lives of both rural and urban poor whites, and traditionally liberal writers —like Paul Green, Charlie May Simon, and Eugene Armfield— continued to endorse more limited, pragmatic reforms outside the context of any mental or material apocalypse. Yet, in 1939 a novel of poor whites appeared that not merely glorified their revolutionary capacities but created literary characters with an unmatched social and moral appeal for the American public. In *The Grapes of Wrath*, John Steinbeck achieved with uprooted Oklahoma sharecroppers what no southern writer had been able to do with the same class of poor white subjects—a proletarian novel that was aesthetically satisfying, philosophically acceptable, and popularly appealing.

CHAPTER IX

Steinbeck's Retreat into Artfulness

Less tied to the more unsavory aspects of the poor white tradition than Faulkner and Caldwell, less committed to violent, revolutionary politics than the Gastonia novelists, less dedicated to the absolute power of documentary truth than Agee, Steinbeck displayed a combination of literary genius and pragmatic contrivance in the creation of his pioneering Okies. A number of critics have suggested that the novel's warm reception was the direct product of its sociological context—that the work is the fortunate outcome of the coincidence of Steinbeck and the dust bowl storms. They argue, "It took seven books and a regional disaster before the country awakened to the fact that it had found in John Steinbeck its chief literary chronicler";[1] "its tremendous vogue is founded partly on what we call an accident—the fact that it concerns itself with one of the major economic problems of our day, the problem of seasonal labor in California, and with . . . the dustbowl";[2] "*The Grapes of Wrath* was not the inclination of his own temperament, but the tremendous pull of the social situation upon him"; "when the national consciousness of the depression had reached its height and the country was supporting the New Deal as its remedy, Steinbeck combined elements of both *Of Mice and Men* and *In Dubious Battle* into a social novel of larger canvas and happier ending."[3] This emphasis on the topicality of *The Grapes of Wrath* and the ripeness of public sympathy for such a project may seem curiously misplaced in view of the widespread indifference to the proletarian novels of the first half of the 1930s, which dealt with national crises at least as tragic and imperative as Steinbeck's subject. These were greeted with apathy or hostility, while *The Grapes of Wrath*, published four years after the dust bowl storms and six after the worst depression horrors and the inauguration of the New Deal, was a runaway best-seller. Perhaps the westward-trekking Okies and Arkies were more traditionally attractive than the North Carolina lintheads; perhaps the nature of the dust storms added a superhuman element to the disaster that avoided guilt and blame; perhaps America was already comfortably sentimental about its suffering years—but more than physical disasters were needed to ensure this notable success.

Walter Rideout finds the key to it in the literary rather than the social history of the decade. "Not only is it unthinkable that *The Grapes of Wrath* would have been enthusiastically received at the beginning of the thirties, but it is even unlikely that Steinbeck . . . could have written the book without being aware of the efforts, crude or otherwise, made by the actual proletarians to solve the problems of ideological literature."[4] What Steinbeck learned from these "laboratory experiments" and from his own Communist strike novel, *In Dubious Battle*, makes his book not the culmination of the leftist trend of poor white literature in the thirties but in many ways a radical retreat from precise political solutions and social documentaries. The book was often initially compared in popularity and impact to *Uncle Tom's Cabin*: like it, it provides powerful human images around which to crystallize the confused emotions of a turbulent era. Mrs. Stowe's novel—published only four years after the *Communist Manifesto*—permitted the argument that "there is a mustering among the masses, the world over; and there is a *dies irae* coming on, sooner or later" and "the same thing is working in Europe, in England and in this country";[5] unlike it, *The Grapes of Wrath* steers clear of any international revolutionary implications for its people. Here are no mustering masses but a group of loyal Oklahomans who dream of possessing their own share of private property and boast of their exclusively American genealogy. The heroes are spectacularly lacking in those qualities of dispassionate and impersonal organization that betoken the superior among the Marxist ideologues in the Gastonia novels. The people's predicament is further distanced from Communist appropriation by being very precisely restricted in time and location to a singular ecological catastrophe. Steinbeck avoids any political programs in a situation fraught with partisan sympathies and concentrates instead on a vaguer philosophical resolution. The resulting ideology, a kind of transcendental agrarianism, seems feasible only in a preindustrial utopia, and for this the plot takes a suitably nostalgic course. By setting the poor white finally in motion, no matter how involuntary, on the pioneer trail to the Pacific, Steinbeck could explore the relevance of seemingly outmoded nineteenth century ideals to the current situation and at the same time cast off some of the more antiheroic vestiges of the poor white's literary tradition.

This retreat into the American past, where the traditional character of the people seemed more compatible with revolutionary activity, was not undertaken without a notable prior effort to confront a contemporary political solution to the misery of the same migrant workers, whose unresolved plight would reappear in *The Grapes of Wrath*. This was the novel *In Dubious Battle*, published in 1936, which concerns the attempts of two Communists to organize a strike among California fruit pickers. It represents virtually a negative draft of the more successful novel—an empirical study of the workers' least appealing attitudes and characteristics, which will not be permitted to mar the compassionate tenor of the Joads' saga.

In Dubious Battle is a powerful indictment of the dehumanizing, totalitarian tendencies inherent in communism, placed against a background of ruthless capitalist extortion that is supported morally by the agencies of the government and physically by gangs of bloodthirsty vigilantes. Trapped between the tyranny of principled fanatics, zealots who subvert life itself to propaganda and rejoice in the unifying effect of a striker's murder, and the mounting vindictive fury of the Fruit Growers' Association against whom the only effective weapons appear to be propaganda and solidarity, is the composite human animal that the migrant workers constitute. This monstrous creature has little in common with the colorful and carefree paisanos of *Tortilla Flat* or the noble and enduring people of *The Grapes of Wrath* who respond to adversity with the resolution, "Worse off we get, the more we got to do." This is a group organism that moves and breathes in unison from hunger to treachery and from satiety to savagery. It can be manipulated by rhetoric and by the regulation of its physical conditions, but it possesses dangerous energies that are more easily unleashed than curbed or directed. An analysis of mob behavior provides the central philosophical quest of the novel—what is group man? The unanimous answer comes from a variety of mutually hostile sources—he is both monolithic and bestial. The only issue at debate is how to train the beast. There is no attempt to suggest that the camp of strikers in *In Dubious Battle*, organized to demand the barest subsistence wage from their employers, is any different in kind, despite their reasonable purpose, from the frenzied marauding bands who attack them. There is none of the distinction between union and mob that Mary Heaton Vorse was so careful to make in *Strike!* In her novel the same class of people, influenced by opposing ideologies, is capable of extremes of either nobility or baseness; in Steinbeck's a group's activities bear no relation to logic or mental impetus but only to physical and emotional prodding by its leaders.

The political dialectic of the novel is voiced by Mac, the dedicated Communist party organizer and empirical amateur psychologist, and Doc Burton, self-styled "dreamer, mystic, metaphysician," who is "'too Goddamn far left to be a Communist'"[6] and derives his behavioral theories from cell biology. The entire course of events in the novel is the vehicle for exhibiting Mac's beliefs: since the strike he organizes among the apple pickers is his method of training the young party protegé Jim Nolan, his didactic theories are constantly put to the test. From the outset he speaks of all men in contemptuous animal analogies: soldiers are "stupid cattle"; his training of Jim is "kind of like teaching hunting dogs by running them with the old boys"; brothels are invariably "cat-houses"; and the first casualty of the strike, an old man, provokes the comment, "The old buzzard was worth something after all." His conviction that groups of men can be turned into a single brutal animal—unified by mutual sacrifice and suffering, fortified by food, and enraged by some gratuitous bloodletting—is witnessed repeatedly. Before the strike he expounds theoretically to Jim the principle of the value of slaughter by the National Guard and the subsequent public funeral of strikers. "He was breathing hard in excitement . . . 'Christ Almighty! If we can only get the troops called out'" (39). Later, when the necessary martyr turns out to be Mac's friend, he examines the corpse carefully to see if it is sufficiently gory to prod the weary strikers into renewed efforts. "'We got to shoot some juice into 'em some way'" (209). He stages all manner of incidents to stimulate fear, fury, loyalty, and blood lust, from the initial use of a bunch of fruit tramps to help deliver a baby to the final gruesome display of the faceless body of Jim. He has absolute faith in the herd instinct of men and their need for " 'some guy that kind of tells 'em where to put their feet' " (53). Of the puppet boss London, through whom he directs the strikers, Mac can say—apparently without conscious irony—" 'He's the natural leader. We'll teach him where to lead. Got to go awful easy, though. Leadership has to come from the men' " (66).

Mac refuses to see his masterly expediency with human emotions as anything other than the most practical means to a highly justified end. " 'You see a guy hurt, or somebody like Anderson smashed, or you see a cop ride down a Jew girl, an' you think, what the hell's the use of it. An' then you think of the millions starving, and it's all right again. It's worth it' " (337). Mac's consuming purpose in life is to organize the masses—not perhaps an irrational or apocalyptic goal—but nevertheless a final end that vindicates for him all the cruelty and duplicity he is conscious of in the means. That his assessment of the mob's nature is largely accurate and his methods of agitation highly effective is borne out repeatedly in their objective results in the plot. After the strikers have devoured huge pieces of half-raw meat, they are " 'cocky'r'n hell. They think they run the world now. They're going out and clean up on somebody. I knew it would happen' " (248). When London whets their appetite for blood by brutally beating a rebellious striker, they shout hysterically, " 'Bust his jaw clean off. That's blood out o' his brain. . . . Killed 'um. Busted his head off' " (320). Suddenly, they become one ferocious mechanism. "A long, throaty animal howl went up. London held up his hands. 'Who'll follow now, and knock hell out o' that barricade?' The crowd was changing rapidly. The eyes of the men and women were entranced. The bodies weaved slowly, in unison. No more lone cries came from lone men. They moved together, looked alike. The roar was one voice coming from many throats" (321).

The capacity to verify Mac's theories obviously lies in Steinbeck's hands. Should he choose to depict the strikers as more noble, independent, or generous than Mac's portrayal, then the Communist's whole methodological superstructure must crumble. Instead, he marshals all his narrative and descriptive resources to create a proletariat as personally repulsive as possible: careless workers, who are cowardly toward their superiors and cruel to their inferiors and deliberately gross in their physical habits, refusing to take even the most trivial precautions necessary for the sanitation of their outdoor toilets and blowing their noses into their fingers.[7] The women in the novel are presented as having only two functions: whores or nursing mothers. They play no active role in the strike and are perhaps dangerously counterrevolutionary, since sex is depicted as the cause and result of uncontrolled violence. Lust is aroused by the grisly amateur slaughter of some cows, and after a short time in the camp, the women are the source of much divisiveness. " 'One of the guys tried to make another guy's woman. An' the first guy come in an' stuck him with a pair of scissors' " (181). Mac's animal metaphors are extended generally into Steinbeck's language, so that "the women crawled like rodents from the tents" (257), Al is as "inwardly-thoughtful looking as a ruminating cow" (52), and his father is "totally unlike Al, small and quick as a terrier" (115). The reader's first introduction to the migrants is when they board the same boxcar in which Mac and Jim are traveling. A dispute arises with Mac over a cushion of papers on which he is sitting, and he equably agrees to share it with his challenger; the worker's only response to such fairness in distributing property is to try to take the whole thing. Apparently intimidation, not decency, is the only way to operate. Only Bolter, the president of the Fruit Growers' Association, asserts to the Communists that "American working men aren't animals" (250) and should therefore settle for the starvation wages they are being offered by the corporation. Thus the stature of the working man is assailed and degraded from all sides, and the only defense is the hypocritical self-interest of employers who would do everything to prolong that debasement.

The moral dilemma of the novel, then, does not rest on the competence of the workers to achieve revolutionary ends by organizing themselves to fight. If such a goal is a valid one, then clearly the vicious, inhuman opportunism of Mac is the only way to achieve it. The dialectic with Doc Burton is not particularly on the validity of *Communist* ends but on whether any teleological philosophy is likely to improve the condition of men. Doc is the poet-philosopher, skeptical of human aspirations that overreach man's self-knowledge and therefore of any "scientific" ideology based on such a volatile and mysterious entity. " 'There aren't any beginnings. Nor any ends. It seems to me that man has engaged in a blind and fearful struggle out of a past he can't remember, into a future he can't foresee nor understand. And man has met and defeated every

obstacle, every enemy except one. He cannot win over himself' "
(259). Doc's perception of mass behavior is almost identical to
Mac's, but he emphasizes that it is based only on the tentative
evidence of his senses, unblinkered by any moral concepts of right
and wrong:

"I want to watch these group-men, for they seem to me to be a new
individual, not at all like single men. A man in a group isn't himself at all,
he's a cell in an organism that isn't like him any more than the cells in your
body are like you." [150–51]

"It might be like this, Mac: When group-man wants to move, he makes a
standard. 'God wills that we recapture the Holy Land'; or he says, . . . 'we
will wipe out social injustice with communism.' But the group doesn't care
about the Holy Land, or Democracy, or Communism. Maybe the group
simply wants to move, to fight, and uses these words simply to reassure
the brains of individual men. I say it *might* be like that, Mac." [151]

Doc's observations further fit the totalitarian policies Mac would
practice by suggesting that he, as leader, takes on the status of a cell
with a special function, like an eye, which is both the master and
the servant of group-man. The crucial difference lies in the fact
that what Doc hypothesizes, Mac has already turned into political
dogma; Mac thereby negates any possibility of exploring further
toward the truth. Doc therefore refuses to commit himself to
actions that he sees are brutal and violent and may well prove
meaningless. Instead he maintains the role of observer, assisting the
strikers only by personal medical services to them. Voicing humanitarian dissent in quizzical chuckles and enigmatic remarks, he is
always lurking in the background of Mac's most callous schemes.
Yet, despite his popularity among the men, who see him as a saintly
altruist,[8] there is also a certain expediency about his strike following
in order to satisfy his intellectual curiosity. Toward the end of the
novel, Doc disappears completely and mysteriously; some critics
have suggested (on no real evidence) that he became a martyr to the
vigilantes, but it seems more likely that in the final battles between
Communists and capitalists, his personal rejection of teleological
thinking seems irrelevant.

Thus, despite the fact that Doc is in the mold of the heroic figure
in other Steinbeck novels,[9] in this book a situation is deliberately
created where there is no simple moral choice between brutal
tyranny and fraternal survival; Mac's solution yokes the two together and Doc can offer no alternative. That Steinbeck, in the

writing of this book, was aware of the likely commercial results of such an attempt at intellectual integrity is evidenced frequently in his comments on it: "a conscientious piece of work"; and "we've gone through too damn much trying to keep the work honest and in a state of improvement to let it slip now in consideration of a little miserable popularity."[10] Mac's inhuman morality is given the most credible defenses, because he is, as Doc says, " 'the craziest mess of cruelty and hausfrau sentimentality, of clear vision and rose-colored glasses I ever saw' " (212); he is sickened by his own violence—yet passionately aware of its rationale. Steinbeck is meticulously fair in giving the Communists their share of persuasive rhetoric:

"They say we play dirty, work underground. Did you ever think, London? We've got no guns. If anything happens to us, it don't get in the newspapers. But if anything happens to the other side, Jesus, they smear it in ink. We've got no money, and no weapons, so we've got to use our heads, London. See that? It's like a man with a club fighting a squad with machine-guns. The only way we can do it is to sneak up and smack the gunners from behind. Maybe that isn't fair, but hell, London, this isn't any athletic contest. There aren't any rules a hungry man has to follow." [290–91]

By illuminating the moral and political weaknesses of all ideologies, Steinbeck felt that he had created a "brutal book, more brutal because there is no author's moral point of view."[11] However, although Steinbeck curiously felt his shaping hand was absent from the moral scheme, it certainly appears more subtly in the personalities of the main characters and in many ways helps anticipate the changes that would give *The Grapes of Wrath* more than a "little miserable popularity."

The archetypal Party organizer's personality belongs in this novel not to Mac, who is subject to such human weaknesses as lust, revenge, and revulsion, but to his young assistant, Jim Nolan, who shows toward the end a capacity to out-Herod Herod in unfeeling dedication. Jim is the stuff of which great Party men are made: his family background has given him a profound hatred of the present system; his self-education has equipped him with a knowledge of Plato, Herodotus, Gibbon, Macaulay, Spinoza, Hegel, Kant, Schopenhauer, Nietzsche, and Marx; and, most important, he needs no opiate other than knowing he is working "toward something"— neither tobacco, liquor, drugs, sex, nor religion. Jim is in fact quite boring, since all he acquires in the course of the novel is a knowledge of methodology; his orientation was firm from the outset, and his opinions are parroted from Mac. There are signs, however, that Jim has reached an even more advanced stage of group-man's leadership than Mac, with fewer reserves of sentiment of any kind and an even greater capacity for textbook orthodoxy at any cost. At the end Jim has almost transcended his body to become a pure, calculating cell. " 'I'm stronger than anything in the world, because I'm going in a straight line. You and all the rest have to think of women and tobacco and liquor and keeping warm and fed.' His eyes were as cold as wet river stones" (280). Ironically, it is his pitifully mutilated body that finally serves the cause, when Mac displays it to the crowd and begins his customary elegy " 'This guy didn't want nothing for himself—' " (349).

Apart from the mob-animal and Doc, the student of human affairs, there is one other predominant personality type opposed to this inhuman selflessness in the novel: this is that of the sturdy individualist, represented by the Andersons, father and son. Each is his own boss in a small but satisfying way—Al, the compassionate owner of a lunch wagon that offers good meals at low prices to the fruit pickers, and the father, one of the few independent small farmers left among the giant fruit corporations of Torgas Valley. Great care is lavished on descriptive details of the two men about their work—Al cooking his hamburgers, his father making coffee for the strike leaders on his immaculate farm. "From a paper bag the old man took out a handful of carefully cut pine splinters and laid them in the stove, and on top he placed a few little scraps of pitchwood, and on top of those, three round pieces of seasoned apple wood. It was so well and deftly done that the fire flared up when he applied a match. The stove cricked, and a burst of heat came from it. He put on a coffee-pot and measured ground coffee into it. From a bag he took two egg shells and dropped them into the pot" (117–18). The old man is a model of the frontier virtues of self-reliance and wide-ranging competence: his farm, an idyllic haven, is maintained with hard work and pride. Taking only a modest profit, Al runs his business with initiative and kindness. We sense that this is how Steinbeck wishes things could be, but in the course of the strike, Al's lunch wagon is destroyed and his father's apple barns burned to the ground. In this novel there must be no ideal way out.

In Dubious Battle was, as Steinbeck had anticipated, not a great popular success, although critical revaluations have tended to rate it very high indeed among his works. It is a deeply pessimistic novel about the plight of the worker in America, which places all its emphasis on methods of coping with the situation, their compatibility with traditional ideals of life, liberty, and the pursuit of happiness and also with traditional fictional concepts of heroism and nobility. *The Grapes of Wrath* can only move back from the brink of despair that Steinbeck approaches in this novel by evading any entanglement with the intolerable moral choices of rival political systems and emphasizing instead vaguer and less compromising religious and philosophical ideals; it can only reaffirm faith in the people by concentrating on the Andersons of its world rather than the destructive and savage mob-man of *In Dubious Battle*.

From the testing ground of Steinbeck's own "Communist" novel and the acrimonious neglect of earlier proletarian literature, it is now possible to posit some of the ideological and aesthetic problems of leftist fiction that existed—independent of the talent of the individual writer—and were challenged in *The Grapes of Wrath*. The most fundamental problem was the carefully fostered antithesis between Marxism and Americanism, an opposition that the enemies of the left found happily exacerbated by the identification of communism with the Russian example and thence with everything undeniably alien. The standard accusation, made at every level from the *Gastonia Gazette* to the Fish committee, was that "Marxism, whether we see it as science, judgment, myth, or plan of action, rushes into head-on collision with almost every principle with which Americans have attempted to explain or justify or purify their way of life."[12] At the most primitive level of the southern poor white, this argument was used most effectively to buttress the sanctity of family, church, and individual loyalty against any broader identification of poor people's interests, such as trade unionism. The equally standard methods of rebuttal, both by the proletarian novelists and by the Communist party, had been either to insist that Americanism was a disease of decadence, warped Puritanism, and greed (e.g., *Beyond Desire* and *The Shadow Before*)—which could be cured by communism—or to prove, with some sleight of hand, that the two attitudes were absolutely identical by making dubious parallels with the American Revolution and later communitarian social experiments (e.g., *To Make My Bread* and *Gathering Storm*; or

Earl Browder's 1936 presidential campaign slogan "Communism is Twentieth Century Americanism").[13]

However, one eminent scholar of Marxism, Sidney Hook, suggests a relationship between the two sets of attitudes that makes the eclectic philosophies of *The Grapes of Wrath* seem more acceptable, despite their political vagueness and naiveté, than such artificial extremism. Rejecting both the unbridgeable chasm theory of the right and the duplication theory of the left, Hook sees in Americanism a surrogate socialism that promised opportunities of material advancement for all, equality, and a classless society and had a prior claim on the faith of Americans. He therefore predicted that a democratic form of socialism could emerge in the United States, only without its "compromising terminology" and "superfluous theoretical baggage."[14] How much of the vital political theory must be jettisoned along with the "superfluous theoretical baggage" may be estimated from Steinbeck's novel, which is, as many critics beginning with Frederick Carpenter's seminal essay have pointed out, a blend of "Emerson's self-reliance, Whitman's love of the democratic masses, Jefferson's agrarianism, and William James's pragmatism."[15] With such a diversity of eminent guides to shape our responses, we may feel a little bewildered about the precise course of action to be adopted toward the faceless banks and giant fruit corporations that cause the Joads' sufferings, but we can also feel comfortably uncompromised in the benevolence we feel toward the victims. A good example of such depoliticizing of even the most emotive radical terminology occurs in the famous passage defining a "red":

"Well, they were a young fella jus' come out west here, an' he's listenin' one day. He kinda scratched his head an' he says, 'Mr. Hines, I ain't been here long. What is these goddam reds?' Well, sir, Hines says, 'A red is any son-of-a-bitch that wants thirty cents an hour when we're payin' twenty-five!' Well, this young fella he thinks about her, an' he scratches his head, an' he says, 'Well, Jesus, Mr. Hines. I ain't a son-of-a-bitch, but if that's what a red is—why, I want thirty cents an hour. Ever'body does. Hell, Mr. Hines, we're all reds.'"[16]

Since nothing in the rest of the novel questions the accuracy or completeness of this definition, who could refuse to be a fellow traveler in such a camp? Unless perhaps he wonders if these could be the same "reds" who flattered, manipulated, incited, and terrorized their way through *In Dubious Battle*.

The aesthetic problems reflect both the ideological bias and, once again, the peculiar qualities of poor white literature. The plots of leftist fiction were of necessity restricted to situations where class conflict was most apparent: in effect, this usually meant a strike or a depression picaresque, easy enough to produce among the urban proletariat but more difficult with the land-clinging rural peasants. In characterization there was also a distinct clash between the rational, meticulous Marxist hero, whose highest virtue lay in organization, and the colorful, comic, vigorously independent philanderer beloved in folk tradition. Humor was also a major stumbling block for serious tendentious fiction—not the moral humor of irony but the special mixture of vulgarity and grotesquerie that produces responses rather more complex than economic sympathy. Caldwell had had to shatter his aesthetic distance to contradict the dehumanized antics of his characters with a reminder that they were victims of the system; the Gastonia novelists had largely overlooked the vulgarity and had concentrated on the chill horrors of gothicism robbed of any qualifying whimsy. The general relevance of custom, folklore, superstition, and history was questionable in a world where nostalgia was dangerous and even counterrevolutionary, as in *Call Home the Heart*, though much literary capital might be made of its rejection. The perpetual problem of the credibility of the point of view of a radical or revolutionary poor white novel had involved some drastic solutions for enabling a sophisticated indictment and remedy to be articulated from a naive and uneducated populace. These had included authorial intrusion (Caldwell, Page); an array of bourgeois intellectual characters to clarify the issues over which the workers were dying (Vorse, Burke, Anderson); and one effort, censured from the left and praised from the right, to let the workers' simple analyses stand alone (Lumpkin). Steinbeck had run the gamut of these problems in *In Dubious Battle*: the conventional plot; undesirable heroes; absolute sacrifice of humor in favor of countless tactical debates; a group of migrant workers without individual character or background, remarkable only for their ominous cohesiveness; and an attempt to suspend his own shaping judgment. In tackling what is essentially the same subject—the emergent activism of California fruit pickers—three years later, Steinbeck had evidently decided that sacrifices in political depth and literary realism might be more than countered by the richness of traditionally native myths and philosophies.

A major means by which the political significance of *The Grapes of Wrath* is reduced is by placing the events in a setting that is at once timeless and temporary—a situation hostile to large-scale social planning, as both Fielding Burke and James Agee had acknowledged. The timeless aspect derives from the close relation of events to the natural cycle of the earth, from decay and despoilment to perpetual rejuvenation. The novel opens in the barrenness and drought of summer dust storms, moves through the thankless abuse of the earth's rich harvest in the fall, and ends in the death of winter rainstorms as the Joads descend to the nadir of their miserable experience. However, our final glimpse of their destitution is alleviated not only by Rose of Sharon's act of familial charity but also by the knowledge that outside "tiny points of grass came through the earth, and in a few days the hills were pale green with the beginning year" (592). The Joads' predicament becomes thus muted in the faith in the earth's renewed fertility. Ironically, this is the one point at which Steinbeck chooses not to remind us that the brightening hills have been stolen from the people for corporate profit; instead he gives us the hope that nature will mysteriously provide, as she did for the man starving for milk. This emphasis on the eternal life cycle minimizes the struggles of puny humans existing by its grace; their humility is further enhanced by the precise nature of the ecological catastrophe that initiates the action of the book.

The dust bowl storms are a natural freak, occurring in a specific location (Texas, Oklahoma, Kansas, Missouri, Iowa, Arkansas) and at a particular historical moment. To the bewildered farmers there is little qualitative difference between this natural hostility and that of controllable human origin. "A forty-acre cropper and he ain't been dusted out and he ain't been tractored out?" (12). The distinction between avoidable and unavoidable human agony is precisely what their wandering in the west should teach them, but even in the great crescendo of anger in which Steinbeck makes his most compelling indictment, there is no effort to direct the outrage to anything beyond the immediate horrors of the California situation. "There is a crime here that goes beyond denunciation. There is a sorrow here that weeping cannot symbolize. There is a failure here that topples all our success. The fertile earth, the straight tree rows, the sturdy trunks and the ripe fruit. And children dying of pellagra must die because a profit cannot be taken from an orange. And coroners must fill in the certificates—died of malnutrition—because the food must rot, must be forced to rot" (477). A novelist with more political intentions would have expanded this magnificent accusation to show the economic heart of this unnaturalness, but Steinbeck instead focuses more narrowly on the local identity of his metaphor. "The people come with nets to fish for potatoes in the river, and the guards hold them back; they come in rattling cars to get the dumped oranges, but the kerosene is sprayed. And they stand still and watch the potatoes float by, listen to the screaming pigs being killed in a ditch and covered with quicklime, watch the mountains of oranges slop down to a putrefying ooze; and in the eyes of the people there is the failure; and in the eyes of the hungry there is a growing wrath" (477). The simple trust of rural people in the providence of the land provokes fury among them at its destruction, but the rage, while undirected, is as futile as cursing the dust storms or the seasons.

As revolutionaries, these poor whites have other obstacles in their close relation to the land: they must overcome their devout attachment to their own few acres; even if they are held under no legal right, the small farms they must leave are, in the consciousness of the croppers, part of themselves—the locus of their family and history. They wonder if, in abandoning them, they are not doing grave injury to the very essence of their existence: "'place where folks live is them folks'" (71). "How can we live without our lives? How will we know it's us without our past?" (120). Like Agee's tenants—and unlike the transient mill workers of Gastonia— believing that home is a metaphysical as well as a local reality, they treasure the relics of their history; when Casy tactlessly comments on the return "home" of Tom from jail, he quickly alters the expression to "'to his folks'" (98). For some of the farmers, like Muley Graves and Grampa Joad, the uprooting is too great. Muley haunts the territory of his forefathers like a lost animal: his despair resolves into a slow martyr's death of acceptance; Grampa dies before the family has even left Oklahoma—and was spiritually dead from the moment when he was borne, drugged, off his own land. For the rest of the family, there is the prospect of a new start in life as hired laborers, the first step toward the proletarian unity of the dispossessed. However, when these backward-looking peasants occasionally forsake their communal thinking, relapse into nostalgia for their own private plots, and even attempt to establish their personal roadside vegetable gardens, it is apparent that Steinbeck is perfectly in sympathy with them. This tends to refute some of the collectivistic fervor of the interchapters and the frequent reminders that the present corporate enterprises grew from just such quasi-legal beginnings in dubious nocturnal squattings.

It is sometimes necessary to distinguish Steinbeck's professed reforming zeal from his own strong sentiment for the idyllic agrarian life of the past. His attitude to machinery may serve as an illustration: he is well aware that if the farm laborers are to triumph against their exploiters, they must remove machines from private hands and possess them themselves (385). The most potent of all these machines is the tractor; yet Steinbeck seems more dismayed by the use of this "evil" instrument on the land, regardless of which of the contending groups is controlling it, than the Okies, who merely see it as threatening their traditional livelihood. Steinbeck's description of the tender love with which a man will cherish the land and the savage rape of it by sophisticated farm machinery seems at odds not merely with any Marxist joy in controlled mechanical energy but with his own acknowledged need for a change in ownership. "Behind the harrows, the long seeders—twelve curved iron penes erected in the foundry, orgasms set by gears, raping methodically, raping without passion. . . . And when the crop grew, and was harvested, no man had crumbled a hot clod in his fingers and let the earth sift past his fingertips. No man had touched the seed, or lusted for the growth. Men ate what they had not raised, had no connection with the bread. The land bore under iron, and under iron gradually died; for it was not loved or hated, it had no prayers or curses" (49).

The physical identity of the people with their homes, of the farmer with the land he plows and tends, is extended also into a series of analogies between people and land animals—rarely with the savage beasts that characterized the masses in *In Dubious Battle* but now with creatures noted for resilience and the instinct for survival. The most enduring is the land turtle, doggedly persisting in his southwesterly direction despite all obstacles, his "fierce, humorous eyes" (20)—imagery very reminiscent of the Joads—staring always ahead, while his tough body assists the natural regenerative processes of the earth. "Lying on its back, the turtle was tight in its shell for a long time. But at last its legs waved in the air, reaching for something to pull it over. Its front foot caught a piece of quartz and little by little the shell pulled over and flopped upright. The wild oat head fell out and three of the spearhead seeds stuck in the ground. And as the turtle crawled on down the embankment, its shell dragged dirt over the seeds" (22). Earlier, Steinbeck had noted the variety of seeds along the roadside, waiting only for dispersal by the hem of a woman's skirt or a man's trouser cuff. The use of pets and domestic animals in the novel as an index to their owner's condition is detailed at length in one critical article,[17] which notes that the closeness to their animals is not a debasing factor for the migrants but a sign of their continuing humanity. Even when they are leading a life whose external quality is close to bestial, Ruthie and Winfield long to lavish their care on a dog. These symbolic details, incidentally, are utterly at odds with what Agee had observed about the relationship of poor whites to their domestic animals—an attitude wholly practical, devoid of affection, and often rather sadistic in appearance to people with more luxurious sensibilities. Such sacrifices in realism were as necessary to Steinbeck's literary portrait of the poor white as they were to the Communist writers.

One means by which Steinbeck restores to the poor whites the dignity, resourcefulness, and vigor that writers from all areas of the political spectrum agreed had been drastically diminished by their undernourished and brutalized existence is the plot itself. The emulation of the great westward trek of a heroic pioneer folk is a denial of the boundless hospitality of a rich continent and a sad elegy for an exhausted frontier. These discoveries are crucial in shaping the wrath that must demand a new way of allocating America's plenty. However, at the same time, the Joads' journey is a reaffirmation of all the qualities that founded a nation in the wilderness. From the long-range perspective of the interchapters, we see the migrants, crawling like insects in their ancient cars, driven from their land by powers that they do not comprehend, and trapped at the mercy of sophisticated exploiters. But in the chapters with the Joads, we are aware not of victimization but of the astonishing fortitude and ingenuity that they maintain in the face of overwhelming odds. Instead of the vacant anesthesia of Agee's tenants and Caldwell's croppers and the docile dependence on others of Vorse's strikers, the Joads maintain noble standards of charity, decency, and even hygiene. For them there is to be a thin line between hunger and fury, not the usual inertia that was elsewhere linked to malnutrition and required all the resources of left-wing propaganda to agitate.

The frontier movement of the plot is an opportunity not only for Steinbeck to relinquish the more undesirable poor white qualities but also to add traditional virtues through association with historical and mythic precedent. Much has been made of the biblical echoes of the plot—the vision of California as a new Canaan or promised land, the exodus of a people from a plague-ridden situation, and the resistance they must meet before the promise can be fulfilled—but the parallel seems more significant when it is recognized as an echo of the first American experience, which was also imbued with such hints. Thus it is a recasting of events that are themselves a radical reordering of the original movement of a chosen people; attempts to tie these mythic overtones too closely to Christian doctrine are not persuasive and are perhaps even offensive to the orthodox.[18] One of the lessons in pragmatism that *The Grapes of Wrath* teaches is the danger of clinging too desperately to any variety of faith, except perhaps for an enduring trust in humanity.

The details of the Joads' journey emphasize the particularly American rather than Hebraic aspects of their experience, and they bring just enough of their history and folk traditions with them to remind us of their proud ancestry. " ' We're Joads. We don't look up to nobody. Grampa's grampa, he fit in the Revolution' " (420). Of Steinbeck's list of revolutionary leaders, they are certainly closer in temper to Jefferson and Paine than to Lenin and Marx, and any possible international implications of the unfairness of California's agricultural system are curtly dismissed with the claim, " 'We ain't foreign. Seven generations back Americans, and beyond that Irish, Scotch, English, German. One of our folks in the Revolution, an' they was lots of our folks in the Civil War—both sides. Americans' " (317–18). Instead of the strains of The Internationale and Solidarity Forever, the Okies and Arkies make country music on their guitars and harmonicas and hold square dances that are a rhapsodic celebration of a purely local folk culture.

Look at that Texas boy, long legs loose, taps four times for ever' damn step. Never seen a boy swing aroun' like that. Look at him swing that Cherokee girl, red in her cheeks an' her toe points out. Look at her pant, look at her heave. Think she's tired? Think she's winded? Well she ain't. Texas boy got his hair in his eyes, mouth's wide open, can't get air, but he pats four times for ever' darn step, an' he'll keep a-goin' with the Cherokee girl.
The fiddle squeaks and the guitar bongs. Mouth-organ man is red in the

face. Texas boy and the Cherokee girl, pantin' like dogs an' a'beatin' the groun'. Ol' folks stan' a-pattin' their han's. Smilin' a little, tappin' their feet. [449]

Steinbeck's skill in catching the rhythm of the square dance caller in this passage is reflected generally in the superb richness and variety of native dialect in the novel. The migrants themselves are very sensitive to any variation of speech and accent, and families from Oklahoma and Kansas gossip wonderingly about the strange tones of someone from Massachusetts; but these aliens who become reconciled through common suffering are all Americans—they still have a common fund of English, unlike the multilingual workers of *The Shadow Before*. Their wanderings lead them into a more profound questioning of their national inheritance than of broader economic principles. One man recalls to a crowd of eager listeners in the firelight the hollow success of shooting an Indian; two women exchange regional superstitions for cutting birth pains—one places a paring knife under the mattress, because " 'our folks always done it,' " while the other says, " 'We used a plow point' " (597). This knowledge of both the fullness and the failure of American life is sufficient for Steinbeck's purpose; of a world beyond their own circumscribed one, the people have only the confused impressions they bring back from a rare trip to the movies: "An' they was a newsreel with them German soldiers kickin' up their feet—funny as hell" (447).

The expansion of the Okies' experience from parochial and provincial to national—though not international—is paralleled by the shrinking of tolerance for them among the Californians. These white, Protestant descendants of the earliest American pioneers are finally confronted with the bigoted platitudes that they believed they, at least, were immune to: " 'Them goddamn Okies got no sense and no feeling. They ain't human. A human being wouldn't live like they do. A human being couldn't stand it to be so dirty and miserable. They ain't a hell of a lot better than gorillas' " (301). Later, as the migrants become desperate, fear and hatred solidify: " 'Why, Jesus, they're as dangerous as niggers in the South! If they ever get together there ain't nothin' that'll stop 'em' " (322). " 'Okies are dirty and ignorant. They're degenerate, sexual maniacs. Those goddamned Okies are thieves. They'll steal anything. They've got no sense of property rights' " (386). This is fairly rampant didacticism, as is the picture of near-perfect communal living in the government camps; yet when Tom questions a watchman as to why conditions that permit any degree of human decency are so rare, the man answers evasively, "'You'll have to find that out yourself!'" (393). There is of course no obligation, either aesthetic or ideological, on Steinbeck to find any cure for the disease whose symptoms he portrays in such a masterly fashion, but one senses a reluctance to investigate even the nature of the malaise. From the interchapters there are strong condemnations of the accumulation of property in the hands of a few and ominous prophecies of great armies of the poor seizing violently land they have a moral right to; in the chapters with the Joads, it seems that effective strikes for higher wages and a program of healthy sanitary shelter by the federal government would keep the workers pacified. A considerable indecisiveness emerges from the novel about how radical the problem is: whether the circumstances of class war exist—likely from the interchapters—or whether there is a clear-cut villain in the Farmers' Association with no broader implications—likely from the chapters and their limited point of view. The problem is partly compounded by the pragmatism of the Joads themselves, in many ways admirable in the face of degenerating circumstances but also dangerous in their willingness to lower their expectations: at the beginning Ma Joad dreams of a white house in California—after a few months on the road, she hopes they may one day afford a tent that does not leak; Rose of Sharon plans early in her pregnancy a comfortable future for her child—at the end she is sulking for a little milk so that her baby may be born alive. The disadvantages of nonteleological thinking are apparent when the result is a perpetual readjustment to straitened conditions: while we are told that the metaphysical grapes of wrath are ripening for the vintage, what we see among the poor is stoicism, sacrifice, and one supreme act of charity.

The rhetoric of cumulative fury that works so effectively on the reader—and promises the metamorphosis of hunger into anger—finally recruits Tom Joad to its service, but it is apparent that it is Casy's gory murder, rather than his unionizing ardor, that is behind the conversion. When Tom carries the message back to Ma, hailed by so many critics as the proletarian mother *par excellence*, she says only, "'I wisht you didn' do it. I wisht you wasn' there'" (535)—this after she has witnessed the worst that California can offer. Rose of Sharon berates her brother hysterically for his violent act of commitment, Ruthie boasts of his daring courage; no one responds to it as principle. At last the discrepancy between the ideal rebellion of the interchapters and the "real" reaction of the Joads verges on irony: in the final interchapter the women anxiously watch their men to determine if they will break or resist under the terrible strain. "And where a number of men gathered together, the fear went from their faces, and anger took its place. And the women sighed with relief, for they knew it was all right—the break had not come" (592). In the final chapter the Joad men have lost both hope and authority, and Pa can only plead humbly with Ma, "'Did we slip up? Is they anything we could of did?'" (604). The interchapters, which began by paralleling on a more general level the events and experiences of the more personal chapters, diverge from them increasingly in the quality of their rebellious response. They become finally a kind of ideological-practical dialogue, demonstrating on one side the moral justification for radical action and on the other the powerful obstacles to it among the people. There is no synthesis of the two: Steinbeck directs us to be fully in sympathy with each point of view while he gradually polarizes them. However, he does place a number of characters in the novel who are capable of building bridges between the two extremes, and it is therefore on these individually heroic people that we are forced to place our hopes for any eventual links.

These characters emerge from the people in the course of the book—there are no professional organizers or parties—and their attitudes are no more politically precise than a vague but strong humanitarianism. Ma, Casy, and Tom have few of the conventional qualities that both dehumanize and elevate a mass leader, but they are richly endowed with traditional folk qualities—a humorous, bossy matriarch; an erstwhile lecherous wandering preacher; and a prodigal son made good but still retaining his more popular vices. Although Ma never commits herself to any kind of program or organization, she is instrumental in overseeing the most important transition in the novel for the Joads, the movement from a family unit to integers in a wider group. The change is significant, for from the outset it is Ma who is most determined that the family will stay together and take precedence in their loyalties, although she is the first to break her own rules. Before she ever appears in the novel, we have from her son Tom a portrait of a Dickensian figure, larger than life, towering above the family in moral stature yet also wholly of it in comedy and error. Casy hears the ghastly gothic tale of her mistake in leaving the gate unlocked, so that the pig escaped and ate a neighboring baby; he hears the ludicrous yarn of this tough woman beating a peddler with a live chicken; but he finds when he meets her that she is the first to insist that he join their already overloaded wagon for the trip west. "'One more ain't gonna hurt; an' a man, strong an' healthy, ain't never no burden'" (139). The rest of the family take their cue from her; so later it is Tom and Al who suggest that they team up with the Wilsons and Pa who says of them "'We got almost a kin bond.'"

All alterations in the family structure are given a special significance, since we are shown that the family is almost sacred in this culture. After Muley Graves gives his impassioned defense of staying behind, Casy says grimly, "'You shouldn't of broke up the fambly'" (65); and before the Joads set out on the road, they have a final clan meeting, rigidly patriarchal in its structure and highly formal in its rules of rank and precedence. With the journey begins a process of attrition that depletes the group of its members and the men of their traditional power. At the first pause for gas, the family dog is killed, and before the day is out, Grampa has died in the Wilsons' tent. However, the countermovement to the loss has already begun, for Grampa's death is recorded symbolically on a page torn from the Wilsons' family Bible, and the next day the two families travel on together. Losses follow rapidly now, from Noah's defection down the river to Granma's death (apparently a calculated choice by Ma between her welfare and the family's survival) and Connie's cowardly disappearance. Ma does not acquiesce readily to this fragmentation and stages a dramatic revolt against Pa and the sons by threatening them with a jack handle to prevent any further breakup in the group. However, she is forced to admit after a succession of disasters, "'Family's fallin' apart'" (294), and is finally faced with the consequences of her loyalties when she has the unpleasant choice of sharing a meager meal with a group of starving children or giving her family enough food. She feeds the children and receives only bitter reproach from their mothers— jealous of their own children's loyalty—although gradually the campers do become more willing to share their few possessions. Nevertheless, there is no dramatic recognition by the people of their common interests, and there is always a powerful sense of regret for the institution that is being relinquished.

Ma's own primacy in the family, though she is eminently fitted for its leadership, is emphasized as a temporary necessity. The rule of women is as unnatural as the rotting oranges and starving children, and there are frequent hints that when the natural order returns, Ma will retire again from her emergency role to the "great and humble" position she formerly occupied. "Pa complained, 'Seems like the man ain't got no say no more. She's jus' a heller. Come time we get settled down, I'm a-gonna smack her.' 'Come that time, you can,' said Ma" (357). When Tom, the most beloved son, must leave, Ma articulates her growing confusion over the validity of the family concept, " 'They was the time when we was on the lan'. They was a boundary to us then. Ol' folks died off, an' little fellas come, an' we was always one thing—we was the fambly—kinda whole and clear. An' now we ain't clear no more. I can't get straight. They ain't nothin' keeps us clear' " (536). This is the beginning of Ma's painful rejection of the central values hitherto held in her life. When Al announces his departure and Rose of Sharon's baby is born dead, she is the source of energy for all to carry on as part of a wider brotherhood. " 'Use'ta be the fambly was fust. It ain't so now. Worse off we get, the more we got to do' " (606). Her determination is realized in her daughter's final symbolic act, the shocking extension of the most basic family metaphor. Ma Joad, the supermother whose immense strength is the mainstay against chaos in the novel—more powerful than Tom's determination or Casy's vision—marks the final abandonment of realism in the depiction of the poor white; yet as a fictional character she is wholly credible and consistent. While Tom and Casy are drawn increasingly into a visionary mysticism, Ma remains always the spokesman for the life force of the common man. " 'Why, Tom, we're the people that live. They ain't gonna wipe us out. Why, we're the people—we go on' " (383). She is saved by Steinbeck from the real danger of saintliness by her sharp tongue and comic capacities; when Pa bemoans the need to leave the unwonted plumbing luxuries of the government camp, Ma replies sharply, " 'We can't eat no toilets' " (312); and Steinbeck makes her the object of a fine comic scene—when the camp ladies' committee visits her, Ma receives them with the casual grandeur of a high-society hostess.

Humor—macabre, gross, immoral—is used in the novel to balance sentimentality, although occasionally it contributes to a somewhat condescending cuteness, particularly about the minor characters, as in the description of Grampa and Granma:

A cantankerous, complaining, mischievous, laughing face. He fought and argued, told dirty stories. He was as lecherous as always. Vicious and cruel and impatient, like a frantic child, and the whole structure overlaid with amusement. He drank too much when he could get it, ate too much when it was there, talked too much all the time.
Behind him hobbled Granma, who had survived only because she was as mean as her husband. She held her own with a shrill ferocious religiosity that was as lecherous and as savage as anything Grampa could offer. [105]

However, for the most part the humor is effective in presenting a people charitable but not wholly unselfish, decent but not genteel. The scene in the truck stop, illustrating the generosity of the owner to some migrants, ends with a glimpse of his stealing the jackpot from his own slot machines. Tom and Casy both share the traditional comic qualities of the poor white hero—easygoing but ready for a fight; homely and humorous philosophers but not intellectuals; sensual, extravagant, blunt, and loyal—all in notable contrast to the Machiavellian Communist leaders, Mac and Jim, in *In Dubious Battle*.

These two heroes rapidly become identified as spokesmen for important ideological attitudes, and little is made of their colorful backgrounds beyond the fact that the two are already established touchstones in the community: the preacher and the killer. The concept of the brutish group-man is rejected here in favor of the Emersonian self-reliant man and the noble and enduring people who are the source of Ma's faith. Extensive analyses have been written of the transcendentalism, Jeffersonian agrarianism, and pragmatism of these spokesmen for the people, though in the rush to defend Steinbeck from accusations of alien influence, relatively little has been said of the regretful note of nostalgia that accompanies such philosophies. They are so intimately connected with the fruitless modern emulation of a no longer realizable nineteenth-century dream that whatever sorrow Steinbeck may have for the decay of heroic individual possibilities, he is bound by the exigencies of the plot to admit that they exist in some tension with current political and economic necessities. Thus it is possible to detect a slight movement away from the rhapsodic transcendentalism that Casy expresses early in the novel and away even from the insistent pragmatism that refuses to look beyond the immediate situation. Tom's early advice to Ma to " 'jus' take ever' day' " (124) is followed solemnly by her; yet there is some ironic qualification for the reader in the knowledge that this "nonteleological advice" is based on his experiences in prison, when dreaming of an impossible release only made the captivity more intolerable. If this is an analogy to the closed frontier, then there is certainly little hope, and Casy later contests this circumscribed denial of anything other than immediate significance. " 'They's gonna come somepin outa all these folks goin' wes'—outa all their farms lef' lonely. They's gonna come a thing that's gonna change the whole country' " (237). By the end of the novel, Casy has decided in some degree what this undetermined change is going to be, since he is working as a strike leader, and is convinced of the power of organized group action. Yet when Tom questions him about these newfound purposes, he receives only the evasive reply he had from the watchman in the camp: " 'Maybe I can't tell you. Maybe you got to find out' " (522). A similar change in attitude seems to occur from the early rejection of notions of good and evil—" 'There ain't no sin and there ain't no virtue. There's just stuff people do' " (32)—to the situation at the end, where there is clearly evil abroad in the universe, even if Steinbeck hedges about defining it too closely as capitalism or the Farmers' Association. Thus some possibility is offered, if a very slender one, that these older American ideals may be transmuted in the service of a displaced people. However, the clash between this modification of Joad attitudes and the insistent revolutionary emphasis of the inter-chapters on the power of wrathful unity—a stance that suggests immediate insurrection—is still far from being reconciled. Whether there is any final hint that this wrath is transferable to the Joads, whether they finally begin to merge with the anonymous people of the interchapters, is decided not in the narrative of the novel but in the much more ambiguous world of its symbols: in the seemingly contradictory relationship of the grapes of wrath to the literal milk of human kindness.

The final chapter of the novel is turned over so utterly to enig-matic symbolic statements that there is no obvious answer to this. The family experiences its last loss in their son Al, the driver, and are thus forced back to walking; but Al's departure is also part of the widening of their circle, since he is to marry the Wainwrights' daughter, thus affirming continuity for these destitute families. While Rose of Sharon labors to give birth, Pa makes a desperate effort to rally unity among the weary and starving men in the camp by enlisting them in the arduous task of building a dike to keep back the floodwaters. These two events could turn the tide of disaster, but the climax of the expectation of life that we have followed through the book with Rose of Sharon is the birth of a dead baby; and when the dike collapses soon afterwards, the men turn their bitterness and wrath on Pa. Uncle John, given the grim task of burying the stillborn child, instead also makes a symbolic gesture of it by floating it down the river to the town in an apple box—a futile political act but a powerful aesthetic and emotional token of resentment. The mood of the family is extremely somber: anger seems to be reserved for each other as Ma and Pa quarrel over their last loaf of bread and Ruthie and Winfield fight viciously over, ironically, a flower. Even Ma's eternal optimism is strained and exhausted; when she whispers, almost trancelike. " 'They's changes—all over'" (605), her own volition seems scarcely to be involved. The final image certainly epitomizes the people's power of endurance—they draw sustenance literally from one another— but in spite of Rose of Sharon's mysterious smile, the act is ambivalent. It is also the culmination of the unnaturalness of the book, from the dust storms to the rotting fruit to the enervation and preempting of the men. Both Ma and Rose of Sharon appear to have reached an advanced stage of consciousness by the end of the novel, but Steinbeck makes no commitments for them, no form of activism beyond the most personal. The Joads' wrath does not appear likely to mature for any harvest, although they have given Tom to fight for the workers.

Thus *The Grapes of Wrath* represents the final depoliticizing and remythologizing of the poor white social novel. Real economic conditions are not distorted, but instead of challenging them with real economic or political solutions, Steinbeck alters the people to make them more competent to deal with the situation by returning to them traditions of courage and generosity and philosophies of optimism and endurance. He selects the best of both the poor white heritage and native American schools of thought and uses them to establish a powerful emotional stimulus to the reader's wrath without providing compromising political precedents for his behavior. By relocating the poor whites a couple of states further west, Steinbeck manages to shake off two centuries of social disrepute and literary extremism. He finally divorces the repulsiveness of poverty from the repulsiveness of the poor and demonstrates that they need not be forever linked, although this, like William Rollins's picture of the inevitable triumph of the hearty proletariat over the decaying middle class, is shown persuasively only outside a southern context.

CHAPTER X

The Transformation of the Poor White in the Depression

Shields McIlwaine abandons his chronicle of the southern poor white at the onset of the thirties, with the assumption that the last extremity of horror and despair has been reached, the lurid depths of the tradition finally plumbed: "Across forty miles of Mississippi roads, simple, degenerate old Anse Bundren hauled and finally buried the corpse of his wife. But on Tobacco Road in Georgia, Jeeter Lester reached the dead end of the sharecropper's row."[1] Yet in North Carolina, Ishma Hensley, Bonnie McClure, and Marge Crenshaw were about to rise from the abyss of misery to lead the striking lintheads at Gastonia; in Alabama the Gudgers, Rickettses, and Woodses were quietly affirming the sanctity of enduring tenant poverty; in Oklahoma the Joads were preparing their battered truck to move off the sharecropper's row and onto Route 66. Flem Snopes, the most sinister of all the con men to emerge from the backwoods, had yet to move into his ascendancy; the grotesquely violent Popeye would challenge the last vestiges of that southern code that had fostered the clownish and degraded image of its peasants; Red Oliver and many youthful victims of the depression would be thrown on the road to explore anew the folkways of regional and national poverty; and a vast array of sharecroppers, weavers, cotton pickers, miners, shopgirls, meat packers, derelicts, and chain-gang convicts would pose for the cameras and pour their intimate lives into the notebooks of New Deal writers and sociologists.

[184]

The literary tradition that McIlwaine feared exhausted showed a remarkable capacity to respond to the eclectic political and aesthetic attitudes of a decade and a region equally noted for the variety of their extremism. However, the response was perfectly appropriate to the complex nature of the tradition, for the literature continued to be one of paradoxes and the frequent unwitting disclosure of details that ran counter to the author's known ideological perspective. The closer a writer came to revealing the essence of the poor white, the more inhibiting did that revelation become to any solution to the poor white's predicament—for the very conception "poor white" is an oxymoron. It insists on the irreconcilable nature of its two parts; the unnaturalness of their yoking assumes a world view in which to be white is to be assured of a satisfactory share of personal resources. When whites are discovered deprived of these—as was most dramatically the case in the South—they take on the status of freaks, to be reviled, cured, pitied, accepted, or mocked. Thus the incongruous is an essential element of their literary constitution, no matter what the ideology of the author. The ways in which this grotesquerie of the southern poor white was reconciled or integrated into a social vision in a period of great national crisis show that the tradition itself was flexible, but within clearly circumscribed limits.

Faulkner used the ludicrous fanaticism of the poor white, both as comic and villain, to mirror modern decadence but also to reaffirm individualism. Caldwell vented his outrage against an economic system that had debased and starved its peasants by creating alien and almost inhuman caricatures, not so different from those William Byrd had discovered two hundred years earlier—yet no longer so amusing in their lassitude and lechery. After Caldwell's revelations, the laughter provoked by their antics could never be quite so smug or wholesome again. Agee responded to the remote poverty of three tenant families by trying to wring dignity from their debasement, but in the process he continued to verify the brutal truths of their accumulated history. He humbled himself before the repellant physical quality of such an existence, but to document it accurately he was forced to catalogue once more its mixture of shames and absurdities. The Gastonia novelists contributed most to the neglected task of exploring the urban experience of the poor white. They found him less a convenient doctrinal cipher than the *New Masses* or the *Daily Worker* had suggested but also a richer source of literary stimulation than might be discovered among the northern poor. Appalling poverty was allied to regional and folk characteristics, and while the intellectual and spiritual loyalties of the poor whites provided some difficulty in their lingering mysticism and superstition, the radical writers created a curious aesthetic compromise by placing the rational Communist utopia in a familiarly Christian eschatology. This was supported by an apparatus of signs, songs, symbols, and slogans that gave the political movement the quality of a religious cult, though its justification in ideology, if not aesthetics, remained dubious. The problems of the comic absurdity and ineptitude of poor whites as proletarians and their dangerous tendency to retreat from urban class warfare back to the temporary soothing powers of nature were ominous ones for "reasonable" authors, but the best of them turned these problems into a dialectical debate that did not impose solutions that were patently false to the circumstances. These were the writers who most significantly expanded the range of the poor white tradition in the thirties, by exploring urban and industrial situations from which non-Marxists prudently averted their eyes. Both Agee's hostile reaction to their problem-solving acumen and Steinbeck's successful retreat from their difficulties were possible partly because of the Communists' experiments, errors, and revelations.

Such widely varied contributions and alterations to the poor white's fictional history do not, however, indicate that the southern sharecropper and linthead were mere literary chameleons whose infinite changeability might be appropriated by every random ideology. Limits existed to the process of attrition and assimilation of the poor white's experience, set on one side by the realities of his contemporary rural and urban situation, and on the other by the strength of the literary tradition itself. Thus one of the most prominent southern literary groups of the decade was forced, by its idealization of archaic regional and rural values, to ignore the present misery of tenants and croppers while inveighing against industrialism as the destroyer of native folk arts and culture. The Agrarians, the most eminent group of writers to emerge as conservative opponents of progress, found every aspect of the poor white's current condition and literary history antithetical to their model of a regional culture. The tenants' eagerness to desert the grueling and unrewarding agonies of cotton farming for the meager regularity of factory cash seemed to mock any schemes for returning the South to a tranquil rural economy; the vulgarity of the fictional cult jarred with Agrarian memories of a more elegant past. Donald Davidson, in a survey of southern literature for *Culture in the South*, decided he would pass over all books dealing with poor whites, since they were the result of a state of mind that was "not quite healthy."[2] Like Davidson, Robert Penn Warren felt that the artist would be likely to find more stimulation in a stable agrarian society than in an industrial culture, but Warren went beyond this to draw up a series of comparisons of the literature that tended to emerge from each of these two backgrounds. This juxtaposition of the contrary qualities of regional and proletarian literature helps isolate some of the reasons why the southern literary consciousness was inevitably at odds with reforming instincts and also why the poor white was an alien figure to regionalists and proletarians alike.

Warren argued that the regional movement involved "the attempt of a writer to reason himself into the appropriate relation to the past; the proletarian movement, as the attempt to reason himself into the appropriate relation to the future."[3] In fact, those who wrote of the poor white in the thirties, whether from a more regional or proletarian bias, were dealing with an even more unlikely task: the attempt to reason their hopelessly unreasonable subject out of the past and into any acceptable relation with either the present or the future. Even among those writers who abjured the more drastic solutions of the radicals, none sought salvation in the southern past. Faulkner, for all the virtues he saw in that more heroic age, exposed its tainted origins and the inevitability of corruption. Agee, though loathe to tamper with the delicate integrity of tenants' lives, nonetheless looked to a future revolution in consciousness and condemned their historic victimization. Caldwell attempted most strenuously to assess the relationship of the traditional stereotype to the contemporary sociological plight. These writers were neither yoked to the past, like the Agrarians, nor chained to the rational solutions of the future, like the Communists. They did not have to posit solutions that must be demonstrably effective outside as well as within their aesthetic context, and therefore they could explore more deeply the myths of nature, the manifestations of frenzied Christianity, and the power of family hierarchy without being forced to rationalize their rejection. It was perhaps Steinbeck who, in *The Grapes of Wrath*, came closest to Warren's definition of a regional writer, despite his appeal to national rather than southern traditions. These were the traditions that were in fact better able to support a cult of folk heroism, of land hunger, and what Warren called "the fusion of the simple economic fact of ownership with the entire emotional life" (631). In the South, however, if literary regionalism was to mean anything more than local color writing—and certainly the Agrarians hoped for much more than that—it would have necessitated as sweeping a revision of the real conditions there as the Marxists were prepared to undertake in their literature. The poor white would certainly be an even more alien figure in such a conservative revolution than he was in organizing textile and sharecropper unions and conducting successful strikes. The primacy of religion, land, and family among his values could not disguise the fact that poverty was the only constant in his tradition, in all its oscillations between sentimental pity and coarse ridicule. The 1930s was scarcely the time to sing its merits or emphasize the southern poor white's role in a return to the antebellum way.

By the end of the decade, autopsies were being furiously performed and elegies gloatingly written over the regional and proletarian literary movements alike; but, with their usual dogged tenacity, the poor whites survived. They reappear frequently in the southern fiction of the following years as comic villains and industrial victims, as unionizing sharecroppers and mob supporters of rabble-rousing politicians, and even still, as quaint and colorful mountain peasants.[4] But it was the era of the depression that proved unusually rich and significant in the accumulating literary history of this oldest American folk figure, for in the political climate of that period, the poor white had transcended the local limits of his culture and had become a symbol for the distress and failure of the nation. The paradoxical attributes of his poverty represented a complex moral, aesthetic, and political challenge to writers in an age when polemical certainty might easily have become the rule. Instead, the poor white became a tool for exploring the past mistakes of the country (most vividly represented in the savage history and rapid industrialization of the South); he became the means for a more profound scrutiny of the role of its artists than ever before; and finally, he became the agency for questioning revered traditions of independence, self-sufficiency, and stoicism to see if they were any longer worth preserving.

NOTES

PREFACE
1. Leonard W. Doob, "Poor Whites: A Frustrated Class," in *Caste and Class in a Southern Town* by John Dollard, p. 447.
2. A. N. J. Den Hollander, "The Tradition of 'Poor Whites,'" in *Culture in the South*, p. 403.
3. Allison Davis, Burleigh B. Gardner and Mary R. Gardner, *Deep South*, Chapter 3 and particularly table on p. 65.

CHAPTER I
1. William Byrd, *The Prose Works of William Byrd of Westover*, p. 85.
2. Ibid., p. 205.
3. Clare de Graffenried, "The Georgia Cracker in the Cotton Mills," *The Century Magazine*, February 1891, p. 498.
4. Marshall W. Fishwick, *Virginia: A New Look at the Old Dominion* (New York: Harper & Brothers, 1959), p. 216.
5. Frank Lawrence Owsley, *Plain Folk of the Old South*, p. 8.
6. Elizabeth Madox Roberts, *The Time of Man*, p. 143.
7. Shields McIlwaine, *The Southern Poor-White: From Lubberland to Tobacco Road*, p. 32.
8. Augustus B. Longstreet, *Georgia Scenes, Characters, Incidents &c., in the First Half Century of the Republic*, pp. 43–44.
9. Johnson J. Hooper, *Simon Suggs' Adventures*, p. 12.
10. Ibid., p. 65.
11. Edmund Wilson, *Patriotic Gore: Studies in the Literature of the American Civil War* (New York: Oxford University Press, 1962), p. 510.
12. D. W. Brogan, quoted in Editorial Notes, *The Lovingood Papers*, ed. Ben Harris McClary (Knoxville: University of Tennessee Press, 1964), p. 49.
13. George Washington Harris, *High Times and Hard Times*, p. 184. Subsequent references to this edition will be made in the text.
14. Kenneth S. Lynn, *Mark Twain and Southwestern Humor*, pp. 54–58.
15. George Tucker, *The Valley of Shenandoah*, 1:131.
16. McIlwaine, *Southern Poor-White*, p. 20.
17. Ibid., p. 36.
18. A. N. J. Den Hollander, "The Tradition of 'Poor Whites,'" in *Culture in the South*, quoting James Sterling, p. 417.
19. Ibid., quoting Hinton Rowan Helper, p. 419.
20. James R. Gilmore, "The 'Poor Whites' of the South," *Harper's New Monthly Magazine*, June 1864, pp. 115, 124.
21. Ibid., p. 124.
22. Merrill Maguire Skaggs, *The Folk of Southern Fiction*, pp. 3–6.
23. C. Vann Woodward, *Origins of the New South, 1877–1931*, p. 154.
24. Joel Chandler Harris, *Mingo and Other Sketches in Black and White*, p. 21. Subsequent references to this edition will be made in the text.

25. Joel Chandler Harris, *Free Joe and Other Georgian Sketches*, p. 235. Subsequent references to this edition will be made in the text.

26. McIlwaine, *Southern Poor-White*, pp. 125–27.

27. Richard Malcolm Johnston, *Dukesborough Tales*, 1968. Foreword.

28. Carvel Emerson Collins, "Nineteenth Century Fiction of the Southern Appalachians, *Bulletin of Bibliography* 17, no. 9 (September–December 1942): 186–91 and 17, no. 10 (January–April 1943): 215–18.

29. Skaggs, *Folk of Southern Fiction*, pp. 40, 57, 116–17.

30. W. J. Cash, *The Mind of the South*, pp. 146–49.

31. G. K. Holmes, "The Peons of the South," *AAPSS* 4 (September 1893): 265–74.

32. Den Hollander, "Tradition of 'Poor Whites,' " p. 423.

33. John William DeForest, *A Union Officer in the Reconstruction*, p. 80. Subsequent references to this edition will be made in the text.

34. Gerald W. Johnson, quoted by Cash, *Mind of the South*, p. 178.

35. Lala Carr Steelman, "Mary Clare de Graffenried: The Saga of a Crusader for Social Reform," in *Studies in the History of the South 1875–1922*, 3:60.

36. De Graffenried, "The Georgia Cracker," p. 491. Subsequent references to this article will be made in the text.

37. Cash, *Mind of the South*, pp. 145–85, *passim*.

38. Ibid., p. 201.

39. Woodward, *Origins of the New South*, p. 211.

40. Cash, *Mind of the South*, p. 211.

41. Horace Kephart, *Our Southern Highlanders*, p. 309.

42. Cash, *Mind of the South*, p. 200.

CHAPTER II

1. William P. Trent, "Tendencies of Higher Life in the South," *Atlantic Monthly* 79 (1897): 768; John Raper Ormond, "Some Recent Products of the New School of Southern Fiction," *South Atlantic Quarterly* 3 (1904): 287.

2. C. Vann Woodward, *Origins of the New South, 1877–1913*, p. 435.

3. H. L. Mencken, "The Sahara of the Bozart," in *The American Scene*, p. 157.

4. John M. Bradbury, *Renaissance in the South, passim*. I am indebted to Bradbury's book, particularly his categories and summaries in chapters 3, 4, and 5 for my account of the revival of southern writing in the 1920s.

5. Elizabeth Madox Roberts, *The Time of Man*, p. 321. Subsequent references to this edition will be made in the text.

6. Edith Summers Kelley, *Weeds*, p. 195. Subsequent references to this edition will be made in the text.

7. Quoted by Earl H. Rovit, *Herald to Chaos*, pp. 24–25.

8. Ellen Glasgow, *Barren Ground*, p. 7. Subsequent references to this edition will be made in the text.

9. Dorothy Scarborough, *In the Land of Cotton*, p. 364.

10. Dorothy Scarborough, *Can't Get a Red Bird*, p. 75. Subsequent references to this edition will be made in the text.

11. John D. Wade, "Two Souths," *Virginia Quarterly Review* 10 (1934): 616–19.

12. T. S. Stribling, *Birthright*, p. 219–20.

13. Ibid., pp. 128–29, 290.

14. T. S. Stribling, *Teeftallow*, pp. 70–71.

15. T. S. Stribling, *Bright Metal*, p. 451.

16. Robert Penn Warren, "T. S. Stribling: A Paragraph in the History of Critical Realism," *American Review* 2 (1934): 463–86.

17. Shields McIlwaine, *The Southern Poor-White*, p. xxiv.

18. Harvey O'Connor, "Carolina Mill Slaves," *New Masses*, May 1929, p. 7.

19. Ibid.

20. Bill Dunne, "Gastonia: A Beginning," *New Masses*, July 1929, p. 5.

21. Jessie Lloyd, "Gastonia Law," *New Masses*, October 1929, p. 5.

22. Ella Ford, "We Are Mill People," *New Masses*, August 1929, p. 3. The same point is made by Broadus Mitchell in Chapter 3 of *The Rise of the Cotton Mills in the South*.

CHAPTER III

1. Frederick L. Gwynn and Joseph L. Blotner, eds., *Faulkner in the University*, p. 177.

2. William Faulkner, *The Hamlet*, p. 5. Subsequent references to this edition will be made in the text.

3. William Faulkner, *As I Lay Dying*, p. 41. Subsequent references to this edition will be made in the text.

4. M. Thomas Inge, "William Faulkner and George Washington Harris: In the Tradition of Southwestern Humor," *Tennessee Studies in Literature* 7 (1962): 47–59.

5. Olga Vickery, "The Dimensions of Consciousness: *As I Lay Dying*," in *William Faulkner*, pp. 232–47.

6. William Faulkner, *Sanctuary*, p. 268. Subsequent references to this edition will be made in the text.

7. Irving Howe, *William Faulkner*, p. 59.

8. Edmond L. Volpe, *A Reader's Guide to William Faulkner*, p. 147.

9. William Faulkner, *Collected Stories*, p. 153. Subsequent references to this edition will be made in the text.

10. Gwynn and Blotner, *Faulkner in the University*, p. 97.

11. Elmo Howell, "Faulkner's Wash Jones and the Southern Poor White," *Ball State University Forum* 8, no. 1 (Winter 1967): 12.

12. William B. Stein, "Faulkner's Devil," *Modern Language Notes* 76 (December 1961): 732.

13. Faulkner, *Collected Stories*, p. 5. Subsequent references to this edition will be made in the text.

14. Howe, *William Faulkner*, p. 79.

15. See Faulkner's description of the Snopes invasion in *Sartoris* (New York: Random House, 1956), pp. 172–73.

16. Gwynn and Blotner, *Faulkner in the University*, p. 80.

17. Faulkner, *Collected Stories*, p. 53. Subsequent references will be made in the text.

18. M. E. Bradford, "Faulkner's 'Tall Men,'" *South Atlantic Quarterly* 61 (Winter 1962): 39.

19. Hyatt H. Waggoner, *William Faulkner*, p. 17.

CHAPTER IV

1. Erskine Caldwell, *Tobacco Road*, p. i.

2. Philip Henderson, *The Novel Today*, p. 150.

3. Caldwell, *Tobacco Road*, p. 32. Subsequent references will be made in the text.

4. Alfred Kazin, *On Native Grounds*, p. 380.

5. Oscar Cargill, *Intellectual America*, p. 392. Despite this comment, however, Cargill is one of Caldwell's few generally sympathetic contemporary critics.

6. Jack Conroy, "Passion and Pellagra," *New Masses*, April 1932, p. 24.

7. Joseph Warren Beach, *American Fiction 1920–1940*, p. 226.

8. Martin Esslin, *The Theatre of the Absurd* (Garden City, N.Y.: Doubleday & Company, Inc., Anchor Books, 1961), p. 301.

9. See Milton Rickels, *George Washington Harris* (New York: Twayne Publishers, Inc., 1965), pp. 89–90.

10. W. M. Frohock, *The Novel of Violence in America*, p. 144.

11. Beach, *American Fiction*, p. 231.

12. Erskine Caldwell, *God's Little Acre*, p. 12. Subsequent references to this edition will be made in the text.

13. Lawrence Kubie, "*God's Little Acre*," *Saturday Review of Literature* 11, no. 19 (November 1934): 305–12.

14. Edwin Rolfe, "God's Little Acre," *New Masses*, February 1933, p. 26.

15. James Korges, *Erskine Caldwell*, p. 40. Caldwell's 1940 novel, *Trouble in July*, is a partial exception to this generalization. It exhibits serious social concern for racial atrocities, perpetrated mostly by poor whites on blacks, and for the exploitation of women. However, there is no longer any effort to unite the poor into an oppressed group with common interests or to hint at the existence of a potential revolutionary class.

16. Erskine Caldwell, *Kneel to the Rising Sun and Other Stories*, pp. 153, 154–55. Subsequent references to this edition will be made in the text.

17. Erskine Caldwell, *Some American People*, pp. 261–62.

18. Erskine Caldwell and Margaret Bourke-White, *You Have Seen Their Faces*, p. 151. Subsequent references to this edition will be made in the text.

CHAPTER V

1. Liston Pope, *Millhands and Preachers*, p. 45.

2. The description of the events at Gastonia and press reaction is based largely on Pope's book, *Millhands and Preachers*, and Fred E. Beal's *Proletarian Journey*, as well as the coverage given to southern industrial strikes and disturbances during 1929 and 1930 by the *Nation*, *New Republic*, *New Masses*, and *Outlook and Independent*.

3. Quoted by Pope in *Millhands and Preachers*, pp. 303, 304.

4. Paul Blanshard, "Communism in Southern Cotton Mills," *Nation* 128 (24 April 1929): 501.

5. Paul Blanshard, "One-Hundred Per Cent Americans on Strike," *Nation* 128 (8 May 1929): 556.

6. See Daniel Aaron, *Writers on the Left*, p. 158; Howard Zinn, "A Comparison of the Militant Left of the Thirties and Sixties," in *The Thirties: A Reconsideration in the Light of the American Political Tradition*, ed. Morton J. Frisch and Martin Diamond (DeKalb: Northern Illinois University Press, 1968), pp. 27–43; and Alfred Kazin, *On Native Grounds*, pp. 409–10.

7. James Burkhart Gilbert, *Writers and Partisans*, p. 90.

8. Murray Kempton, *Part of Our Time*, p. 136.

9. Quoted by Broadus Mitchell in *The Rise of the Cotton Mills in the South*, p. 167.

10. Georg Lukacs, *Realism in Our Time*, p. 113.

11. Leslie Fiedler, "The Two Memories: Reflections on Writers and Writing in the Thirties," in *Proletarian Writers of the Thirties*, pp. 13–14, 15.

12. Walter B. Rideout, *The Radical Novel in the United States 1900–1954*, p. 207.

13. Mary Heaton Vorse, *Strike!*, p. 324. Subsequent references to this edition will be made in the text.

14. Walt Carmon, "*Strike!*" *New Masses* 6–8 (November 1930): 18.

CHAPTER VI

1. Walter B. Rideout, *The Radical Novel in the United States 1900–1954*, p. 174.

2. Shields McIlwaine, *The Southern Poor-White*, pp. 200–12.

3. Ann Firor Scott, "After Suffrage: Southern Women in the Twenties," *Journal of Southern History* 30 (August 1964): 305.

4. Olive Tilford Dargan, *The Mortal Gods and Other Plays*, p. 93.

5. Fielding Burke [Olive Tilford Dargan], *Call Home the Heart*, p. 2. Subsequent references to this edition will be made in the text.

6. Georg Lukacs, "Propaganda or Partisanship," *Partisan Review* 1 (April–May 1934): 36. This article is an effort to define the difference, not a commentary on Burke's novel.

7. Elmer Davis, "The Red Peril," *Saturday Review of Literature* 8 (16 April 1932): 662. See also the reviews by Jonathan Daniels, p. 537, and Amy Loveman, p. 684, in the same volume.

8. Fielding Burke [Olive Tilford Dargan], *A Stone Came Rolling*, p. 269. Subsequent references to this edition will be made in the text.

9. A. B. Magil, "*To Make My Bread*," *New Masses* 8–9 (February 1933): 19–20.

10. Grace Lumpkin, *To Make My Bread*, p. 61. Subsequent references to this edition will be made in the text.

11. Liston Pope, *Millhands and Preachers*, p. 263.

12. See Rideout, *The Radical Novel*, p. 311.

13. Grace Lumpkin, *A Sign for Cain*, p. 364.

14. See the following reviews: *Books*, 27 October 1935, p. 4; *Boston Transcript*, 26 October 1935, p. 5; *Nation* 141 (23 October 1935): 480; and *Saturday Review of Literature* 13 (9 November 1935): 10.

15. Flannery O'Connor, quoted by C. Hugh Holman, "The View from the Regency-Hyatt: Southern Social Issues and the Outer World," in *Southern Fiction Today*, p. 30.

16. Esther Lowell, "*Gathering Storm*," *New Masses* 8–9 (May 1933): 29.

17. Dorothy Myra Page, *Gathering Storm*, p. 28. Subsequent references to this edition will be made in the text.

CHAPTER VII

1. Daniel Aaron, *Writers on the Left*, p. 168.

2. Frederick J. Hoffman, *Freudianism and the Literary Mind*, p. 60.

3. Ibid., p. 229.

4. Ibid., p. 241.

5. Sherwood Anderson, "How I Came to Communism: Symposium," *New Masses* 8–9 (September 1932): 8.

6. Sherwood Anderson, *Marching Men*, p. 222.

7. Sherwood Anderson, *Memoirs*, p. 187.

8. See Alfred G. Meyer, *Marxism*, pp. 69, 164–65.

9. Sherwood Anderson, *Perhaps Women*, p. 57. Subsequent references to this edition will be made in the text.

10. Frederick J. Hoffman, "The Voices of Sherwood Anderson," in *The Achievement of Sherwood Anderson*, p. 233.

11. Irving Howe, *Sherwood Anderson*, p. 219.

12. Ibid., p. 231.

13. Oscar Cargill, *Intellectual America*, pp. 683–84.

14. Reinhold Niebuhr, "Still on Probation," *World Tomorrow* 15 (30 November 1932): 525.

15. Sherwood Anderson, *Beyond Desire*, p. 9. Susequent references to this edition will be made in the text.

16. Granville Hicks, "Red Pilgrimage," *New Republic* 73 (21 December 1932): 169.

17. Walter B. Rideout, *The Radical Novel in the United States 1900–1954*, p. 219.

18. William Rollins, Jr., *The Shadow Before*, pp. 128–29. Subsequent references to this edition will be made in the text.

19. Rideout, *The Radical Novel*, p. 209.

20. Ibid.

21. Will Herberg, "The Christian Mythology of Socialism," *Antioch Review* 3 (Spring 1943): 125. A similar argument is made in Albert T. Mollegen's article, "The Religious Basis of Western Socialism," in *Socialism and American Life*, 2 vols., 1:109–10.

22. Fielding Burke, *Call Home the Heart*, p. 326.

CHAPTER VIII

1. James Agee and Walker Evans, *Let Us Now Praise Famous Men*, p. xv. Subsequent references to this edition will be made in the text.

2. See also William Scott, *Documentary Expression and Thirties America*, Part Three, "The Documentary Nonfiction of the Thirties."

3. Selden Rodman, "The Poetry of Poverty," *Saturday Review of Literature* 24 (23 August 1941): 6.

4. Noted by Alan Holder in "Encounter in Alabama: Agee and the Tenant Farmer," *Virginia Quarterly Review* 42 (Spring 1966): 203. I am indebted to many of the ideas in this excellent essay as points of departure for my comments.

5. George Barker, "Three Tenant Families," *Nation* 153 (27 September 1941): 282.

6. Lionel Trilling, "Greatness with One Fault in It," *Kenyon Review* 4 (Winter 1942): 102.

7. Fielding Burke, *A Stone Came Rolling*, p. 368.

8. David Martin, "R. D. Laing: Psychiatry and Apocalypse," *Dissent* 18 (June 1971): 236–37.

9. James Agee, *Agee on Film*, 2 vols. (New York: Grosset & Dunlap, 1967), 1:143.

10. Federal Writers' Project, *These Are Our Lives*, p. 11.

11. John M. Bradbury, *Renaissance in the South*, p. 152.

12. Carson McCullers, *The Ballad of the Sad Cafe*, pp. 287, 159, 423.

CHAPTER IX

1. Leo Gurko, *The Angry Decade*, p. 212.

2. Joseph Warren Beach, *American Fiction 1920–1940*, p. 309.

3. Edwin Berry Burgum, "The Sensibility of John Steinbeck," in *Steinbeck and his Critics*, pp. 112, 105.

4. Walter B. Rideout, *The Radical Novel in the United States 1900–1954*, p. 288.

5. See John R. Adams, *Harriet Beecher Stowe* (New York: Twayne Publishers, Inc., 1963), p. 52.

6. John Steinbeck, *In Dubious Battle*, p. 151. Subsequent references to this edition will be made in the text.

7. Peter Lisca, *The Wide World of John Steinbeck*, p. 124.

8. Lester Jay Marks, *Thematic Design in the Novels of John Steinbeck*, p. 52. Marks's book has a fine general discussion of the novels; he also elaborates the nonteleology theory in most detail.

9. Ibid., p. 19.

10. Lisca, *The Wide World*, pp. 114, 109.

11. Ibid., p. 114.

12. Clinton Rossiter, *Marxism*, p. 7.

13. Rideout, *The Radical Novel*, p. 315.

14. Sidney Hook, "The Philosophical Basis of Marxian Socialism in the United States," in *Socialism in American Life*, 1:450–51.

15. Marks, *Thematic Design*, p. 66.

16. John Steinbeck, *The Grapes of Wrath*, p. 407. Subsequent references to this edition will be made in the text.

17. Robert J. Griffin and William A. Freedman, "Machines and Animals: Pervasive Motifs in *The Grapes of Wrath*," *JEGP* 62 (1963): 569–80.

18. Martin Staples Shockley, "Christian Symbolism in *The Grapes of Wrath*," in *Steinbeck and his Critics*, p. 266.

CHAPTER X

1. Shields McIlwaine, *The Southern Poor-White*, p. 245.

2. Donald Davidson, "The Trend of Literature: A Partisan View," in *Culture in the South*, p. 204.

3. Robert Penn Warren, "Some Recent Novels," *Southern Review* 1 (Winter 1936): 629. Subsequent references to this edition will be made in the text.

4. John Bradbury, *Renaissance in the South*; this summary of the role of the poor white in southern literature after the 1930s is based on chs. 5, 6, and 7.

SELECTED BIBLIOGRAPHY

Aaron, Daniel. *Writers on the Left: Episodes in American Literary Communism*. New York: Harcourt, Brace & World, Inc., 1961.

Agee, James, and Evans, Walker. *Let Us Now Praise Famous Men: Three Tenant Families*. Boston: Houghton Mifflin Company, Riverside, 1960.

Anderson, Sherwood. *Beyond Desire*. New York: Liveright Inc., 1932.

_____. *Kit Brandon*. New York: Charles Scribner's Sons, 1936.

_____. *Marching Men*. Cleveland: Case Western Reserve University Press, 1972.

_____. *Perhaps Women*. New York: Horace Liveright, Inc., 1931.

_____. *Sherwood Anderson's Memoirs: A Critical Edition*. Edited by Ray Lewis White. Chapel Hill: University of North Carolina Press, 1966.

_____. *Windy McPherson's Son*. 1922. Reprint. Chicago: University of Chicago Press, 1965.

Barker, George. "*Three Tenant Families*." *Nation* 153 (1941): 282.

Beach, Joseph Warren. *American Fiction 1920–1940*. New York: Macmillan Company, 1941.

Beal, Fred E. *Proletarian Journey: New England, Gastonia, Moscow*. New York: Hillman-Curl, Inc., 1937.

Bertelson, David. *The Lazy South*. New York: Oxford University Press, 1967.

Bradbury, John M. *Renaissance in the South: A Critical History of the Literature, 1920–1960*. Chapel Hill: University of North Carolina Press, 1963.

Bradford, M. E. "Faulkner's 'Tall Men.'" *South Atlantic Quarterly* 61 (1962): 29–39.

Browder, Earl. *Communism in the United States*. New York: International Publishers, 1935.

Burke, Fielding [Olive Tilford Dargan]. *Call Home the Heart*. New York: Longmans, Green and Co., 1932.

_____. *A Stone Came Rolling*. New York: Longmans, Green and Co., 1935.

Burke, Kenneth. *The Philosophy of Literary Form: Studies in Symbolic Action*. Baton Rouge: Louisiana State University Press, 1941.

Byrd, William. *The Prose Works of William Byrd of Westover: Narratives of a Colonial Virginian*. Edited by Louis B. Wright. Cambridge, Mass.: Harvard University Press, Belknap Press, 1966.

Caldwell, Erskine. *God's Little Acre*. New York: Grosset & Dunlap, 1933.

_____. *Kneel to the Rising Sun and Other Stories*. New York: Viking Press, 1935.

_____. *Some American People*. New York: Robert M. McBride & Company, 1935.

_____. *Tobacco Road*. New York: Duell, Sloan and Pearce, 1932.

_____. *Trouble in July*. Boston: Little, Brown and Company, 1940.

_____, and Bourke-White, Margaret. *Say Is This the U.S.A.* New York: Duell, Sloan and Pearce, 1941.

_____, and Bourke-White, Margaret. *You Have Seen Their Faces*. New York: Modern Age Books, Inc., 1937.

Calmer, Alan. "Portrait of the Artist as Proletarian." *Saturday Review of Literature* 16 (1937): 3–4, 14.

Cargill, Oscar. *Intellectual America: Ideas on the March*. New York: Macmillan Company, 1941.

Cash, W. J. *The Mind of the South*. New York: Alfred A. Knopf, 1941.

Coles, Robert. *Migrants, Sharecroppers, Mountaineers*. Children of Crisis, vol. 2. Boston: Little, Brown and Company, 1971.

Core, George, ed. *Southern Fiction Today: Renascence and Beyond*. Athens: University of Georgia Press, 1969.

Couch, W. T., ed. *Culture in the South*. Chapel Hill: University of North Carolina Press, 1935.

Dargan, Olive Tilford. *The Cycle's Rim*. New York: Charles Scribner's Sons, 1916.

_____. *Highland Annals*. New York: Charles Scribner's Sons, 1925.

_____. *The Mortal Gods and Other Plays*. New York: Charles Scribner's Sons, 1912.

_____, and Preston, Frederick. *The Flutter of the Gold Leaf and Other Plays*. New York: Charles Scribner's Sons, 1922.

Davidson, Donald. *Southern Writers in the Modern World*. Athens: University of Georgia Press, 1958.

Davis, Allison; Gardner, Burleigh B.; and Gardner, Mary R. *Deep South: A Social and Anthropological Study of Caste and Class*. Chicago: University of Chicago Press, 1941.

Davis, Elmer. "The Red Peril." *Saturday Review of Literature* 8 (1932): 661–62.

DeForest, John William. *A Union Officer in the Reconstruction*. Edited by James H. Crowshore and David Morris Potter. New Haven, Conn.: Yale University Press, 1948.

De Graffenried, Clare. "The Georgia Cracker in the Cotton Mills." *Century Magazine*, February 1891, pp. 483–98.

Dollard, John. *Caste and Class in a Southern Town*. 2d. ed. New York: Harper & Brothers, 1949.

Draper, Theodore. *The Roots of American Communism*. New York: Viking Press, 1957.

Eaton, Clement. *The Mind of the Old South*. rev. ed. Baton Rouge: Louisiana State University Press, 1967.

Egbert, Donald Drew, and Persons, Stow, eds. *Socialism and American Life*. 2 vols. Princeton, N. J.: Princeton University Press, 1952.

Faulkner, William. *As I Lay Dying*. New York: Random House, 1964.

_____. *Collected Stories*. New York: Random House, 1950.

_____. *The Hamlet*. New York: Random House, 1940.

_____. *Sanctuary*. New York: Random House, 1958.

Federal Writers' Project. *These Are Our Lives*. Chapel Hill: University of North Carolina Press, 1939.

French, Alice. *Knitters in the Sun*. 1887. Reprint. New York: Garret Press, 1969.

French, Warren. *A Companion to "The Grapes of Wrath."* New York: Viking Press, 1963.

Frohock, W. M. *The Novel of Violence in America: 1920–1950*. Dallas: Southern Methodist University Press, 1950.

Gilbert, James Burkhart. *Writers and Partisans: A History of Literary Radicalism in America*. New York: John Wiley and Sons, Inc., 1968.

Gilmore, James R. *My Southern Friends*. New York: Carleton, 1863.

———. "The 'Poor Whites' of the South." *Harper's New Monthly Magazine*, June 1864, pp. 115–24.

Glasgow, Ellen. *Barren Ground*. Garden City, N.Y.: Doubleday, Page & Company, 1925.

Griffin, Robert J., and Freedman, William A. "Machines and Animals: Pervasive Motifs in *The Grapes of Wrath*." *Journal of English and Germanic Philology* 62 (1963): 569–80.

Gurko, Leo. *The Angry Decade*. New York: Dodd, Mead and Company, 1947.

Gwynn, Frederick L., and Blotner, Joseph L., eds. *Faulkner in the University: Class Conferences at the University of Virginia 1957–1958*. Charlottesville: University of Virginia Press, 1959.

Hagood, Margaret Jarman. *Mothers of the South: Portraiture of the White Tenant Farm Women*. Chapel Hill: University of North Carolina Press, 1939.

Harris, George Washington. *High Times and Hard Times: Sketches and Tales*. Edited by M. Thomas Inge. Nashville: Vanderbilt University Press, 1967.

Harris, Joel Chandler. *Free Joe and Other Georgian Sketches*. 1888. Reprint. Ridgewood, N. J.: Gregg Press, 1967.

———. *Mingo and Other Sketches in Black and White*. 1884. Reprint. Upper Saddle River, N. J.: Gregg Press, Literature House, 1970.

Hart, Henry, ed. *American Writers' Congress*. New York: International Publishers, 1935.

———., ed. *The Writer in a Changing World*. New York: Equinox Cooperative Press, 1937.

Henderson, Philip. *The Novel Today: Studies in Contemporary Attitudes*. London: John Lane, 1936.

Henneman, John B. "The National Element in Southern Literature." *Sewanee Review* 11 (1903): 345–66.

Herberg, Will. "The Christian Mythology of Socialism." *Antioch Review* 3 (1943): 125–32.

Hicks, Granville. *The Great Tradition: An Interpretation of American Prose Literature Since the Civil War*. New York: Macmillan, 1933.

———. *Where We Came Out*. New York: Viking Press, 1954.

Hoffman, Frederick J. *The Art of Southern Fiction*. Carbondale: Southern Illinois University Press, 1967.

_____ . *Freudianism and the Literary Mind*. 2d. ed. Baton Rouge: Louisiana State University Press, 1957.

Holder, Alan. "Encounter in Alabama: Agee and the Tenant Farmer." *Virginia Quarterly Review* 42 (1966): 189–206.

Holman, C. Hugh. *The Roots of Southern Writing*. Athens: University of Georgia Press, 1972.

Holmes, Edward M. *Faulkner's Twice-Told Tales: The Re-Use of his Material*. The Hague: Mouton and Co., 1966.

Holmes, G. K. "The Peons of the South." *Annals of the American Academy of Political and Social Science* 4 (1893): 265–74.

Hooper, Johnson J. *Simon Suggs' Adventures: Late of the Tallapoosa Volunteers*. 1846. Reprint. Americus, Ga.: Americus Book Co., 1928.

Howe, Irving. *Sherwood Anderson*. New York: William Sloane Associates, 1951.

_____ . *William Faulkner: A Critical Study*. 2d. ed. rev. New York: Random House Inc., Vintage, 1952.

Howell, Elmo. "Faulkner's Wash Jones and the Southern Poor White." *Ball State University Forum* 8 (1967): 8–12.

Inge, M. Thomas. "William Faulkner and George Washington Harris: In the Tradition of Southwestern Humor." *Tennessee Studies in Literature* 7 (1962): 47–59.

Johnston, Richard Malcolm. *Dukesborough Tales: The Chronicles of Mr. Bill Williams*. 1871. Reprint. Ridgewood, N. J.: Gregg Press, 1968.

Karanikas, Alexander. *Tillers of a Myth: Southern Agrarians as Social and Literary Critics*. Madison: University of Wisconsin Press, 1969.

Kazin, Alfred. *On Native Grounds: An Interpretation of Modern American Prose Literature*. New York: Harcourt, Brace and Company, 1942.

Kelley, Edith Summers. *Weeds*. 1923. Reprint. Carbondale: Southern Illinois University Press, Feifer & Simons, Inc., 1972.

Kempton, Murray. *Part of Our Time: Some Ruins and Monuments of the Thirties*. New York: Simon and Schuster, 1955.

Kephart, Horace. *Our Southern Highlanders*. New York: Outing Publishing Company, 1913.

Killian, Lewis M. *White Southerners*. New York: Random House, 1970.

Korges, James. *Erskine Caldwell*. Minneapolis: University of Minnesota Press, 1969.

Kroll, Harry Harrison. *I Was a Share-Cropper*. New York: Bobbs-Merrill Company, 1936–1937.

Kubie, Lawrence. "*God's Little Acre*." *Saturday Review of Literature* 11 (1934): 305–12.

Lange, Dorothea, and Taylor, Paul Schuster. *An American Exodus: A Record of Human Erosion in the Thirties*. New Haven, Conn.: Yale University Press, 1969.

Larson, Erling. *James Agee*. Minneapolis: University of Minnesota Press, 1971.

Lewis, Henry Clay. *Old Leaves from the Life of a Louisiana Swamp Doctor*. 1843. Reprint. Upper Saddle River, N.J.: Gregg Press, Literature House, 1969.

Lisca, Peter. *The Wide World of John Steinbeck*. Brunswick, N.J.: Rutgers University Press, 1958.

Longstreet, Augustus B. *Georgia Scenes, Characters, Incidents &c., in the First Half Century of the Republic*. 1835. Reprint. New York: Sagamore Press, Inc., 1957.

Lukacs, Georg. *Realism in Our Time: Literature and the Class Struggle*. Translated by John and Necke Mander. New York: Harper & Row, 1962.

———. "Propaganda or Partisanship." *Partisan Review* 1 (1934): 36–46.

Lumpkin, Grace. *A Sign for Cain*. New York: Lee Furman, Inc., 1935.

———. *To Make My Bread*. New York: Macauley Company, 1932.

Lumpkin, Katherine DuPre. *The South in Progress*. New York: International Publishers, 1940.

Lynn, Kenneth S. *Mark Twain and Southwestern Humor*. Boston: Little, Brown and Company, 1959.

Lyons, Eugene. *The Red Decade: The Stalinist Penetration of America*. Indianapolis: Bobbs-Merrill Company, 1941.

McCullers, Carson. *The Ballad of the Sad Cafe: The Novels and Stories*. Boston: Houghton Mifflin Company, Riverside, 1951.

McDonald, Lois. *Southern Mill Hills*. New York: A. L. Hillman, 1928.

McDowell, Frederick P. *Ellen Glasgow and the Ironic Art of Fiction*. Madison: University of Wisconsin Press, 1960.

McIlwaine, Shields. *The Southern Poor-White: From Lubberland to Tobacco Road*. Norman: University of Oklahoma Press, 1939.

Madden, David, ed. *Proletarian Writers of the Thirties*. Carbondale: Southern Illinois University Press, 1968.

Marks, Lester Jay. *Thematic Design in the Novels of John Steinbeck*. The Hague: Mouton, 1969.

Martin, David. "R. D. Laing: Psychiatry and Apocalypse." *Dissent* 18 (1971): 235–51.

Marx, Karl, and Engels, Frederick. *Literature and Art: Selections from Their Writings*. New York: International Publishers, 1947.

Mencken, H. L. *The American Scene*. New York: Alfred A. Knopf, 1965.

Meyer, Alfred G. *Marxism: The Unity of Theory and Practice: A Critical Essay*. Cambridge, Mass.: Harvard University Press, 1964.

Mitchell, Broadus. *The Rise of the Cotton Mills in the South*. Baltimore: Johns Hopkins Press, 1921.

———. "Why Cheap Labor Down South?" *Virginia Quarterly Review* 5 (1929): 481–91.

Nation. All editions for years 1929 and 1930.

New Masses. All editions for years 1926–1935.

New Republic. All editions for years 1929 and 1930.

Niebuhr, Reinhold. "Still on Probation." *World Tomorrow* 15 (1932): 525.

Ormond, John Raper. "Some Recent Products of the New School of Southern Fiction." *South Atlantic Quarterly* 3 (1904): 285–89.

Owsley, Frank Lawrence. *Plain Folk of the Old South*. Baton Rouge: Louisiana State University Press, 1949.

Page, Dorothy Myra. *Gathering Storm: A Story of the Black Belt*. New York: International Publishers, 1932.

Panichas, George A. *The Politics of Twentieth Century Novelists*. New York: Hawthorn Books, Inc., 1971.

Pells, Richard H. *Radical Visions and American Dreams*. New York: Harper & Row, 1973.

Pope, Liston. *Millhands and Preachers: A Study of Gastonia*. New Haven, Conn.: Yale University Press, 1942.

Potwin, Marjorie. *Cotton Mill People of the Piedmont*. New York: Columbia University Press, 1927.

Rahv, Philip. "Proletarian Literature: A Political Autopsy." *Southern Review* 4 (1939): 616–28.

Raper, Arthur F., and Raper, Ira. *Sharecroppers All*. Chapel Hill: University of North Carolina Press, 1941.

Reed, John Shelton. *The Enduring South: Subcultural Persistence in Mass Society*. Lexington, Mass.: D. H. Heath and Company, Lexington Books, 1972.

Rideout, Walter B. *The Radical Novel in the United States 1900–1954: Some Interrelations of Literature and Society*. Cambridge: Harvard University Press, 1956.

Robb, John S. *Streaks of Squatter Life, and Far West Scenes*. Edited by John Francis McDermott. 1847. Reprint. Gainesville, Fla.: Scholars' Facsimiles and Reprints, 1962.

Roberts, Elizabeth Madox. *The Time of Man*. New York: Grosset & Dunlap, 1926.

Rodman, Selden. "The Poetry of Poverty." *Saturday Review of Literature* 24 (1941): 6.

Rollins, William, Jr. *The Shadow Before*. New York: Robert M. McBride & Company, 1934.

Rossiter, Clinton. *Marxism: The View from America*. New York: Harcourt, Brace and Company, 1960.

Rovit, Earl H. *Herald to Chaos: The Novels of Elizabeth Madox Roberts*. Lexington: University of Kentucky Press, 1960.

Rubin, Louis B. *The Faraway Country: Writers of the Modern South*. Seattle: University of Washington Press, 1963.

———, and Jacobs, Robert D., eds. *Southern Renascence: The Literature of the Modern South*. Baltimore: Johns Hopkins Press, 1968.

Scarborough, Dorothy. *Can't Get a Red Bird*. New York: Harper & Brothers, 1929.

———. *In the Land of Cotton*. New York: Macmillan Company, 1923.

Scott, Ann Firor. "After Suffrage: Southern Women in the Twenties." *Journal of Southern History* 30 (1964): 298–318.

Seib, Kenneth. *James Agee: Promise and Fulfillment*. Pittsburgh: University of Pittsburgh Press, 1968.

Sheppard, Muriel Early. *Cabins in the Laurel*. Chapel Hill: University of North Carolina Press, 1935.

Skaggs, Merrill Maguire. *The Folk of Southern Fiction*. Athens: University of Georgia Press, 1972.

Steelman, Lala Carr. "Mary Clare de Graffenried: The Saga of a Crusader for Social Reform." *Studies in the History of the South 1875–1922*. Vol. 3. Greenville, N.C.: East Carolina Publications in History, 1966.

Stein, William B. "Faulkner's Devil." *Modern Language Notes* 81 (1961): 731–32.

Steinbeck, John. *The Grapes of Wrath*. New York: Viking Press, 1939.

_____. *In Dubious Battle*. New York: Covici, Friede, 1936.

Stewart, John L. *The Burden of Time: The Fugitives and Agrarians*. Princeton, N.J.: Princeton University Press, 1965.

Stott, William. *Documentary Expression and Thirties America*. New York: Oxford University Press, 1973.

Stribling, T. S. *Birthright*. New York: Century Co., 1922.

_____. *Bright Metal*. Garden City, N.Y.: Doubleday, Doran & Company, Inc., 1928.

_____. *The Forge*. Garden City, N.Y.: Doubleday, Doran & Company, Inc., 1931.

_____. *The Store*. Garden City, N.Y.: Doubleday, Doran & Company, Inc., 1932.

_____. *Teeftallow*. Garden City, N.Y.: Doubleday, Page & Company, 1926.

_____. *The Unfinished Cathedral*. New York: Literary Guild, 1934.

Sutton, Walter. *Modern American Criticism*. Englewood Cliffs, N.J.: Prentice Hall, Inc., 1963.

Tandy, Jeanette R. *Crackerbox Philosophers in American Humor and Satire*. New York: Columbia University Press, 1925.

Tannenbaum, Frank. *Darker Phases of the South*. New York: G. P. Putnam's Sons, Knickerbocker Press, 1924.

Tedlock, E. W., Jr., and Wicker, C. B., eds. *Steinbeck and his Critics: A Record of Twenty-Five Years*. Albuquerque: University of New Mexico Press, 1957.

Thompson, Edgar T., ed. *Perspectives of the South: Agenda for Research*. Durham, N.C.: Duke University Press, 1967.

Thompson, William Tappan. *Major Jones' Scenes in Georgia*. Philadelphia: T. B. Peterson and Brothers, 1843.

Thorp, Willard. "Suggs and Sut in Modern Dress: The Latest Chapter in Southern Humor." *Mississippi Quarterly* 13 (1960): 169–75.

Thorpe, Thomas Bangs. *The Mysteries of the Backwoods*. 1846. Reprint. Upper Saddle River, N.J.: Gregg Press, Literature House, 1970.

Tindall, George Braun. *The Emergence of the New South 1913–1945*. A History of the South, vol. 10. Edited by Wendell Holmes Stephenson and E. Merton Coulter. Baton Rouge: Louisiana State University Press, 1948–1967.

_____. "Beyond the Mainstream: The Ethnic Southerner." *Journal of Southern History* 40 (1974): 3–18.

Trent, William P. "Tendencies of Higher Life in the South." *Atlantic Monthly* 79 (1897): 766–78.

Trilling, Lionel. "Greatness with One Fault in It." *Kenyon Review* 4 (1942): 99–102.

Trotsky, Leon. *Literature and Revolution*. Ann Arbor: University of Michigan Press, 1960.

Tucker, George. *The Valley of Shenandoah*. Southern Literary Classics Series, 2 vols. 1824. Reprint. Chapel Hill: University of North Carolina Press, 1970.

Turner, Arlin. "Seeds of Literary Revolt in the Humor of the Old Southwest." *Louisiana Historical Quarterly* 39 (1956): 143–51.

Twelve Southerners. *I'll Take My Stand: The South and the Agrarian Tradition*. New York: Harper and Brothers, 1930.

Vance, Rupert B. *Human Geography of the South: A Study in Regional Resources and Human Adequacy*. 2d. ed. Chapel Hill: University of North Carolina Press, 1935.

Vickery, Olga W. "The Dimensions of Consciousness: *As I Lay Dying*," in *William Faulkner: Three Decades of Criticism*. Edited by Frederick J. Hoffman and Olga W. Vickery. East Lansing: Michigan State University Press, 1960.

Volpe, Edmond L. *A Reader's Guide to William Faulkner*. New York: Farrar, Straus and Company, 1964.

Vorse, Mary Heaton. *Strike!* New York: Horace Liveright, 1930.

Wade, John D. "Two Souths." *Virginia Quarterly Review* 10 (1934): 616–19.

Waggoner, Hyatt H. *William Faulkner: From Jefferson to the World*. Lexington: University of Kentucky Press, 1959.

Warren, Robert Penn. "Some Recent Novels." *Southern Review* 1 (1936): 624–49.

———. "T. S. Stribling: A Paragraph in the History of Critical Realism." *American Review* 2 (1934): 463–86.

White, Ray Lewis, ed. *The Achievement of Sherwood Anderson*. Chapel Hill: University of North Carolina Press, 1966.

Woodward, C. Vann. *Origins of the New South, 1877–1913*. A History of the South, vol. 9. Edited by Wendell Holmes Stephenson and E. Merton Coulter. Baton Rouge: Louisiana State University Press, 1948–1967.

INDEX